BIG BEACON

Foreword by Rt Hon. Grant Shapps MP

SEVEN DIALS

First published in Great Britain in 2023 by Seven Dials,
an imprint of The Orion Publishing Group Ltd,
Carmelite House, 50 Victoria Embankment,
London EC4Y 0DZ

An Hachette UK company

1 3 5 7 9 10 8 6 4 2

Images courtesy of Baby Cow/BBC p.6, 7, 8, 9, 10, 11, 12 (bottom); Baby Cow/Dave
Lambert p.5; Colin Hutton p.3; Getty Images p.2, 4, 12 (top), 13, 14, 15, 16 (top)

A CIP catalogue record for this book is
available from the British Library.

ISBN (Hardback) 978 1 3987 1921 7
ISBN (Export Trade Paperback) 978 1 3987 1922 4
ISBN (eBook) 978 1 3987 1924 8
ISBN (Audio) 978 1 3987 1925 5

Typeset by Input Data Services Ltd, Bridgwater, Somerset

Printed in Great Britain by Clays Ltd, Elcograf, S.p.A.

www.orionbooks.co.uk

Contents

FROM
'THE RIME OF THE
ANCIENT MARINER'

The ship was cheered, the harbour cleared,
Merrily did we drop
Below the kirk, below the hill,
Below the lighthouse top.

The light came on Oh! How it shone
As the keeper flicked the switch
It casts its spell, the rocks were quelled
The sea was now his bitch

by
Samuel Taylor Coleridge (first verse)
and Alan Partridge (second verse)

A LETTER FROM THE AUTHOR

he[1] book you are about to read isn't like other books. It employs a daring structure known as a dual narrative.

What's a dual narrative? Well, it comes from the words 'dual', meaning two, as in dual carriageway or dual nationality. And 'narrative', meaning story or narrative.

It's a device you'll be familiar with from the world of film. In a popular movie, we might follow a character in childhood and then see that *same* character played as an adult by Keira Knightley. Now, when people pay to watch Keira Knightley, they ain't gonna sit there for an hour while a child actor has a go at the role. A paying punter and fan of Knightley will spend that hour thinking, quite rightly, and excuse my language so early in the book, What the fuck is this?

---

1 I've always wanted to start a book with a big monk's letter and make it quite saucy. I was advised I can't do that in the current climate but my assistant suggested if I include a muscly man it would keep the moaning minnies at bay. If I can keep it up, I hope to start every chapter with one of these.

People simply don't *sit* in a movie they're not enjoying, not in a cineplex that has air hockey on site or a ten-pin bowling alley next door. You have to grab them by the short and curlies (pubes) and enthral them from the get-go. If not, they'll vote with their feet and skidaddle, maybe grab a Frankie & Benny's and try to win a big teddy from a basketball game with an undersized hoop. No disrespect to the child actor – I'm sure they're very good and they've been in *Holby* or the stage version of *Matilda* – but we're here to see Knightley. We want Knightley. Where's Knightley?

How does a filmmaker square that circle? How can he (or increasingly she! 👍) incorporate the childhood section of the story without angering their Keira-hungry audience? They do it by using a *dual narrative*, with the storylines running, if you like, 'side by side' – a phrase a lot of you will be familiar with. With the stories placed in parallel, the filmmaker can flit between the two at will. Bit of the child actor, bit of Knightley, bit of the child actor, bit of Knightley. Oftentimes, love that word, they'll pop the date on screen to indicate to the audience that we've swapped from one period of time to another. It's something we've all seen, and if you're thinking, Hmm, doesn't ring a bell, trust me, you will have seen it, you just can't remember right now.[2]

So, we *know* it works in films, but incredibly it's never been tried in a book before – until now. In *Big Beacon*, each strand of the dual narrative will tell a different story of resurrection. One follows the pursuit of a simple dream, the struggle to resuscitate a career as a TV personality. Will I succeed?[3] The second follows a very different quest – one in which I spurn the world of broadcasting for a more humble life spent restoring a dilapidated lighthouse, and in doing so, in scenes that are often quite

---

2 *Jumanji.*
3 [SPOILER] Yes.

moving, tenderly breathing new life into both the abandoned seaside building and, in a funny kind of way, my own soul.

A simple rule of thumb is that the chapters alternate between the narratives. So it goes TV career, lighthouse. TV career, lighthouse. TV career, lighthouse, TV career, lighthouse. You get the idea. If you read the book, it's really quite easy to follow. You come to realise that if you're reading about my TV career, the next chapter is gonna be about the lighthouse. And when that's over, you'll be back on the TV career. Then it's lighthouse again. I'm making it sound like you need a pen and paper. It's really not that hard. My assistant's read it and she doesn't even have an O Level.

Please enjoy this book. Pop a bookmark in this page if you'd like to return to it as a ready-reference tool. Any bookmark will do, but I'd ask you not to fold back the corner of the page, as it creates dog ears.

Thank you.

PRODOGUE

wo candy flosses, please!'

I sniff deeply and let the sticky air waft up from the drum and fill my nostrils. I've always enjoyed the taste of these sugary pink puffs and buy them whenever I see a stall. Tucking into this wispy, coloured nest might feel like you're eating an old woman's hair on a stick, but my God, she is one *delicious* lady.

It's 11 June 2021. The funfair's come to Chapelfield Gardens in Norwich and we are going to *rock*. I've enjoyed the evening so far, nodding at people who recognise me from my BBC One show *This Time* and just forgiving those who don't.[4]

I've come with my dog, Seldom, to stretch (a) his legs, and (b) the patience of everyone else at the funfair. Seldom's

---

4 For those who are interested and do want to approach me:

'Hey Alan, where's Jennie?' = BAD

'Hey Alan, my uncle isn't very well, can you record a birthday message for him on my phone?' = BAD

'Mr Partridge, sorry to bother you, I don't want a selfie, I just want to say nothing more than I admire and respect what you do.' = GOOD

a rambunctious presence, preferring to walk through people rather than round them and snarling if he feels disrespected – even when restrained by a lead lashed to my arm, supported by a two-shouldered, concealed harness fitted with an emergency ripcord.[5]

But the fact is, he becomes more cross if left alone in the house. Of course, I prefer to come to the fair without him, but when I got home the other year he smelt fried onions on my clothes and went *berserk*. So this year I've taken no chances. He's had his eggs, he has his ear defenders on, and, as long as they don't play banjo rock – e.g. Mumford & Sons – I like to think *everything will be fine*.

The vendor hands me my flosses and I hold my card against the contactless console to pay – it feels odd using a modern payment system to buy a snack that should have been banned in about 1970, but no one else raises an eyebrow so I just chuckle and stroll.

I look round for Seldom but there's no sign. He's probably gone to get a burger. He learnt last year that if he kicks open the cool box behind the burger van, he can get at the discs of frozen mince and feast.

I wait for a minute for him to return, allowing myself a brief daydream in which he meets a female dog who just *gets* him and is able to bring out his softer side, the two of them eventually living at the oasthouse with me – so wrapped up in each other that I can have visitors again. Another minute passes. I've finished my floss and his is beginning to droop. This isn't like him.

A single white balloon floats upwards. I watch its silent rise. Then back to the action.

---

5 After some trials in a field using a quad bike as a dog substitute, this emerged as the best solution.

I start to walk around, calling Seldom's name, gently at first but then more urgently: 'Seldom? Seldom!'

Another minute passes. I'm frantic now. Where is he? I'm stopping people. 'Have you seen my dog? He's big and brown. I don't know – he's just a big, brown dog.' But no one's seen him.

Now I'm running, pushing past duck-hookers, coconut hurlers. 'Seldom! Seldie!' I pray he's not got on a dodgem. Like the nearby town of Sheringham, he welcomes careful drivers *only*. Seldom, where are you?

I hand his candy floss to a young boy whose mother tuts – Oh, *fuck off*, I think – and hurtle through the throng of giggling families. I'm spinning round, the funfair now a blur of neon and tat. And then . . . I see him, lying peacefully a few yards away.

Relief gushes through me and I put my hands on my knees, partly to steady myself and partly to wipe on to my trousers *any* trace of candy floss. I smile and walk towards him. He's having a nap in between the helter-skelter and the waltzers.

'Where the hell did you go, you daft bugger?' I say, although I skip 'the hell' and 'you daft bugger' bits.

He's not moving. I approach him, making a clicking noise with my tongue like a Geiger counter so as not to suddenly surprise him with one loud noise when I'm beside him. 'Seldie?'

He's very still. I stare at him. He's not breathing. Something's wrong. I push him hard – the acid test. Either he retaliates with extreme prejudice or he's dead.

Oh my God, I think he's dead. I know in that moment the image of this hulking dark form next to the lighthouse-shaped slide would be seared onto my brain *for ever*.

'Seldom! Seldom, no. Please, Seldom. No, Seldom, Please, Seldom. No, Seldom.'

Two fairground workers look over, resembling a pair of

thick-set Morrisseys. 'We can shift him, no problem,' says one. 'We've shifted bigger weights than that before now.'

I don't ask. Seldom would have liked them.

I watch as they roll him into the jaws of a digger, and it suddenly hits me: he's gone. I howl at the heavens. 'Nooooo!' I see the balloon rising ever higher – as if his very soul is taking flight.

'Seldom!

'Seldom!

'Seldom!

'Seldom!

'Seldom!

Seld—'

I realise a woman is standing next to me, handing me back the candy floss I'd gifted to her son. I take it, wait for her to leave, then, before the tears begin, I plunge my face into it – and eat.

SOMETHING IN THE MIDDLE

21st June, 2021

[6] man strides down a corridor in BBC Broadcasting House with an almost rhinocerine confidence. It's ten days PS[7] and he's a presenter at the top of his game – with no idea he's about to lose even more than he's already lost.

'I'm gonna need breath mints, a big banana and some coffee.'

The man is I, Partridge.

'Caf or decaf?' My assistant holds up two flasks as she jogs to keep up – her replacement hip, a Chinese one crudely shaped out of PVC composite by twelve-year-olds, earning its money with every step.

'Caf. No, decaf. No, *caf*. Extra caf. *Maximum* caf. I want the amount of caffeine Jason Statham would order.'

'So a very strong black coffee?'

'Precisely. A very strong black coffee with milk.'

---

6 Calligraphy and erotica are rarely intertwined. But when I saw the opportunity, I seized it, and I think you'll agree the results are mostly good.

7 Post-Seldom.

It's an hour after we've aired the latest episode of *This Time* and I am motoring, having been summoned to a meeting with the show's producer, the head of content for BBC One and representatives from the corporate communications department and HR. I am not surprised. Moments earlier, I had created a nationwide campaign, exactly the kind of 'big tent' idea the badly listing show badly needed. All of a sudden, da big dogs got shit to *talk* about.

Faster I stride. Faster and faster. To my left, a wall adorned with empty BBC slogans; constant, constant pictures of Pudsey Bear (well done, you raise money for needy kids, *we get it*); and maps of fire exits and muster stations.

I begin to perspire. My assistant, whose nostrils are attuned to detect any fluctuation in my odour, looks up at me. 'Roll on?'

'Roll on.'

She hands me the Mitchum antiperspirant and I reach under my untucked shirt to slather it beneath my left arm. I hand the tube back to her and raise my right arm for her to do that side, as I've not been able to reach there since hurting the rotator cuff in my left shoulder at the weekend. My own fault! I'd attempted to dislodge a wasps' nest from the side of my house using an old swing-ball I'd found in the shed. Wielding the pole like a medieval mace had been *incredibly* satisfying – the tennis-ball end acted as a miniature wrecking ball and pissed the wasps *right* off – but it had played merry hell with my shoulder.

My assistant does as instructed, removes any stray hairs from the applicator ball and replaces the lid. Moments later, she hands me the coffee. She's recently got into coffee bags, as she finds the Nespresso intimidating and this way she can employ a system she already understands from the world of tea bags. On this occasion she's squeezed the coffee bag a bit too hard and it's ruptured, leaving a layer of sedimentary silt at the bottom of the flask. Still, she's a good worker and was only trying to extract maximum flavour from the bag, albeit cackhandedly.

Besides, I am in a very good place, for in the last few minutes of the show, something special had happened. An unscripted moment of daring improvisation that had spawned a movement, one that was already making waves and/or inroads across the nation.

* * *

'I am hopping mad and I want something in the middle.'

Eleven words. Forty-two letters. One *hell* of a rally cry. Uttered by me, live on BBC One, at 9.26 p.m. on 21 June 2021, this primal scream landed in an echoey TV studio like liver on a butcher's slab. A cold, fat plop. But my God, it fizzed down cables into the nation's living rooms where it prompted a very different reaction. And suddenly – boom! – everything changed.

Odd to think I'd said these words just a week earlier after a hairdresser had left a big gap in my fringe. Then, no one had batted an eyelid, yet these very same words delivered down the lens of a camera, encapsulating the frustration of the viewing public, had tonight gone off like a nuclear bomb and catapulted me to the vanguard of a nationwide movement.

It was a simple call for reasonableness – pithy, clear and almost musical in its rhythms. There was a poetry to these words that made them resonate and linger. Ross Kemp said later he was pretty sure they were a haiku but he wasn't certain. And the sentiment itself – a rejection of extremism, plus a request to have more programmes on TV like *Goodnight Sweetheart* and *Antiques Roadshow* – was surely irrefutable. Little wonder it had created a groundswell of public feeling.

The public was the ground; I was the swell.

Revisionists will try to understate how seismic this was – and that's cool, that's cool, that's cool – but the facts are these: in the days that followed, 'I am hopping mad and I want something in the middle' became every bit as ubiquitous as 'Hands, Face, Space' or (my personal favourite) 'See It, Say It, Sorted'. It captured the public imagination, certainly in towns with a high C2/D social demographic (skilled, semi-skilled and un-skilled manual workers). Trust me, that heady summer those words were *everywhere*. You couldn't move without seeing them retweeted by a single dad who likes the England flag, or chanted by a gaggle of aggressive mums outside a Portsmouth school. For three weeks they were daubed on a motorway bridge on the M6 as you approached Preston.

It gave the people hope, something to believe in, an issue over which they could come together. Families that had been fractured by one brother sexting another brother's fiancée, a gran saying something overtly racist to a grandson's mixed-race girlfriend, or an uncle grabbing a nephew by the collar because he sneered at Brexit, could finally sit down for a roast dinner and say, 'Hey, what about that something in the middle campaign?'.

For the first time, I was the face of something. The leader of a people. An iconic figure with an army of acolytes in lockstep behind me. I was like Christ donkeying through the streets of Galilee. I had *heft*.

We arrive at the meeting room. I enter.

I don't know it yet, but I'm walking into an ambush, an HR mugging in which I'll be told I've already completed my final television appearance. My last ever episode of award-winning[8]

---

8 CHECK.

BBC magazine show *This Time*. I am effectively going to be crucified like (yes, him again) Lord Jesus Christ.

* * *

'Do you mind if I don't high five you, Alan?' Howard Newman, the show's producer, is avoiding my eye, not to mention my hand, which now hangs in the air, as limp and redundant as the mistletoe in Rod Liddle's conservatory. I slowly lower it.[9] I know this to be a bad sign. No five should ever go unhighed. My rotator cuff twinges in sympathy.

I'm surrounded by fretting BBC staff and a producer (Howard) who looks like a heart attack in a Burton shirt – a coterie of panicky pen-pushers, covering arses and baying for blood.

Howard speaks again: 'I think we need to look at your role, going forward.'

I nod. A less intelligent mind might have processed this as, They want to look at me roll, going forward, and launched into a judo roll in the middle of the meeting room. But although *slightly* panicking, I am an altogether sharper intellect and realise what was meant just *before* initiating a roly-poly.

I feel no rancour towards Howard. It is obvious to me that the role is too big for him and he is struggling. He'd joined the corporation from E4, the channel famous for bringing us Japanese stunt show *Banzai*. Well done them – but *Banzai* was twenty-two years ago. What have they done since? Nothing.

This is not what I expected – and *certainly* not what I deserve. I have sat on the famous sofa hundreds of times and been a loyal servant of the show and a kindly presence for our audience, using simple language to help less able viewers understand potentially

---

9 My hand, I mean. Rod's mistletoe's been up since 2010 and gone black.

difficult concepts such as inflation or the House of Lords.

Away from the studio, I've been a passionate defender of both the show's output and the BBC's wider public-service remit, and will confront critics at dinner parties, putting them straight on a few things – and once even loosening the top of the salt cellar so that a guy from *The Times* had his risotto swamped with excess seasoning.

Today's show hasn't been without its crumples, I admit that. I am my own worst critic, if you don't count the guy from *The Times*. But I'm certain the audience won't have noticed. In that studio I'm a watchword for unflappable professionalism. There's a serenity to the way I broadcast. Amol Rajan says I'm like a swan in a suit. And this is a man who knows about a breezy style of broadcasting, since he has a chronic mumble and lazily runs two, three, sometimes four words together at a time – a trait that sounds like poor diction but is in fact a deliberate affectation to appear more chilled out. In real life he couldn't be clearer and has a clipped manner reminiscent of the speaking clock.

Was it all plain sailing? Have I been 100 per cent perfect? Yes. So it feels a bit odd – not upsetting, just odd – to be here in a room full of concerned voices, and even concerneder faces.

Howard, however, sees things differently, reminding me that Her Royal Highness the Princess Royal Princess Anne had been in the studio and insisting that I've embarrassed the croissant-haired royal. I chuckle calmly. This is Her Royal Highness the Princess Royal Princess Anne we're talking about – she has three brothers who are moooore than capable of doing that, from Princes Andrew and Edward to our new king, Prince Charles.

But Howard is now saying I've made the show look bad – interesting! Made them look bad? Did I make them 'look bad' in the VT when I was visiting Chelsea Pensioners and handing out book tokens to thank them for their service? Did I make them 'look bad' when I launched Britain's Fittest PE Teacher? Did I make them 'look bad' when I and the *This Time* Pick-up Squad collected discarded cans worth £125 and used the cash to carpet a Scout hut? Did I make them 'look bad' when I dressed up as Pudsey Bear for *Children in Need*, lending a spry physicality to the partially sighted teddy bear?

Why are they being like this? So I went off-script – biiiiiiig deal. Presenters are given *licence* to embellish the show with spontaneous riffing. For example, Jennie is able to tell an anecdote about yoga if one occurs to her, which it does maybe eight times a month. Or she might nudge me playfully without my prior say-so. Or she might add a 'ba-bye' even though 'Alan says Goodnight' is the last line on the autocue. Things like that.

'We can't have this,' drones Howard. 'Today was meant to be a special show and as per usual you've made it all about you.'

I take exception to this. 'As per usual?'

'"I'm hopping mad and I want something in the middle",' he scoffs. ' I mean, what was that?'

'It was a campaign to improve the BBC,' I say.

'Yeah, with your face all over it,' he scoffs.

My voice lowers to a croaky hiss, like the sister's boyfriend from *Happy Valley*: 'You might be surprised, Howard, but for some of us broadcasting isn't about boosting our own profile. It's about helping the public.'

I look round, expecting a few nods of appreciation, but instead Howard just extends his hand – and *not* for a high five. 'HR will be in touch,' he says. 'But listen – thank you.'

'You're sacking me? You can't do that.'

'I can, as a matter of fact. Just … think of it as a chance to spend a bit more time with your—'

'What, dog?'

'Well, yeah.'

'Dog's dead.'

The snapping reminder of Seldom's face discharges a pang of anguish – a panguish – and briefly transports me back to the hours and days after his death: the two fairground Morrisseys helping me to roll his body into the jaws of a digger; the futile calls with taxidermists both here and abroad; the consequent decision to lay him to rest and ringing the fairground lads to ask to borrow their digger again; the giant heaving sobs as I knelt at the graveside using my own arms to doze huge mounds of earth back into the grave[10]; the sullen days thereafter when I'd unthinkingly toss bits of food onto the floor only for them to sit there unsnaffled.

For a second I toy with the idea of leaning into it, of playing the dead-dog card. I am, after all, a grieving man. And many a BBC employee has escaped redundancy for less – IBS, anxiety, mild IBS, think I might be gay, repetitive strain injury, had a bad dad so sad. The BBC knows it has to take complaints seriously. Ever since Operation Yewtree, management has become – I hesitate to say 'touchy feely', that was the bloody problem! – but more alive to potential welfare concerns. However, I ain't gonna lower myself.

'I'd already decided to resign, mate. Drafted the letter this morning.'

'Let's have a look, then.'

'It's not on me. It's in my bag.'

'Your bag's next to you.'

'My other bag.'

'Didn't know you had two bags.'

'Got six bags.'

---

10 An actually quite efficient technique I'd adopted at my mother's funeral, which felt fitting. Seldom could be 'one angry mother', and so could Mum.

'You want to go and get it, then?'

'Nah. I think we're done.'

On that, I am instructed to hand over my lanyard and pass, a brutally cold *sayonara* similar to how I imagine it would be if you left the Church of Scientology or LinkedIn. I open the door and find my erstwhile co-host Jennie Gresham standing near the door. She looks startled to see me – but that may be the botox, because she does use botox.

'Hi, Alan, sorry, just on a call,' she says, pretending to be on the phone.

'There's no one on the phone – I'm not stupid,' I say.

She opens her eyes wider, or tries to, her eyebrows fighting their way through huge tracts of botox in an attempt to look quizzical and adorable.

'Hand it over,' I instruct, and she obeys. I put it to my ear. 'Hello?' I say sarcastically.

'Hello,' says a voice.

'Who's this?'

'Liz Gresham.'

'Who's she when she's at home?' I bark.

'Jennie's mum.'

'You must be very proud – I'll hand you back.'

I return the phone to Gresham.

'Happy?' she says.

'Ecstatic,' I say, then, once she's gone, I add a whispered, 'You fucking cow,' which I regret but also stand by. I march off, reasonably confident my dignity is relatively intact and I can hold my head fairly high. Yes, a good day, all things considered.

What these people don't seem to realise is, I've already left. My departure came an hour and a half ago when I had the camera follow me out of the building, swapping the cold straitjacket of the TV studio for the warm embrace of the public. That was my goodbye. Yes, I'd *physically* returned to attend the meeting I've just described. But the real me? The me deep inside? That dude was last seen striding down Regents Street, swinging his big arms and humming a rock song. Oh, I am *gownnnnnne*. I am *outta* here. It's a shame to be leaving the BBC at a time when most of its senior roles, both exec and non-exec, are finally being given to supporters and donors of the Conservative Party. But leave I must, or rather left I have.

It's the year of our Lord 2021 and my TV career is over.

THE KRAKEN AWAKES

t was the year of our Lord 2011 and I was about to build a TV career.[11]

To explain how, we must go back to a time when I was a broadcaster marooned on local radio, much as a castaway is marooned on a desert island on the popular Radio 4 show *Desert Island Discs*.

So now, come with me. Come back down the years. For we float now though time and space and also in mid-air to 2011. Aaaaaaand, we've landed.

It was January. North Norfolk Digital shone brightly in the Norwich dinge, an incongruous glint of glamour on an otherwise unattractive face. Like Rudolph's red nose[12] or Mick Hucknall's horrible gold tooth.

---

11 This is the dual narrative thing I was on about. (Oh and while we're down here, my editor and I disagreed about the monk's letter that opens this chapter. I felt it should have been a deeply haunting sexually avant-garde work, she didn't. So forgive this rather bland pseudo William Morris protest letter.)

12 Which in my imagination looked glowing and bright rather than bulbous and sore, the latter usually a sad indicator of alcohol dependency, which does tend to be more prevalent in Nordic countries where reindeer like to live. No, I

For what seemed like aeons (but was actually eight years), the station had imbued the city with an unmistakeable elan and was regarded locally as the oracle of what was cool. No one in Norwich liked Ed Sheeran until we put him on the playlist and said, 'Check out this kid, he's special.' We were kingmaker, arbiter, judge and jury.

What we said mattered. If we said chunky knitwear is hot this season, sales of wool and knitting needles would skyrocket. If we said watch Silent Witness *tonight at 9, people would tune in bang on 9. If we said apparently goat's cheese contains salmonella, shoppers would avoid it and boycott goat products more widely. If we said there's a tailback on the A40, by God people would avoid the A40 and find alternative routes. We had* clout.

Trust me when I say/write there wasn't a broadcaster in the land who wouldn't have been creatively satisfied by being part of the NND team. I know I was. Every second of every day, my mind was generating phone-in ideas, competitions, throws to the news and fun features. The jingles alone were occupying huuuuuge amounts of brain space, and new jingles – like a man who's consumed too much Viagra and cornflour – were coming thick and fast,[13] such that I was able to turn almost every sentiment I needed to utter into a short, catchy song. From a jaunty 'Do you want dessert or shall we get the bill?' to a more hard-hitting, current-affairs style 'Denise! Fernando! Your mother's had a fall'.

I was partnered by my on-air friend and real-life acquaintance Sidekick Simon. Ours was a creative partnership at its most vital – the radio equivalent of Simon & Garfunkel in their 1965–70 golden

---

picture Rudolph's nose as more of a red-light bulb, the kind they use in brothels, although I shudder at the image of Rudolph for some reason hoisted up to the ceiling of a knocking shop to light the room against his will, the bewildered mammal frightened and confused by the activity taking place below him, all of which he is inadvertently illuminating with his magic nose.

13 Have to try stand-up one day!

era, but with him *as Garfunkel and* me *as Simon. I (Simon) providing the creative engine, and Simon (Garfunkel) harmonising with what I (Simon) was doing while also adding Simon's (Garfunkel's) own bits.*

The point is, I would find myself calling or texting Sidekick Simon frequently through the day and night, eager to share whatever new idea I'd come up with as soon as possible. And for his part, Simon would text me with ideas he'd had. One or two would fit the bill and find their way into the tail end of the show. Others were interesting but tonally wrong. 'Should we legalise cannabis?' would have been incendiary to a Norwich listenership. And many others – 'Live STD results', 'Simon's poetry slam', and 'Remembrance Day bloopers' all fell foul of my 'interesting but not quite right' filter. Still, together we cooked up a pretty special show on a pretty special radio station.

That was before.

Fast forward three months and there had been a sea change at the landlocked radio outfit. One day, waiting for the traffic lights to change on the drive to work, I caught sight of myself in the window of a tanning shop, the reflection of my face framed by a halo of shiny brown buttocks. I was struck by how old I looked. The pleasant chub of my cheeks and lips had given way to a pinched, angular quality like a wooden crow.

What had changed? I wondered. Where was the cheery broadcaster who used to drive to work singing popular songs of the time? Back in the day, I'd drive to work full of vim, entertaining myself with a neat game I called Speed Magnet. I'd do my darndest to stick exactly to the speed limit, gently teasing the accelerator to hover at exactly 30mph (if in a 30 zone), and the second it became a 40, I'd zoom to close up the 10mph shortfall before hovering there, praying to God almighty that a tractor wouldn't pull out and ruin the game. If that sounds less than thrilling, think again! Passing through a rural village containing a primary school would see me slam on the anchors, screeching down from the 60mph national speed limit riiiiight the way down to 30 before plunging again, just yards later, to the 20mph school zone limit. At the town limits, you'd better believe I'd get up to 60 again just as soon as I could! It was daredevil exhilaration and the best thing was: it was 100 per cent legal!

But there was a sullenness to me on this drive. Something at North Norfolk Digital had changed. No longer the beating heart of the Norfolk music scene, it had vacated its HQ in a prime central Norwich location and relocated to a faceless business park some four miles away, alongside a number of other potential HQs that sat empty because no serious corporation wanted to plonk themselves on a site marooned so far from a town or motorway.

It was a poorly planned development. A long road punctuated every 30 yards by yet another mini-roundabout, these annoying white mounds coming down the track like beads of my assistant's rosary. These roundabouts served no function, their exits leading to blunt dead ends, since the development had stalled due to lack of demand. Which is why I used to simply drive over them – until the owners in their wisdom put paid to that, replacing the painted mounds with flower beds. The drive had consequently become a painful stop-start affair and I never didn't arrive at work in a bad mood.

Why on earth did we move? I'd often find myself in the middle of Norwich looking up at the building that used to be NND's home. Now a Roman-style 24-hour massage sauna, it was a seedy, crumbling relic of our once glorious past. Although I'd never seen inside such a place, I could nonetheless imagine that the walls echoed to the sound of Eddie Shepherd coughing news into his microphone, Barbara Bickerton recounting one of her long stories, yours truly telling a single mum she has won £50 of Iceland vouchers, or the ghost of Wally Banter haunting the corridors, although I knew the real Wally Banter could often be found in there as well, certainly on the days his ex had the kids.

And now here we were, so far out of the hustle and bustle of Nor-
wich life that we might as well not exist. It was largely for this reason
that North Norfolk Digital was locked in a spiral of decline.

The move also had a disastrous effect on the quality of guest we
were able to attract. It's one thing to convince Joe Wicks or Sandi
Toksvig to come on the show when the studio's a stone's throw from
the train station – Simon will run to Costa and grab you a coffee
while we're on air, we'd say; he can take your coat to the dry cleaner
as well if you want, we'd say – but if you think Joe Wicks is going
to sit in a minicab for twenty minutes to come and talk about kettle
bells, forget it. Ain't gonna happen. Sandi would still come but she
would not be happy about it, and my God that came over on air. You'd
quickly realise why her agent called her Sandy Toxic.

Suddenly we were no longer treating listeners to must–hear inter-
views with TV stars and social media 'influencers'.[14] Instead we were
desperately filling airtime with a man who got an asbo for practising
his tuba or personalityless local–wine expert Rosie Witter. One day
our star interviewee was a man from Dyno-Rod who was only in
the building because the disabled toilet had backed up – turned out

---

14 A new type of job invented only in the last few years, 'influencers' are young
people – typically aged between fifteen and twenty-five – who post short online videos multiple times a day in which they speak quickly and loudly about
themselves. For reasons that aren't fully understood, this doesn't infuriate other
young people – it *attracts* them. They come to trust and listen to the views of
these young people who speak quickly and loudly about themselves, not even
being put off by the fact that they say 'in hopes of' rather than 'in the hope of', or
'inside of' rather than 'inside', or 'super excited' rather than 'very excited'. Businesses pay these 'influencers' to endorse their products. And it works because
millennials would rather follow what they're told by someone who has no expertise about a product and is only endorsing it because they are being paid to do
so over the views of a professional reviewer at a reputable publication providing
an assessment that is genuinely independent. What's my view on all this? Don't
have one, never really thought about it.

he knew a lot about fatbergs, which, to be fair, was actually quite interesting.

The office was a largely unwelcoming place. There was the faceless grey architecture, the mini-roundabouts issue, not to mention an air-conditioning system that made a drrrrrrrrrrrrrrrr noise so persistent that you continued to hear it long after leaving the office, so you'd find yourself frantically fingering your earhole at home, or while on a date with a woman and you'd have to pretend it'd got water in from the swimming pool.

Would you put up with that? Would you stand for the greyness, the roundabouts, the drrrrrrr? Not many would. And yet I did. I <u>settled</u>. I stuck where I should have twisted. I relaxed into the folds of the rut I was in. The dreams I'd had began to extinguish and sputter – not all at once, but one by one, gradually, like the candles on an asthmatic child's birthday cake.

You come to accept that this is who you are: a local digital DJ with only one car and a physique laden with a ring of fat around the middle, like a human Saturn.

Every now and then, I'd feel a rumble deep within. A yearning for a new purpose, as if there was something out there I needed to do. I just knew there was a new chapter of my life, waiting to be written – like Ross Kemp's sci-fi novel Robosoldier. But what would it be?

I could never quite pin it down. It was like trying to recall the dream you had last night. The more you run towards it, the further away it seems to get.

Think, Alan. Think. Think! THINK.

'And now Australia's finest export, apart from beef: Olivia Newton-John. Although someone told me recently she's from Greece. Never knew that. She doesn't look Greek, maybe she shaves her arms. This is "Xanadu"!'

It was April 2011 and I was at work again. I pulled down the fader, took off my 'cans'[15] and reached for the mailbag, hoping that, before the song finished, I could find an interesting letter to bulk out the next hour of the show. I wouldn't usually dip into the few letters we got — what had once been a large woven-plastic mail sack was now simply a big pencil case — but that day's edition of Consumer Champion had been pulled at the last minute because the complaint was from a woman who got locked in a tanning booth that wouldn't switch off and the owner of the salon happens to be a friend.

Reaching into the mailbag, I felt something smooth and cylindrical, not much bigger than a fig roll. It was a golden woggle. One word left my lips: 'No.'

Followed by: 'No, please.'

I fumbled around inside the padded envelope and found a note. It had no name on it, merely the words 'Fall in, troop. Fall in! Aaaaaat ease.'

My mouth went dry, but I managed to bleat: 'Simon? Take over.'

I grabbed my coat and walked out of the studio. I bustled through the office, heading for the exit.

'Have you told Gavin you're going?' said a marketing woman called Sue.

'Nope.'

'Well, you have to.'

'You tell him.'

'Nope.'

'Guess he ain't getting told, then.'

And I was gone. The people in the corporate side of the business could be teeeeeedious busybodies sometimes. But they just worked in a different culture. Disc jockeys and sidekicks should be given more licence to do as we please, as we have creative sensibilities that need

---

15 What twits/twats called headphones.

to be cosseted. So, for example, the office guys had to stay until 5 p.m.; we could knock off whenever.

They weren't allowed to heat up smelly food in the microwave, but we could put a piece of salmon on full whack and forget about it over the weekend with relative impunity. Things like that. But I wasn't thinking about office dynamics. I was thinking about what the arrival of the golden woggle meant.

It meant Peter Flint was in trouble.

In 1988, I presented a bi-monthly radio show called Scoutabout *on* Radio Norwich. Scoutabout *was the tip-top, non-stop, hot-to-trot one-stop shop for British Cubs, Scouts, Venture Scouts and, to a lesser extent, Girl Guides (not Brownies). That was my description and I own the copyright* to *that description.*

I was brought in alongside regular presenter Peter Flint, and for a time we were a double act that fizzed like a car battery in a puddle. We co-presented for no more than six months, but in that time a bond was formed that nothing could ever break, a brotherhood cemented one day when we were given a pair of golden woggles by the Chief Scout. A woggle, for the uninitiated, is a fastener for the neckerchief, often made from plastic or leather. These ornamental woggles were cast in gold and awarded in recognition of our support for the wider Scouting movement, a truly humbling honour. Owners of a golden woggle become part of an elite group, one that pledges to always be there for the others, to be a beacon in times of darkness, a trusted ally in times of strife. And it also means you must never tell on one another, which isn't for any nefarious reason, although now I come to type it, it does sound a bit weird.

Let me tell you something about Peter. He was special. The kind of broadcaster who comes along once in a generation. Peter reminded me of a young Chris Evans or a straight Kenny Everett, a brash, confident force of nature with bags of talent. Peter could have been anything he wanted to be. He was the enfant terrible of regional broadcasting – he would tease an Akela or hoik up a quick rope swing (also known as a tarzy rope) without even asking who owned the tree or whether the branch would withstand the fat kids. He'd be seen with a girl on his arm at the opening of a new leisure centre or opticians. He'd be a fixture in nightclubs and sometimes hosted barbecues down at the marina, on a boat he sometimes borrowed from his wife's brother.

He was keen to take Scoutabout *to TV and wowed the BBC Children's department with his sheer vivacity; however, kids TV supremo Biddy Baxter did not like him and the show fell into development hell, later emerging on Children's ITV as* Fun House, *presented by the bad-haired Pat Sharp. Peter was despondent, both that Pat had pipped him to the presenting gig and that the show had almost no connection to the Scouting movement whatsoever.*

When Peter was removed from Scoutabout *for getting drunk in his garden on the Queen's birthday, I was hugely disappointed in him. Nonetheless, we remained friends. He knew we could never be seen together, and that contact between us had to cease. The Scouts would never have permitted me to consort with a man who had got drunk on the Queen's birthday.*

On parting, we clasped hands like blood brothers. He gave me his golden woggle, and I gave him mine, although seeing as they were identical we could have just kept hold of the ones we had. We pledged that if either of us were ever in trouble we should send the golden woggle with the Scoutabout *catchphrase, and the other would – nay, <u>must</u> – spring to their aid at once.*

Years passed. Peter settled into a succession of lower-key roles on local radio, the wattage of his broadcasting abilities dimmed by the need to throw to the travel news or read out a statement from the council about where to get the flu jab or about a spate of spent condoms being left on a towpath. Radio Ipswich, All Anglia Radio, Calling Canterbury, Peterborough Community Radio and Paddock

FM all benefited from the sheer fucking <u>magnetism</u> of Peter's on-air personality – sorry for swearing. I'd long since lost touch with him but from afar he'd always seemed happy enough. Give him a box of CDs and a £25 book token to give away and he will give you three hours of wonderful radio.

But here was Peter sending up a distress flare in the form of a golden woggle.

I arrived at his home to find a bevy of cars parked outside. Not wanting to park down the street and walk back, I parked in front of his driveway, having cannily clocked that the car parked in it hadn't been driven for a while. You can tell from the brown leaves that have collected on the front wipers. I do that a lot when I don't want to park down the street and walk back.

The house had one of those PVC front doors with a door handle so you can let yourself in – why do people have those? – and I made my way inside. In a downstairs bedroom I saw the very thing I had dreaded. Peter was in bed, eyes closed, surrounded by his family. His loyal wife Kathleen sat beside him, a more buxom presence than the former model who went round pubs in Norwich with a holster full of cigarettes for sale, but still lovely looking.

'Peter!'

One of his family shushed me.

I mouthed to Kathleen, 'How is he?'

She pursed her lips and did a small shake of the head.

Then . . . 'Alan?'

I looked down. Bravely, Peter had opened his eyes. He reached for my hand and I allowed him to clasp it, subtly nudging Kathleen aside with my hip/the side of my bum until I was sitting in the bedside chair instead of her.

'Hello, old friend,' gasped Peter. 'Fall in, troop. Fall in.'

And then together we said, 'Aaaaaaat ease.'

It was an incredible moment of stunning emotion, which might not be coming across on the page, but take my word, it was quite something. Two former presenters of regional Scout-based magazine show Scoutabout *reciting the catchphrase after many years of not doing that. Quite, <u>quite</u> something.*

'Long time no see, old friend,' I said. Then added: 'What the hell were you doing getting drunk on the Queen's birthday?'

He looked crestfallen and I regretted bringing it up.

'You asked for my help,' I said, eager to move on.

'There's only one way you can help,' he said.

'Name it.'

He pulled my ear close to his lips.

'Make the most of what you have,' *he said.* 'Don't do what I did, don't settle for second best. I beg you, Alan, do everything in your power to give yourself the platform that your talent deserves. For talent is like a flower; it needs light and water but most of all guts.'

I'm paraphrasing slightly – I did want to record what he was saying on my iPhone, but the sombre mood in the room told me that would have been frowned upon. He definitely said the thing about flowers needing guts, because I remember thinking that was quite odd.

'What, you mean . . .?'

'Television, Alan. It's where you belong.'

'Nah! That was years ago.'

'Promise me, Alan,' he said, more urgently, squeezing my hand hard, which hurt, actually. 'Promise you'll do everything you can to get back on TV.'

He started coughing.

'Alright, love, that's enough,' said Kathleen.

He closed his eyes. Silence. Then a male voice at the back: 'Does someone here drive a Vectra? They've blocked me in the bloody drive.'

I left the house, Peter's words chiming around my head, the solemn plea from a man on his deathbed. Although I've just remembered he did actually get better after that. Retrained as a financial adviser and apparently made a shitload of money in 2022.

But still. A promise was a promise.

In that moment I decided I was going to get myself back on BBC Television within twelve months. And while I ended up taking slightly longer (it was more like eight years), I would one day achieve that feat.

And yes, enemies of mine say this noble vow sounds like a made-up literary device to justify my clamour for TV work, a fig leaf behind which resides the unsightly cock and balls of my own ambition.

What I will say is that attitude is <u>exactly</u> why Brexit isn't going very well.

SEEING THE LIGHT

July 2021

'I could email the man from Dolphin. He'd buy you lunch if he thought you wanted a bathroom.'

'I'm talking about a *proper restaurant lunch*. Last time he drove me to a retail park and bought me a Whopper. Ended up telling me about his divorce with the windscreen wipers on.'

In the weeks after my departure from the BBC, my assistant has been trying to bulk out my schedule. This is a tough time for me.

I am a man who enjoys structure. I like to be busy, or appear busy. People around me know this. Sometimes I'll open my calendar app to see the shape of my day and say to my assistant, 'What the hell's this? Where's the structure?' By which I mean there should be one to two activities in the morning, a scheduled lunch, and then something in the afternoon. Evenings are either a social or work event, or she's meant to leave out a ready meal and write in the diary 'meal, ready'. Just because I don't like seeing the phrase 'ready meal' written down in my diary.

If no lunch is planned, my assistant will do a ring-round, see if there are gala lunches or charity buffets in the local area, or agree for me to meet with a salesman I'm stringing along so that *he* can buy me lunch.

I joked to my friend that my diary contained so much white it looked like a blizzard.

He said, 'It's good you can laugh about it.'

I said, 'Kieran, that's a hallmark of my career. If you joke about something it stops it being a threat.'[16] But the fact is, my diary is empty and neither I nor my assistant have much clue how to fill it.

Obviously, dog walking is off the menu (God, I miss him). I can't even attend my usual racquets club because a complaint I've made is under investigation and I've been asked not to attend until that has been completed, which I respect.[17]

But with squash off-limits and no job to go to, I'm struggling to fill my days. This is one of the first times in my life I have been genuinely unemployed. On the other occasion the BBC let me go, in 1994 after I discharged a firearm in the studio and killed a man, I still enjoyed a rich seam of corporate work, even doing a tongue-in-cheek photoshoot to promote a local paint-ball range, which, to use the vernacular, went down like a shit sandwich with the dead man's grieving relatives. Fair enough, shouldn't have done that. The fact that he was universally dis-liked even by his own family didn't change the fact that I had taken the man's life – even someone who, as I say, was universally disliked.

---

16 But the truth is, I hate making deprecating jokes about myself. I tried it for a while when I entered the pub for the weekly quiz, making quips such as 'here he is, the bad smell' or 'I'd look good next to a tramp', but even though it was me making the jokes at my own expense they started to wear me down.

17 Long story short: a female cleaner who had been allowed to clean the male changing rooms on account of her blindness had been spotted, by me, reading a magazine in her sister's car. It was clear to me, and all the men I told, that her disability had been a cunning smokescreen so that she, a woman, could enter a world of freshly showered men and businessmen and have a good old butcher's at us as she cleaned. We bravely spoke up, as early proponents of a fledging movement that went by the hashtag #HeToo. And Christine was suspended (later reinstated).

But right now, in 2021, commercial work is sparser. Every now and then, sure, I'll don some gardening trousers for a promo shoot, or host a Q&A where members of the public can fire questions at the CEO of a flexible-office provider. Or present a one-on-one with a crypto specialist where I'll say, 'What do we mean when we say bitcoin?' and then have to nod furiously until it's my turn to speak again. But these engagements are far and few between.

I move listlessly around my home, stopping periodically to drape myself over one of my three sofas, but even the leather one I had imported from Pakistan feels scratchy and lumpy. I'm at a loose end and I don't like it.

I ask Alexa how she is, in the hope that her programmers at Amazon HQ have prepared an amusing answer for her to say, but they haven't so I say, 'Alexa, stop,' and she goes quiet again.

The radio, then. It's preset to my old station North Norfolk Digital. Three days a week, my former colleague Simon Denton still sidekicks on the show, despite also working on *This Time* (for now). Still, I enjoy hearing his wisecracks on the radio. The guy's just a *talent* – something you can't say about his on-air partner and the lead DJ of my erstwhile mid-morning slot Chase McPhail. Chase is absolutely *awful*. I mean, he Stinks. The. Place. Out.

'You're listening to *Mid Morning Matters* on North Norfolk Digital.' No shit, Chase. 'It's Monday, 7 June, which means it's – drum roll, please! – Sir Tom Jones's birthday! In a glittering career, Sir Tom scored thirty-six UK hits and nineteen in the United States – an incredible fifty-five hit singles. So today, Simon, whadda we asking?'

A jingle booms: 'Today's Big Q!'

And then Simon pipes up: 'Yes, today we're asking for your

favourite Tom Jones songs. What's your fave song by Sir Tom? If you don't know any, maybe you can think of a song by someone else called Tom. Tom Petty or Tom Waits, maybe.'

'Love it, love it, love it. So, line one, who's there?'

'Alan in Norwich.'

I can hear Chase's tone change as soon as he recognises my voice. But I'm a listener and I've every right to call in if I want to.

'Alan Partridge!' gushes Chase. 'Once of this parish, always a treat . . . What your favouri—'

'How are you, Simon? All going well on *This Time*?' I didn't bother letting Chase finish.

'Yeah, good, good.'

'Anything juicy coming up?'

'Bits and bobs,' he says. 'We're thinking of doing this returning feature where we renovate a lighthouse and get Princess Anne to open it. She was telling Jennie she's a Patron of the Lighthouse Board so—'

'Which lighthouse?'

'Abbot's Cliff in Kent.'

I pull a 'whatever' face, but you can't see it on the radio.

'You should come in slightly quicker after the "Today's Big Q" jingle,' I say. ' Quite a bit of air in there.'

'Thanks, Alan.'

'And Chase?' I say.

'Yip?'

Who says yip? 'Thirty-six UK hits and nineteen US hits doesn't make fifty-five hit singles. They double up. It was probably thirty-six UK hits, of which nineteen were also hits in America. Rather than thirty-six hits here then another nineteen different songs that were hits in America.'

'Just reading what it says, buddy! Got a favourite Tom Jones song?'

'Nope'
'OK, then . . .'
'Alright, bye.'
'Bye, Alan,' says Simon.
'Bye, Simon.'

* * *

Three days later and things are no better. Incredibly, I find myself helping my Filipino housekeeper Rosa to ball up my socks, just for something – anything – to do. Later, I hold one end of the bedsheet and she the other, meeting in the middle so that she can fold the sheet, like a sedate version of a Morris dance.

If my friends could see me now, I think, helping a woman to do the very work I'm paying her to do? Why, they'd pee themselves laughing, and they'd be right to piddle themselves. My assistant isn't laughing. She clomps past theatrically as we work, later observing sniffily that 'presumably madam will be getting her full wage for doing half the work?'

I know Rosa is humouring me for fear of having her visa revoked or whatever it is she keeps going on about, but I think she gets something out of it too. I sometimes make suggestions that, applied correctly, would improve the workflow of certain tasks. For example, Rosa hadn't realised that when taking clean crockery from the dishwasher to the cupboard, she could bring dirty crockery back on the return trip, almost halving the amount of journeys required and leaving the dirty tableware beside the dishwasher ready for entry once the clean plates were put away. I tell her it's all about finding small efficiencies, and although she goes and gets the anchovies from the fridge having mistaken the word 'efficiencies' for 'fishies', I think she gets it.

Throughout all this, the kerfuffle I've lit under the BBC is smouldering. I am very much a Guy Fawkes figure, lighting a fuse under The Establishment and then blowing the whole thing sky high, although I remember as I type that Fawkes didn't manage to do that and was pulled to pieces by horses. Still, the same kind of idea.

But it just isn't enough. Time dribbles on. Seconds turn to minutes, turn to hours, turn to days, turn to weekends, turn to long weekends, turn to weeks.

What I needed was a purpose. This couldn't be the end of Alan Partridge. No, I would not go gentle into saying, 'Goodnight!' If I could just work out what I should be doing! But it was like – and I'll say it again because it's a good phrase and I think you should be allowed to use good phrases more than once – trying to recall the dream you had last night. The more you run towards it, the further away it seems to get.

And then one morning in September, I arise at dawn. I put on good socks, new ones, ones I've been saving. Something is compelling me to *walk*. And so walking I go,[18] aimless, with neither compass nor sandwich. I'd given my all for the BBC, agreeing wholeheartedly with its public-service ethos and sharing its hatred of advertising, but now, with nowhere to go, I, Partridge,[19] start walking like a nomad.[20]

I have nowhere to be. I have nothing to come home for. I hop on a bus for a bit, or sidle onto a train if I notice a station. All the while, it feels as if something is pulling me onward.

I am in a town now. Now it is countryside. Look, there's a business park. Look, there's the sea. The surrounding topography melts between one form and another. It is starting to get dark.

---

18 Sorry, weird syntax there.
19 ISBN: 9780007449170
20 ISBN: 9781409156703

And then ... there it is. I stop and my eyes go up a bit. Rising from a windy headland overlooking the Channel, or the English Channel as you used to be able to call it, in glorious colour, spattered by waves and bird dung, is a lighthouse.

I feel my back straighten, as if subconsciously aping its posture. Fallen into disuse it may have been/done, but it is standing there nonetheless. It cares nothing for the vagaries of fashion, for the whims of producers or commissioners, for the eddies and floes of popular taste. It simply remains. It is.

I feel a lump form in my throat. What is it? Pride? Respect? A blob of regurgitated sandwich? Previously, I'd always found lighthouses a bit flashy[21] and had often dismissed them as little more than big, hollow torches. And look at it – its walls are pock-marked and peeling, the windows are stained, cracked and one is fully broken, perhaps where youths have thrown stones at it or an errant gull has clattered into it beak-first, poor bastard.

But right here, right now, I am struck by the sheer resilience of lighthouses. While I am attacked, buffeted, nay-said, lighthouses stand tall and unbending. Residents, local businesses, councillors, seagulls, holiday makers – they all come and go, but throughout, the lighthouse remains impassive and permanent. The sniggerers may dismiss lighthouses as little more than architectural phalli, but these admittedly cock-shaped structures are so much more than that. As I look up at the building, it occurs to me that they are lasting relics of a time when people would look out for their fellow man – a proud monument to the simple act of caring. Today, we look to television and radio for guidance. It is broadcasters who shepherd us away from harm – be it the weather forecaster telling us to pop a coat on, the daytime TV

---

21 Gotta try stand-up!

chef warning us off British beef, or a local radio DJ saying, 'Get your money out of Northern Rock *today*.' But in the days before TV and radio, the lighthouse was our broadcaster – a glowing friend who'd say, 'You might want to steer clear of those rocks,' or, 'There's land in this direction FYI.'

Yes, the parallels between broadcasting and lighthousery should now have been made abundantly clear to the less able reader. But what compelled me to come to this place;[22] what exactly has drawn me[23] to this large lantern,[24] to this significant signal,[25] to this, gosh, I dunno . . . this big beacon?[26]

I catch myself. Get a grip, Alan. What is a lighthouse, really? With its conical/cylindrical shape and stripy paintwork, it looks like a camp Dalek with the prong snapped off. No, it is time to head home. Storm clouds are coming in.

I turn to leave but what's that on the breeze? My olfactory system detects the smell, the faintest smell, mind, of . . . candy floss? I turn to look at the lighthouse, but my eye is taken by something remarkable: in this light and from this angle, that giant black storm cloud looks like a dog lying down. And the lighthouse beside it looks like a helter skelter. It is the very image that has been seared into my mind since Seldom died. And then, odder still, a bolt of lightning flashes across the sky, eerily reminiscent of how Seldom would bare his teeth if you smiled at him. Could this be a sign? A sign from Seldom in the afterlife? Is that what has brought me here?

No, I think, this is fanciful. Stop it, Alan, you're being a berk. I chase the thought from my mind like a vicar hosing confetti

---

22 Big moment coming at the end of this sentence, guys.

23 I'm about to use the name of the book within the prose itself.

24 Here it comes.

25 Oh my God, I'm about to say it.

26 Absolutely superb. I am *so* glad I did that.

off a footpath and begin to head home. I have dry cleaning to collect or I'll have nothing to wear for Esther McVey's barbecue in a few days ...

NEW WAYS OF THINKING

October 2011

'Getting Back on TV: A Roadmap? Private and confidential?' boomed the sales assistant with a smirk.

'Here,' I said curtly, aware that every other customer and most of the staff were craning their necks to see who it was for.

It was October 2011 – notice the italics – and I was in a branch of Prontaprint where I'd come to have my latest work printed and leather-bound. The document, a 95-page tome of pure laser-focused strategy, was the product of several weeks of brainstorming, jotting, deleting, rejotting and blue-skying, and I was extremely pleased with it. But not so pleased I wanted it advertised to the world by a bellowing shop boy.

'Private and confidential means classified,' I hissed. 'I'd thank you not to holler it to all and sundry. Do you think the CIA had its dossier on killing Bin Laden shouted out for all to hear?'

'If they had it printed in a Prontaprint, yeah.'

I glared at him. I'd really got into glaring recently, finding it an effective way of losing your temper without having to think of a cutting remark.[27]

---

27 I was also pleased with my use of the 'do you think the CIA did such-and-such when hunting for Bin Laden?' put-down. The bearded al-Qaeda frontman had been killed while resisting arrest five months earlier and comparing someone's efforts unfavourably to those of the CIA was my go-to slag-off for a further twelve months.

'Two hundred and twenty nine, ninety,' he grinned.

I paid, took the book, discarded the plastic bag it had been slotted into by throwing it on the floor of the shop, and whooshed away.

For the next few weeks, that book never left my side/bag. This intensely personal piece of work was my bible, a step-by-step blueprint to re-establish myself as a presence on British TV screens.

I won't go into the specifics – I may want to sell the book for money in the future – but put it this way, as a strategic field guide, it was literally bulletproof.[28] *Under the chapters Focus, Mindset, Objectives, Get Real, Action Points, Refocus, No Surrender, Edmonds, Marketing and Troubleshooting, the book provided a how-to guide outlining what I needed to do and when, with Plans A, B, C, D and E prescribed in forensic detail.*

Essentially, the strategy involved me getting the word out that I'd be amenable to the kind of shitty presenting work I might previously have scoffed at – including online and youth-orientated. With a raft of credits amassed in short order, I could then start to apply for longer-form corporate presentations. This in turn would get me on the radar of talent bookers and producers in regional TV. From there it was guest VTs or stand-in work on the digital channels, before making the leap to similar gigs on the core terrestrial networks. Then it was a hop, skip and jump to my own shows, or anchoring roles on blue-riband titles in the spheres of current affairs, factual or chat. It would be:

1. *Easy*
2. *Peasy*
3. *Lemon, and finally . . .*
4. *Squeezy*

---

28 Although not literally.

I would read passages in bed every night, or as much as I could before sleepiness overwhelmed me and I dropped off with my book and mouth open. I was ready.

I SHALL

'Avast! Avast!' screams the barrowman. 'Land, two points abaft the beam, starboard side. Land, I say!'

With the captain nowhere to be seen, you turn to order the coxswain to change course but he too has abandoned his post. The ship, now a helpless item of flotsam, lurches landwards once again, borne on the big, wet shoulders of a wave. You are far too close to the shore.

'Tis 1793, and as midshipman of the *Amsterdam* – a merchant ship under the banner of the Dutch East India Company – you instantly sense danger. You look round, the weather – wind with bits of rain in it – lashing your cheeks like liquid shrapnel. No matter, for yours is a weather-beaten face – a craggy, bestubbled visage that speaks of decades at sea, with narrowed eyes that both squint and glint.

The captain appears – all smooth skin and large, privileged nostrils. 'Helm down! Let her come up!' he bellows, but there's panic in his voice.

'You helm down like that, fair chance you'll scuttle her,' you say, removing the pipe from betwixt your teeth.

'We'll see, shall we?' brays the captain.

'Happen we will.'

A second later, it occurs. GRAAAAAAAP! The rock cleaves open the belly of the ship, cargo spilling from its underside much as tinned food spills from the burst bottom of a cheap

39

plastic carrier bag. The ship severs into two. The back end – or stern – of the ship is lost for ever in the freezing inky-black waters. And suddenly the front section – or prow – starts its deathly descent into the depths, its plunge almost reluctant, like a hand gingerly reaching into a blocked U-bend at the home of an elderly relative.

The men leap off the stricken boat, their legs doing a running action in mid-air like the Isle of Man logo before they are lost to the waters.

You peer down at the rolling seas. Amid the gloom, you can just make out people dotted between floating crates – human croutons in a massive bowl of cold cargo soup. Barrels of sugar, spices and rum have burst open and bled into the brine, making the ocean spray taste a bit like dandelion and burdock, or a Bacardi and blackcurrant if you're a young woman.

A young woman! you think, and you remember that somewhere on board is Eliza, the flame-haired (i.e. ginger) harbourmaster's daughter you had fallen for back in Exmouth. Yours had been a forbidden love, her waistcoated father adamant that she would never marry a seafarer below officer class. But you had knocked 'pon her window in the dead of night and said, 'Come. Come away with me.' And come away she had, hiding in your quarters where you'd spend nights sharing hopes for the future and having sex.

'Eliza! Eliza!'

'I am here,' she trills and emerges from her cabin. 'What is it, my love?'

And you explain what's happening with the crash and whatnot.

'Will we die?' she says, her timid voice wobbling like a jelly, even though jellies don't exist yet.

You look away, unable to answer. 'I promised you happiness. Seems I have failed you,' you whisper.

She touches your face. 'You have never failed at anything in your life,' the beautiful woman says. 'You're perfect.'

You tell Eliza to jump. Only when satisfied that *all* crew have abandoned ship do you even consider doing the same – that's leadership – at which point you pinch your nostrils closed because you don't have your nose clip and . . . jump.

Whooooooosh! Then silence. You plunge beneath the surface, suddenly at peace as your ears are temporarily jammed by compacted water. Then you emerge, shaking your head so your long hair releases droplets of water similar to a Davidoff advert.

The yelps and hollers of the panicking men temporarily disorientate you – why you can nary hear yourself think. If only it weren't so bloody dark! You're a strong swimmer – excelling especially in backstroke and the newly invented butterfly – and ordinarily you'd be able to cut through the waves and tow Eliza by the chin until you made landfall where, after a brief rest, you could have sex again. But without being able to see . . .

And then . . . *salvation.*

For suddenly – KUKUM! – a light comes on. 'Tis a lighthouse! May God be praised! Suddenly the cartography of the shoreline can be seen by swimmers and drowners alike.

'Land!' you say. 'It's this way!'

But when you turn you see the men are frolicking and playing. 'Now! Come on! You'll die! Get out of the fucking water now!'

'Bloody hell, easy,' says a voice.

'Get out of the water! Get out of the water!'

'Alan, stop.' replies the voice. 'I said stop! Jesus Christ, you're scaring the kids.'

What?

* * *

'I said stop. Please, Alan, the children.'

On that, I look around me – remembering I am not in the ice-cold waters of the English Channel but in the now equally frosty environment of Esther McVey's summer barbecue. In the pool, children are whimpering, some quite pathetically.

All around are the staring eyes of women I recognise from the worlds of broadcasting and politics.[29] Women who wouldn't have stood a chance in dark, freezing water, by the way. Their bushy, blow-dried hair styles would take on huge amounts of water, in the same way a sheep would. The absorbency of wool – it can absorb up to 30 per cent of its weight in water – is why you never see knitted swimming trunks, although I concede there are other reasons too.

I press pause on my shipwreck daydream, parking it for later rather than ditching it completely, because I still want to get to the swimming to shore and having sex bit.

I take stock of my surroundings. My hair is dishevelled, so messy you wouldn't even be able to say with confidence whether I comb to the left or the right. My eyes are wild, my breathing shallow and heavy, if that's possible.

Dermot O'Leary approaches warily and slowly takes something from me. I realise now that I had been holding a lamp, one of those outdoor uplighters that had been trained on a tree – why do people light trees? – and beaming it towards the pool, acting for all the world like a deranged human lighthouse.

But I am not a lighthouse. I am a man who hasn't slept for days and is now concerning guests at Esther McVey's summer barbecue.

I straighten my hair – it's to the right, by the way, the nap of the hair sits flatter in that direction – and mutter some apologies.

---

29 Two realms Esther straddles quite, quite elegantly.

'I should go,' I say. Normally when I say I should go – such as after singing the song from *The Greatest Showman* when a woman has invited me back for coffee, or accidentally letting off in a judo hold – I expect, and receive, a, 'No, don't be silly,' but today not a single person no-don't-be-sillies me. Worse, Esther says, 'You should go.'

'Yeah, I did just say that, Esther,' I snap.

* * *

Everywhere I look over the next few days – whether cooking dinner, looking at pictures of totem poles or having a quiet night in with a cherished friend – I see the lighthouse. It's there in the shape of a pepper mill, a wine bottle, a stick of celery, a totem pole, a Belisha beacon, a sex aid, a church steeple and a swearing finger. Over the course of several evenings, I even find myself forming a lighthouse from compacted bits of mashed potato, but I throw it away when it starts to go brown.

It's as if the lighthouse is trying to force itself into my consciousness. But why?

It is speaking to me. Why? Because lighthouses are *important*. And just because people have gone off them and moved onto younger buildings, it doesn't mean we should leave lighthouses unheralded. No, we should spend money restoring them to former glory.

One of my favourite pieces of writing is this brief essay on lighthouses. It is reproduced here with the kind permission of its author[30] and publisher.[31]

---

30 Me.
31 Me.

They say we don't need lighthouses. They say we have global positioning systems now, we have depth sounders, X-band radar and electronic charting systems. They say a ship's captain could navigate with his eyes closed (and I'm told that is something they do when drunk). Easy peasy, they say. Nothing can go wrong, they say.

BUT WHAT IF IT DOES?

What if a cyber hack causes the world's entire GPS system to fail? What then? What if the Russians invent a nautical radar jammer? What if the charting systems crash? What if someone left the depth sounders on the quayside and they're sitting there now, useless and covered in seagull shit? What then?

Suddenly, shorn of these whizz-bang navigational aids, ships would be literally all at sea. In the pitch black, you'd have oil tankers ploughing towards Portsmouth, ready to shed their gloopy load all over the harbour. And look there, a passenger ferry about to crash into Hastings, spilling immigrants across the beach, something the residents of Hastings – still reeling from the unwelcome arrival of the Normans – famously cannot stand. Yonder, there's a cargo ship full of electric vehicles and it's careering towards Kent, spinning bow-doors first into Folkestone and vomiting its payload of Teslas all over Britain's already-congested roads. A cruise liner full of pensioners somehow drifts into the Solent, crushing yachts and ruining Cowes Week for the braying coked-up idiots who like to attend.

Quickly! someone would say. Let's turn on the lighthouses so people can see where the bloody hell they are. Ah. Just one problem. We forgot about their upkeep. We let them crumble into the sea. Or we demolished them to build an authentic seaside café that sells £15 fish and chips.

Or they've been turned into Airbnbs and there's a bathtub where the giant lightbulb should be. We thought we knew it all and now we're paying the price for our own stupid, stupid arrogance.

An unlikely turn of events? Perhaps. But do you wanna take that risk?

Anyway, aside from their admittedly far-fetched practical use, how about a bit of respect? Chances are, your elderly parents have zero practical benefits either – but you still respect 'em! Would you let granny and grandad fall into the sea, or be destroyed by diggers? Of course not. So it seems insane that we don't afford the same privileges to coastal buildings.

When I look at a lighthouse, I see a certain majesty. A proud defiance. A structure of solemn fortitude that says, Let the rain lash at my flanks, let the wind pummel my face, let the sea feed on my feet, let time ravage my innards. I shall still remain standing. Ready to shine my light.

You may be dazzled by the new. The vagaries of fashion may draw your eye elsewhere, to one of those glass and steel office blocks that for some reason looks like it's leaning because architects think straight lines are naff, or to a high-rise apartment complex because apparently the phrase 'block of flats' is considered shit. By all means, shower these new buildings with acclaim. But here the lighthouse shall remain, distant from other structures, noble, selfless.

Its walls may not house a start-up company that makes apps, or an indoor skate park or a fleet of Mercedes-Benzes. But what does it offer? It helps people. It offers guidance in times of need. Yes, these misunderstood cylinders think only of others. And I reckon it's time we remembered that.

Just a really nice piece of writing. And there are always going to be cynics. People who say, 'Are you really talking about light-houses, or are you talking about yourself because you're worried you're past it?' To which I say, *I'm on about the first one.*

I need to think. *Something* wants me to dwell on all this. Could it be that this is what Seldom wants me to do with my life? Like *Field of Dreams*, but instead of Kevin Costner building a baseball stadium because a ghost told him to, it would be me, Alan Partridge, restoring one of our nation's most important monuments because a dead dog told me to – not actually any more ludicrous than the Costner one.

Nitpickers (e.g. my editor) will doubt the veracity of this vision, or complain that it is broadly the same construct I used to motivate the revival of my TV career, that I'm taking the idea of honouring the wishes of a dying friend and retooling it with a dog – and in adjacent chapters, as well. Think about it, though. Who would structure a book like that? That's how you know it's real.

* * *

The morning after Esther's barbecue, still sheepish at having been asked to leave, I slink back to collect my coat. I'm feeling a little awkward but I have to say Esther could *not* be nicer – she'll bend over backwards for anyone as long as they're not on benefits and speak English as their first language.

She ushers me into the kitchen where, just my luck, several of the previous day's guests, who had stayed the night, are tucking into a cooked breakfast, or rather several cooked breakfasts, i.e. one each. Andrew Castle, Gary Barlow, Liz Kershaw, James Martin, Theo Paphitis and Carole Malone, plus partners – a who's who of people you'd expect to find eating a fry-up at Esther McVey's house.

As they cram the greased food into their mouths, they're having an animated debate about coloured wheelie bins. 'We used to have one metal dustbin for everything and everyone was a damn sight happier,' argues Malone, coherently.

'Yeah! Now it's one bin for paper, one bin for glass and another for . . . oh, I can't remember all the different ones, but I do know it's completely bloody stupid!' attempts Martin, who's less good at this than the others.

'I blame recycling!' chortles Barlow.

Everyone agrees that recycling is annoying, while Castle, with one eye on his talk radio show, frantically scribbles notes and mutters, 'This is gold, this is gold.'

'If you finished with something, get rid,' insists Paphitis. 'Why do we have to bring things we've finished with back to life?'

'I *would* bring back hanging,' muses McVey. Oh, absolutely, they all agree. Hanging's different. No, they're talking more about things you don't use anymore.

I am enjoying the conversation immensely. If I had any plans to mount a TV comeback, 'Esther's Breakfast Bar' or 'Home Truths with Esther' would be at the top of my list. But since I don't, I just join in.

'Mind you, I saw a broken old lighthouse yesterday,' I smile. 'You wouldn't want to bin that!'

'I would,' scoffs Kershaw. 'At least if you do up a cottage in the Cotswolds you get to gut the inside, partition it into a four-bed and turn it into a luxury holiday rental. A lighthouse'll be conservation this, English Heritage that and Grade II listed blah, blah, blah, and everyone having to tiptoe around the place just because it's old. This is what I'd do to the lighthouse.' And on that, she uses the back of a fork to mash a potato waffle into what is left of her beans. I know it is only a waffle, but it feels really mean.

Everyone else is laughing and laughing, their mouths agape like pink cauldrons of laughter and egg and sausage.

'Well, some people like old maritime buildings,' I say. The laughter stops. 'Some people don't agree with any of you, actually. Some people think we should preserve our national treasures. Some people have a bit of respect.'

Silence. The lump is still there in my throat, but I recognise it now as fury – at the state of the lighthouse I'd seen. How dare the locals let it fall into that state. How dare they care so little for a treasured totem of our maritime heritage?

'You rebuild it, then.' This is Barlow.

'I just might, Gary.' And I nod at them in turn. 'Andrew. Liz. Theo. James. Carole.'

'It's Carole with an "e".'

'I know it's with an "e",' I shout. 'They're pronounced the same, Carole! Oh, and the glasses around your neck aren't fooling anyone: you're thick and you know it.'[32]

And I am away, heading for the door.

Esther's Breakfast Bar! I conclude in that moment that any lingering interest I've had in a television career is well and truly gone. I am going to buy and restore an English lighthouse. And I will call it Seldom.

---

32 I later sent Carole some flowers to apologise. On the note I wrote: 'I was in the wrong, you're not thick, you're just an annoying woman who struggles to be funny. Best wishes, Alan Partridge'.

STASIS

January 2012

By the start of 2012, my TV renaissance had borne as much fruit as my assistant eats – none. With every setback, I would slink back to the restorative bosom of North Norfolk Digital in the same way a joey would slink back to the inside of its mother's pouch.

One morning, I asked my assistant to compile a list of TV commissioners, including names, phone numbers and other details such as were they gay, were they a man or woman, and did they have an unusual hobby (e.g. were they gay)? The plan? To do my radio show then spend the afternoon hammering the phones – speaking to the commissioners and offering my services.

By the time I'd got in the car, my assistant had emailed through a list of contact details. A worryingly quick turnaround that suggested she had had a list to hand already. But why? Oh God, no . . .

At lunchtime, I demanded that she hand over her laptop and password.[33] A quick scan of her emails confirmed my worst fears. She had been 'using her initiative' (something her contract expressly forbids) to offer my services to every TV channel she could think of, and a few she couldn't.

The missives were peppered with clumsy attempts at formal phrasing: 'to who it may concern' [my emphasis] and 'I trust this finds you well', but worse – much worse – were her attempts to market me. According to her letters, I was 'presentable, neat, punctual and

---

33 Of course it was 'jesusiscoming'.

good', I would give most things a go 'if medically allowed', and she even told Channel 4 that I could 'do a young person's accent' and 'was prepared to use any of the following swearwords: shit, penis, twit, ass, arse, bloody and the n-word'. As I read them, I could feel my ass/ arse closing up with embarrassment.

Elsewhere, she had culled entire passages from an old online dating profile I'd written so that mixed in with my professional skills were declarations that I enjoyed the company of clean women, preferred 'real chests only, please' and was happy to pay for dinner on dates one, three, five and seven. While accurate, the letters when read together by a prospective employer were nonsense.

Sitting in the North Norfolk Digital studio, things felt bleak. But as I stared at the monitor in front of me, scanning a depressing list of shit-sounding jingles (from 'station ident 1' to 'station ident short' to 'funky jingle v2' to 'news slam intro' to 'news slam outro' to 'weather sponsor with VO' to 'weather sponsor original' to 'sexy jingle do not play before 9 p.m.'), I decided to do something.

There and then, I typed out a text message to accept an invitation to do a piece of sports commentary. I was going back to where it had all begun for me. Yes, this was in many ways a degrading backwards step, but maybe it was the kickstart I needed.

MY TRANSITION BEGINS
(NOT GENDER)

November 2021

I'm glaring at a man. He's standing in my bedroom, staring me down, without a shred of contrition. Honestly, the *nerve* of him. Eventually, I speak.

'Have you got a problem, mate?'

The man says nothing, but he continues to hold my gaze. I take half a step closer. 'I said, "Have you got a fucking problem?"'

The man raises his eyebrows, as if amused, mocking me almost. This guy!

'Because if you do,' I say, 'let's step outside, son. Have a little chat there. Then maybe I'll give your face a problem, how about that?'

The man shows no inclination to step outside. So I make a sudden movement and he does too. I snort in disdain.

'Nah, didn't think so. You know what you are? Chicken shit. You heard. So get your things, and *get out*.'

Then, with my arms out slightly to make myself look wider, I stand there, cock of the walk. God, that felt good.

That little exercise, a scripted tough-guy conversation between me and my own reflection, was taught to me by Ross Kemp and I've never forgotten it. Ross performs a version of this in the full-length mirror in his hallway every time he leaves the house, as a way of reminding himself he's tough and to pump himself up in the pecs. Me? I only tend to do it when I need to steel myself for an important occasion or a big decision.

And boy, am I facing a big decision now. I'm about to embark on a potentially life-altering change of circumstances, bigger even than going vegetarian for a week back in 2019: it will mean leaving behind the cashmere comfort blanket that is Norfolk for a whole new life by the seaside, where I'll do my bit for Britain's architectural heritage. And while my assistant is yet to be convinced, that's very much her problem and not mine.[34]

---

34 Her concern was that I had a tendency to become unhealthily obsessed by things at times of crisis in my life. For example the following relationship, which I am only prepared to discuss here in a footnote. For several weeks in late 2013, I had been romantically entangled with a recently-retired female judoka. Lady A – as she will be referred to in order to conceal her identity – was a woman who knew exactly what she wanted. Between the sheets, feedback was frequent and unambiguous. 'Do it faster.' 'Bounce me slower.' 'You're making that noise again, Alan.' She didn't muck about when it came to physicality, either, the early exchanges of lovemaking typically characterised by an abundance of shoving and grabbing. (In general she would shove and I would grab, though mainly to stop myself falling off the bed.)

Sexy talk was no less forthright. As she entered a state of elevated arousal, Lady A would begin to refer to me using terms that wouldn't so much make a vicar blush as make him just sit there not saying anything for quite a long time, before standing up and saying he has to go now.

The key was not to take it personally. If there were occasions when I felt myself becoming upset, I'd simply say I needed the loo, and (if permission was granted) a few minutes alone reciting positive affirmations would generally right me, before I'd request permission to re-enter and head back to the coalface. For some, having to take this kind of time out would be a real passion killer. Fortunately for me, however, that has never been an issue. For whatever reason, I am one of those men who is relatively quick to stiffen.

With completion achieved (hers, not mine – I tended not to), all mention of me being a worthless subhuman piece of shit who couldn't even keep his family together, or whatever, would instantly cease as she picked up her phone and went back to looking at judo news. Ultimately, though, our flame, which had burned so brightly, was to be snuffed out by Christmas as Lady A left me for a short bald man who used to serve in the SAS. They were just a better fit.

Do I need pumping up? You better believe it. And getting shirty with my own reflection just works. As Ross says, 'If you wanna be a big boy, you've got to *act* the big boy.' And now I feel ready.

Ready to raise the funds needed to purchase a ruin, ready to make the necessary arrangements to move (by instructing my assistant to do that for me), and ready to find the perfect building. In one movement, I grab my car keys, gate fob, phone, wallet, jacket, belt and cap. And then off I go to meet a real estate agent – by which I mean an agent of 'real estate' rather than an 'estate agent' who's real. Important to make that clear.

* * *

'Can you stop talking about *Fraggle Rock* now, please?'

I am in a greasy-spoon café on Sheringham high street, for my second mealtime of the day. I'm eating eggs Benedict, which in this establishment comes with chips and baked beans – but then so does everything else.

Opposite sits Edward, an estate agent with a knot in his tie so egregiously fat I want to reach over and yank it to an acceptable size before he can stop me. But I don't. On the table before me, the particulars for six lighthouses are fanned out. Somerset. Dorset. Yorkshire. Sussex. Cornwall. And Scotland, although I haven't really looked at that one because I'm obviously not going to move to Fife.

Somerset looks promising. Dorset isn't bad. Yorkshire has a dollop of Heinz Beans on it because my assistant distracted me while I was putting the spoon to my mouth. The blurb for Cornwall boasts of its many appearances on the small screen in a much-loved children's show, prompting Edward to launch into a freewheeling and seemingly pointless description of the show *Fraggle Rock*, which is now entering its tenth minute even though my assistant and I have made clear we've never heard of it.

Edward stops talking about *Fraggle Rock*. I look out of the window. 'Do you have anything in Kent at all?' I ask. 'Maybe in and around, say . . . Abbot's Cliff?'

The agent looks surprised. 'Oh, well. There is one right there, yes. But it's currently under offer.'

'Beat the offer,' I say, dabbing at my mouth with a paper napkin before standing up. I shove the chair back with my legs, forgetting it's bolted into the floor, meaning the edge of the seat just digs into the back of my knees. 'Ow.'

The agent finds the lighthouse in question on his phone. Constructed in 1860, for over a century and a half its one giant eye has swivelled this way and that to calmly guide vessels westward towards the port of Folkestone. And though derelict, it has a grace and nobility well beyond the reach of any of the new breed of younger, more fashionable lighthouses that probably have their own social-media accounts. Well, I just fall in love with the place.

Yet my assistant isn't so sure. As she shuffles from foot to foot, emitting the vague smell of jumble sale, I know she has something to say.

'Only thing is, Alan . . .'

Told you.

'I'm just not sure it's the right thing to do.'

'That's exactly what you said about getting a microwave,' I shoot back. 'Now look at you. You can ping and ding with the best of them.'

'It's just . . . if you're trying to get one over on someone . . . let bitterness take hold and it will never let go. It's like *Japanese knotweed*.'

'You don't have to stress the word Japanese,' I retort. 'It's not their fault. And this is nothing to do with anyone else. This is about doing something with meaning, something that takes a rundown ruin and turns it into something special. Look at me, I've never been happier! I'm fizzing around the place like a soluble pain killer. I'm like Solpadeine. You know all about Solpadeine, don't you?'

She smiles and does a little nod. She likes it when she can join in with my similes.

* * *

Later that day, I spin around in my office chair, as it helps me think and looks cool. Then to business: I tot up how much I still need to raise using a calculator that's on the last dregs of its battery. The read-out is incredibly faint and intermittent, but eventually a number swims into view, like a Victorian ghost appearing at a foggy window before disappearing.

I have already begun divesting myself of *some* of my assets. First to be recalled was the start-up loan of £35k I'd given to two models from Brighton who wanted to start a green-juice business. Next to be recouped was my minority stake in race-horse Northern Ireland Protocol. I only invested in it in the first place because I was trying to impress a group of friends who earn more money than I do. My portfolio of shares was the next to be sold off. Shell – gone. BP – gone. Nestlé – gone. HSBC – gone. Amazon – gone. Uber – gone. Bet365 – gone. Shoe Zone – retained.[35]

I also agreed to front an advertising campaign for a Chechnya-based hotel chain. Initially I had been hesitant on account of

---

35 Had no choice, joint investment with assistant.

needing to do a photoshoot in just my swimming trunks. But needs must, and by adding a clause to the contract insisting they digitally deflate my stomach, lower back and chin, and inflate my calves, quads, pecs, hands and lips, I felt comfortable I'd emerge with much of my dignity intact.

With *some* of my assets now liquid, and my pecs and tummy successfully monetised, I have put together a formidable war chest. And while it would be vulgar to discuss exactly how much the shortfall is, I'm not embarrassed to say it is in the medium to high tens of thousands. Am I surprised or upset? No. It's a figure I could still comfortably raise on my own; I'm very well off and one of the shrewdest investors I know. I have a collection of vintage mobile phones in a shoebox that must be worth a few grand. And I estimate I own at least five thousand pounds' worth of good quality bric-a-brac. No, I'm not short of a few bob, not even close, and anyone saying I am is either looking at my accounts for 2010–11 or full of shit.

However, something is nagging at me. If I am to pull this project off, I'll feel pretty damn proud of myself. But then I think: Isn't that quite selfish, to keep all of that pride to myself? What if there was a way of letting other people feel proud as well? If I was to, say, ask the public to donate money as part of a crowdfunding scheme, maybe then, ordinary people could claim a share of that pride for themselves? It feels like the kindest thing I can do, even though, as I say, I don't need to do it because I have plenty of dosh of my own.

I jot down a short blurb, explaining that the lighthouse renovation will be 'funded **by** the community, built **for** the community, and feel like it belongs **to** the community'. The 'feel like' is an important caveat because, of course, legally it will be owned entirely by me, a point I underline at the bottom in a much smaller font.

I illustrate the page with a painting of celebrated lighthouse heroine Grace Darling and add a few hundred words culled from Google on her stunning legacy. Not that she has anything to do with this lighthouse. Hers is in Scotland. Nor is she any more heroic than any other lighthouse keeper. After all, she only saved nine lives, whereas the average for male lighthouse keepers is likely to be in double figures. I don't know, I just feel that in the current climate her inherent 'womanness' will help broaden the reach of the appeal.

To entice donors further, a branded T-shirt, tote bag and mug will be sent to each of them. Designed by me with the help of a millennial employee in Prontaprint who kept taking the mouse and doing it for me rather than just explaining how to do it then letting me learn for myself, the merchandise features a picture of yours truly in the foreground, with the lighthouse behind. And by choosing a photo where I am extending my hand, I have created the illusion that I am holding the lighthouse in my palm, a visual effect taught to me by a holidaying South Korean child at the world-famous tilting Tower of Pisa.[36]

It isn't just the money. No, I enjoy the thought of being a piece of something bigger, part of a wider team of history buffs and kindly philanthropists – leading the way while a thousand back-seat drivers chip in with their twopenn'orth at every opportunity. Yep, cannot wait.

By the end of 2021, when the crowdfunding deadline arrives, I have raised a healthy amount. Is it a shame that the incidental costs (T-shirts, mugs and totes; the price of couriering the merchandise to donors – mainly in Norfolk but one guy is in Malaysia – plus the fee for the Prontaprint professional design service that I had mistaken for Duwaine just showing me how

---

36 Thanks, Do-yun!

to use the computer) came to £6,000? A little, but once I've topped up the pot with a small bridging loan signed off by the team at Bradford & Bingley, I have the money I need.[37]

Six days later, I sit in my conservatory, pen in hand, poised to sign the mortgage contract. As my housekeeper buzzes around taking the official photos under the direction of my assistant – 'chin up slightly', 'very nice', 'bit more teeth', 'not that much teeth', 'tuck in the tummy', 'perfect' – I bring down the pen and sign.

The lighthouse is mine.

I am now quite simply – and it's not a name I will use again because it sounds quite childish – the big beacon boy.

*   *   *

As excited as I am about my new life by the sea, cutting the umbilical cord that tethers me to Norfolk isn't going to be easy. She is thick and she is fleshy, and I am going to need some very big scissors. But just as I will miss Norfolk, so Norfolk will miss me too. Not to toot my own bugle,[38] but I've been one of the biggest dogs in the county for the best part of thirty years. And when someone like that is no longer there, it leaves a hole. I am

---

37 I've always thought Bradford & Bingley sound like the names of two talking dogs in a shit live-action Disney film. Setting up Bradford as an old-school aristocrat type and Bingley as his loyal but long-suffering butler would fail to resonate with the kids of today. A safer bet for Disney would be to make Bradford a boy dog that used to be a girl dog and Bingley a girl dog that used to be a boy dog. Tapping into the prevailing wokeness of modern culture but handling the subject with sensitivity and care would make a surefire success of any such tranny dog franchise. But what do I know?

38 Until recently I'd have started this sentence with 'Not to blow my own trumpet', but I have since been told the phrase is a euphemism for bending double and self-fellating.

a well-known face around Norwich, adding a dash of cheer to people's days. I'll shake hands with a greengrocer, I'll say hello to a butcher, I'll shake hands with a corner-shop owner. I'll chat to (female) beggars, offer feedback to buskers, and be the very visible face of campaigns against any council plans – e.g. the pedestrianisation of Norwich city centre – that are a clear backward step for the community. I don't always have time for shelf stackers, but a nod in their direction as I grab a fresh pack of All-Bran? You better believe it.

However, exiting the county will also pose some fairly hefty administrative challenges, so I sit down with my assistant, and over tea and toast and toffees we begin to map things out. I'm not exactly awash with cash now, and so she suggests, wrongly, that I should put the oasthouse on Airbnb.

'Absolutely no *way*,' is my reply. 'No way will I ever do that. Complete strangers milling about in my house?'

'Yes, but you'll be living in Kent. And the income will—'

'Ain't happening. Some inner-city family I've never met clattering round my house, scratching themselves in my bed? Cutting their toenails perched on the edge of the bath? Sitting in underpants on my sofa without even having the good grace to put down a dog towel? Absolutely not. Not now, not ever.'

With that subject dealt with, it's on to more workaday matters.

First to be tackled is my membership of the David Lloyd Health & Racquets Club. Financially it would make sense to cancel this membership, but socially? No way. You see, whereas London has the Carlton and the Groucho, Norwich has the David Lloyd, and anyone who's anyone is a member there: the movers, the shakers, the gluten-free bakers.[39] Quite simply, the David Lloyd is where things get done. Exchanging business

---

39 Elias Parsons, CEO of NorfoBake.

cards in the steam room. Floating a proposal as you and a senior businessmen talc each other down by the lockers. Looking into the whites of a fellow exec's eyes as you hammer out a deal in the showers.

Calling up manager Richard Juice, I make a bold pitch.[40] My request is that he place my membership on hold while I am out of county, to be re-activated upon my return. Juice gives this short shrift. If I don't want the membership there are plenty who will. I counter: OK, then, will he allow me to put my membership on hold *if* I continue to pay my monthly membership fee? We have a deal.

A more emotional parting comes with my pub-quiz teamers. Familiar faces at the Boxley Wheatsheaf, Tony Blanch, Clive Lambeth, Phil Tin and I have been pub quizzing under the name Cromwell's Bitches since 2007. And we've been through a lot. The final in '09 when we narrowly edged out the Periodic Table Dancers to walk away with the coveted Copper Tankard. The final in '10 when they narrowly won it back again. Phil's wife's cancer. The semis in '16 when a steward's inquiry saw us disqualified for alleged Google use in the disabled bogs. Like I say, a lot. So saying ta-ta hurts.

As for my hair and beauty team, well, I reach an agreement with the Thai lady who burns off my nasal hair that she will make the trip to Kent every two months, while my hairdressers (I have three on rotation in order to foster a healthy sense of competition) will be contacted if I am unable to find suitable arrangements near the lighthouse.[41]

---

40 As a child Richard Juice had been known as Dick Juice but had to rebrand as Richard when a female colleague took offence.
41 Their names are Giovanni, Gianni and Luca, and they are all third-generation Italian (i.e. English).

Finally, it's an email to everyone in my contacts, and I must have started it a dozen times. How to get the tone right when there are so many different people to appeal to? Important people like friends and celebrities, and others like tradesmen and a paediatrician I know. In the end I just force myself to begin and say that if I stop before the email is finished I won't be allowed a treat after my tea. It works better than I could ever have imagined.

Did I know I was going to pen a poem? I can honestly say I didn't, yet what flows from my brain, nay my *heart*, is a piece of writing of which I remain immensely proud. The email is reproduced below.

Pals,
Alas it's time for me to flee
Riding south to Kent and sea
Tears are forming in my ducts
Round fat droplets, fit for ducks
I pray that you keep safe and well
Do not forget my face, my smell
Go raise a glass, sup by the gallon
Ever yours, your good friend Alan.

Then underneath, I write the rubric: 'The above is an **acrostic** poem where the first letter of each line spells PARTRIDGE.'

My assistant feels I should delete that explanation, as if pointing out the acronym somehow makes it feel less good. I disagree, arguing successfully that the small chance someone might not notice what I'd done is simply a risk too far, since, without the acronym, the poem could be seen as potentially shit.

* * *

And then the day comes, 7 February 2022. The day I am leaving Norfolk.

I had aimed to be on the road by about quarter past eight, that way I could get through town before the school run. I was determined to spend today in good spirits but knew this would be impossible if I had to contend with any lollipop ladies. Their total inability to understand that a driver stopping for them is a convention and not the law never fails to wind me up. The right of way remains at all times *with the vehicle on the carriageway*; stopping is at the *driver's* discretion and if they judge that *not* stopping is what they wish to do, a lollipop lady has neither the *legal* recourse to do anything about it, nor the *moral* right to pull her face.

Fortunately for me, I am bang on schedule, and with both car and snacks packed, I close my front door and head to my vehicle. I flick my head round to take one last look at the oasthouse, my chin resting on my shoulder in a way that's accidentally coquettish but does prove I would have been quite sexy if I'd been born a lady.

That thought is disturbed by the ringing noise a telephone makes when it rings. I jog backside the house and pick up.

'Hello, Partridge.'

'What the hell are you playing at?'

I recognise the voice instantly. It's my former *This Time* producer Howard Newman. 'Hello, Howard.'

'You bought our fucking *lighthouse*.'

Oh dear. Howard seems angry and, as you can imagine, that makes me very, very sad. 'Sorry – *your* lighthouse?'

'It was going to be a running feature of the show for the next year. A historic renovation in honour of the Princess Royal, community involvement, Jennie doing the whole *Challenge Anneka* thing,[42] then we donate it to the RNLI.'

---

42 Ooh, modern reference, Howard.

'What, and you think – let me get this straight because I'm real confused right now – you think I've gazumped you and bought the lighthouse . . . out of spite? Oh, Howard, that's hurtful.'

'You're a child.'

'Thank you. I use Oil of Olay to keep my skin plump. Will there be anything else, Howard?'

'You'll regret this.'

Click. He's hung up. To this day, I feel awful about all this. A dreadful misunderstanding seems to have scuttled the centrepiece of my former employers's 2022 editorial output. I am so sad I go and have a Mars bar.

* * *

'I think that's a bloody eagle!'

It was forty minutes later and I was on the A140 noticing something in the corner of my eye – not literally the corner of my eye, that was just a benign growth that appeared the previous Christmas after I'd tried to rinse some grit from my eye using vinegar, but somewhere in my peripheral vision. A dark splodge against the slate-grey Norfolk sky. Shutting my left eye because the Sarson's tumour made it quite hard to focus, the splodge suddenly revealed itself. It was a bird. But not a basic bird – neither a basic boring bird like a sparrow nor a basic rudely-named bird like a tit or thrush – no, this appeared to be nothing short of an eagle.

I had just passed the village of Scole, the last conurbation before exiting Norfolk, and was suddenly overwhelmed by a strong sense that, far from just flying around looking for something to do, this majestic feathered creature had been with me the whole way, guiding me safely to the county border like an avine police outrider.

I lowered my window. 'Farewell, dear friend! Prithee well!'

I considered what to say to it next and quite liked the phrase 'winged guardian', but couldn't think of how to put it in a sentence. Also, I don't like the *Guardian*. I closed the window again.[43]

Yet the message wasn't lost on me. Just as birds emigrate – I think eagles go to Spain – so *I* was emigrating, to Kent.

---

43 When I later relayed this story to an ornithologist friend of mine (to the extent that you can ever *really* be friends with an ornithologist) he said it wouldn't have been an eagle because there are no eagles indigenous to this country. Ultimately, though, he just couldn't handle the fact that something he'd tried to see all year, I'd just seen from my car window and wasn't even that arsed.

GOING PLACES
(OF MY LIFE)

March 2012

I was providing live commentary at a seniors' badminton tournament at Cromer leisure centre. The fee wasn't great, but I needed to swing by anyway to collect my bodywarmer and underpants from the lost-property box.

I wouldn't say I was the world's biggest badminton aficionado, but by the time we got to the semi-finals I had largely mastered the terminology: 'And Clive Kennedy absolutely WALLOPS the cockleshut.'

It was then that I spotted none other than Norwich carpet king-pin Brendan O'Coyle. His chain of CarpetChief stores had been the dominant player in the Norfolk flooring scene for over two decades. Retail or domestic, carpet or laminate, those guys had it covered. Literally. If it was inside and you could walk on it, it was probably CarpetChief.[44]

---

44 In those days CarpetChief was riding high, although more recently things have been tougher. Designed in the 1980s, their logo featured the friendly face of a Native American chief saying, 'HOW can we help you?' Quite clever, really. But these days we live in an era when people are realising they have a problem with things they didn't have a problem with before. And though Norwich is slower to be buffeted by these changing tides than most, buffeted they eventually were, and the logo – featuring the affectionately named Big Chief Carpet Man – was quietly retired. Today he's been replaced by a talking rug. But it's just not as good.

But what was he doing here? He wasn't taking part – the last thing you could describe Coyle as was an athlete. Big gut, large arse and fingers like the sausage rolls that made up the bulk of his diet, he would have made an unlikely badmintine. No, my first thought was that he was here because the rumours that his team was being brought in to carpet the sports hall were true.

And would it have been such a mad idea? Certainly it would have put a stop to the high-pitched noises made by training shoes jamming against the rubber floor (the dreaded 'sports hall squeak'). Carpet would also cushion the falls that were an almost daily occurrence at a facility whose patrons were overwhelmingly geriatric. (The manager once told me they had 999 on speed dial, which to me seemed slightly pointless, but I didn't say that because I knew he was being bullied by his wife – for example, making him wear rubber gloves to do the washing up even when he wanted to do it without.)

As it turned out, sport-hall carpetisation was never to come to pass. The wobbly pensioners would have to take their chances. No, Brendan was there because CarpetChief was the tournament's platinum sponsor, providing a first prize of twenty-five square metres of carpet, laminate or vinyl to the winner in the men's competition and twenty square metres in the ladies'. It was a mouth-watering prize and one that went some way to explaining the ferocity of competition that afternoon.

Not that I was particularly enthused by the sport unfolding before me. By now, there was an unmistakeable half-arsedness to my delivery, even the bits that required oomph: 'Shot of the Morning sponsored by CarpetChief goes to Helga Bellamy for what's described here as a "jumping backhand with shout". Wish I'd seen that, you can imagine the skirt billowing on the way down like a German parachute . . . on one of the very missions, I think I'm right in saying, in which her father sadly died.'

I caught sight of myself in the reflection offered by a vending machine, a man in an Umbro tracksuit carrying a hefty microphone and speaker like a man on day release setting up the karaoke in the corner of a pub for a friend. I sighed, deep and long and hard.

Remember, I'd once presented live coverage of the Tour de France, of World Cup football contests, of Saturday lunchtime wrestling, I used to be a big dog[45] in the world of sports broadcasting, and while my love or tolerance of sport has waned to the point of disintegration over the years, the fact remains: I used to be an extremely successful sports broadcaster. I used to <u>be</u> somebody.

I turned away from the court, where a man was on his fifth or sixth attempt at getting his serve over the net. And I began, quite simply, to natter. Good, honest chat about my surroundings: 'A warm welcome to anyone stepping into Cromer leisure centre for the first time. The facility here has been open since 1997, barring a week in 2010 when it had to be shut down after a glass eye was found bobbing about in a ladies' toilet. This is the sports hall and the panels of composite roofing you can see above were actually taken from a decommissioned poultry factory owned by the late Bernard Matthews. If you look long enough, you can sometimes make out a feather trapped in the steel beams. Often, what looks like a stuck shuttlecock is actually just a bit off a chicken . . .'

I fizzled out. This was hopeless. I caught sight of myself in the vending machine again then accidentally said out loud, 'What the fuck am I doing?' It echoed around the sports hall like a whipcrack. I set down the speaker and microphone and decided that was enough.

I sauntered over to the vending machine, shoved in a quid and punched option zero-four, 'chicken-style soup'.[46] And as fluid filled cup, I realised Brendan O'Coyle was standing next to me.

I nodded at the carpet kingpin, mirthlessly.

---

45 Miss you, Seldom!
46 Or as it was called until recent legislation came in, 'chicken soup'.

'Brendan.'

'Alan.'

'Pleased to meetcha.'

'Ditto.'

It was a crisp opening, something I imagined the out-of-shape businessman enjoyed, although in his case it'd be a Walkers Grab Bag.

As I pushed back the vending machine's coin concealment flap to retrieve my 80p change, conversation began to flow. Brendan explained that he'd enjoyed what he'd heard of my commentary but was particularly taken by my description of the leisure centre. He couldn't help but wonder, if I could bring something so humdrum to life, maybe I could do the same on a much bigger canvas . . .

I could hardly believe my good fortune. He and a group of local business bigwigs[47] had recently got together to launch a project called 'Horizon Norfolk: speedway to growth'. As its name makes clear, the project's aim was to boost tourism in Norfolk as a way to increase revenues for their businesses. The central plank of the campaign was to be a documentary called 'Welcoming, Placid, Lively' about the best bits of the region, which was to air on local digital channel Mustard TV (formerly That's Norfolk). And now he wanted me to narrate it. They'd send a videographer to grab a few shots – the market, the high street, the town hall, some countryside, some leisure facilities – then a guy on their marketing team would write a short script and I'd put my voice to it.

Interesting. Would I get script sign-off? I would not get script sign-off. Could we talk production budget? We could not talk production budget. Was there scope to reimagine the format? There was not scope to reimagine the format.

I could sense he was wary of these questions, clearly concerned that

---

47 Literally, it turned out, in the case of three of them, who had lost the run of their BMIs and wore hairpieces.

I would deviate from the central mission of the project: to get people to move to, and spend money in, the Norwich area. I told him he had no worries there. As far as I was concerned, Norwich was the star. I'd take a back seat.

This was marketing outlay, nothing more, nothing less. We had a shared vision. There was no need for micromanaging.

That seemed to mollify him. So much so that he felt able to loosen the creative straitjacket. I could write my own script, I'd have significant creative input, I could appear on screen in a limited capacity, and if extra budget was needed, we could talk about that. He looked at me then asked, 'Whadda ya say?'

'And action!'[48]

Filming took place over two weeks in April 2012. I had piles for the entire fortnight but I didn't tell anyone and it didn't affect the schedule.

The team got on great, we really did. Of course, looking back now, through the lens of the various hashtags we must obey, it seems appalling how little diversity there was. With the exception of the make-up girl who I can't fully picture but will have been called something like Mandy or Debs, it was a crew of entirely white males. I am a loud and proud supporter of encouraging people of all genders, backgrounds and handicaps into the industry. They may not look like you, they may not sound like you, they may not walk like you, but surely having to put in a little bit of extra effort is a small price to pay for a TV industry rich in different voices and experiences and walking styles. But yeah, as I say, we got on great, we really did. Similar interests, similar senses of humour, all wore bootcut jeans and shoes, it was just

---

48 As the presenter of the programme, saying, 'And action!' wasn't my job. And, in fact, I didn't say it. I've just put it here to provide a bit of impetus to the description of the filming process.

a great, worry-free working environment. Yeah, fantastic.

I formed a particularly close bond with cameraman Pete Smith-sonby, despite the fact that I didn't like his name. My view was that it had too many endings. It should either be Smithson or Smithby, not Smithsonby. If everyone used all the endings they liked I'd be Alan Partridgesonsteinbyov. But I'm not.

Smithsonby had served in the Falklands, and because I like wars and he'd been in one, we buddied up big-style. He'd loved his time in the Malvinas and said on his days off he'd wander down to the beach to see the penguins. He explained that the islands are home to five different types and that his favourite had been the stunning Magellanic penguin, Spheniscus magellanicus, *found all over the Falklands. He added that they typically dig their burrows around the coastlines, preferring areas heavy in tussock. It was at this point that I said I hadn't realised you get days off during a war. He said, 'You don't get a full weekend but you do get one day a week.'*

Something about this didn't ring true to me and, sure enough, when I called bullshit he immediately folded. He knew I was a fan of wars and had just wanted to impress me. And I was fine with that. I've never had a problem with people coming up with lies to impress me. It makes me feel important and that's a feeling I enjoy. Besides which, Pete had a real flair for camera angles and I was determined that the programme should feature absolutely loads of them.

For me, the centrepiece of the episode was an interview I conducted in a leisure centre pool with nervous physiotherapist Annabel Swanson. To the best of my knowledge it was – and remains – the only British television interview ever conducted while treading water.

The idea had come to me the previous Tuesday during Weekly Bath. Weekly Bath is a practice I had begun several years earlier after some friends bought me a hygiene consultation for my fiftieth birthday.

One of the many fascinating things I learned from Debbie that day, during what was a hugely interactive and at times quite emotional session, was that for Alan to be truly clean, showering alone just doesn't cut it.

One word: gravity. You see, showering is hard to beat when it comes to sploshing off grub and grime from the bulk of Alan's body, but there are certain harder-to-reach locations that escape scot-free when gravity is allowed to decide where water goes and where it doesn't. And for these areas, only Weekly Bath will do.

Block out an hour in the diary, half-fill the tub with the hottest water you can bear and it's time to begin. Going at your own pace and taking care to perform the clean just as Debbie showed you, the results really do speak for themselves. Because whether lying on your back with your ankles round your shoulders, or floating on your side with your knees tucked up to your chin, Weekly Bath affords the cleaner a degree of access traditional stand-up showering simply cannot rival.

And it was while performing the first of my chin-tuck arse-cleans that the treading water idea came to me. When I pitched the concept to nervous physiotherapist Annabel Swanson, she wasn't keen, but when I clarified and explained that I wasn't really asking her, I was telling her, she soon agreed.

The screening of the edited show took place at the lavishly carpeted headquarters of CarpetChief Ltd, a former slaughterhouse on the A47 between Norwich and Blofield. Drinks and canapés were laid on before the main event, and even though most members of 'Horizon Norfolk: speedway to growth' were driving, Brendan was friendly with the chief constable so having a few was absolutely fine. I offered to say a few words by way of introduction, but Brendan said there was no need and I was cool with that. And so, with bellies full of champagne and sliders, we entered the boardroom and sat down to watch.

I would say frowns first appeared when the title screen popped up. The title my employers had given the project – 'Welcoming, Placid,

Lively' – had, as things often do in the whirl of the creative process, _slightly_ mutated into something fresher and better. Through various iterations, it had evolved like so:

'Welcoming, Placid, Lively.'

'A Welcoming Place – and Lively!'

'A Welcoming Place to Live.'

'Welcome to the Place to Live.'

'Welcome to the Place You Live.'

'Welcome to the Place of Your Life.'

'Welcome to the Place of My Life.'

'Welcome to the Places of My Life.'

And finally: 'Alan Partridge: Welcome to the Places of My Life.'

Yes, the naming process had gone a bit Chinese whispery back there, but the final title better suited the show I had created, which turned out to be a deeply personal journey around the places that had formed the child I was and the man I had become.

Forty-five minutes later, and as Chumbawamba's 'Tubthumping' boomed out over the final credits (a song choice I maintain was a good one), I began to feel an immense sense of pride; a powerful I-want-to-say-throbbing feeling inside of me that I liked very much indeed. As conceiver-producer- writer-director-presenter, every decision had been mine. And to see my vision realised so superbly was deeply grat-ulating [Lynn, check word].

Yet as I looked around the boardroom table with my eyes, flicking my balls left and then right, something seemed off. Instead of the founders of 'Horizon Norfolk: speedway to growth' whooping and hollering like Ainsley Harriott at his kid's nativity, the room had fallen silent. What I had seen as a love letter to Norfolk – a deeply personal journey around the county I knew best – they saw as a self-serving puff piece, an attempt to promote not Norfolk but brand Partridge. My blood ran cold, much as it must have done for the cattle *who were once slaughtered here for their beef and leather.*

Around the table were all ten members of Horizon Norfolk. I recorded their reactions in my diary when I got home that night:

Sandy Cobb – avoided eye contact; Rory Blench – stared at ground; Pete Grear – slow hand clap; Simon Cottingley-Booth – can't remember; Tim Blair – ate biscuit; Hal Topham – ate biscuit; Len Dingle – ate biscuit; Bob Dingle – drew finger across throat in 'you're dead' gesture; Pat Stonk – ate biscuit.

As for O'Coyle, he was spitting feathers. With his sausage-roll-and-burger hands balled up into meat-and-pastry fists, he fixed me with an Irish glare (I forgot to say he's Irish).

It had been a bruising encounter, metaphorically and literally (Bob Dingle pinched me on the arm as I left). But with a DVD of Places *tucked under my arm, I had a calling card to get me back on the telly.*

FISHERMAN'S FRIENDS

February 2022

'What are we organising, again?'

'The turning of the first sod.'

'Ooh, I like the sound of that.'

The official start of any construction project is the ceremony of 'groundbreaking'. Also known as the turning of the first sod, it's an event with a simple formula. Gather some dignitaries, lay on some canapés, and encourage a smattering of applause as the first spade enters the ground. And it was as my assistant and I discussed this, me in the shower, her outside the bathroom door, that she had put two and two together and – as so often – made about sixty.

Her assumption was that the term 'sod' was a truncation of 'sodomite'. Hence when she'd heard me talking about organising an event to 'turn' a sodomite, she'd assumed it was a reference to the gay-conversion therapies with which she was so fascinated.

Quite why she thinks I'd be organising an event to make gay men straight is anybody's guess, but it has put a spring in her step and I know better than to mess with that. I send her off to the cash & carry to buy a job lot of hot dogs and a nice big shovel.

In the end, a combination of heavy rain on the morning of the event and not getting any replies to my invites means it's called off. And while I'm disappointed not to mark the start of renovations with a little fanfare, I am pleased to be able to give a bit back by donating the two hundred unused hot dog sausages to a local women's refuge.[49]

No, official ceremonies are all well and good, but today is about the start of the build. This is the first day of the rest of my life. And while I also said that on the day I decided to buy the lighthouse, then again on the day the sale went through, I still feel it has a certain amount of validity in this context too.

With one hour until the builders are due to arrive, and with my assistant gamely attempting to dismantle a gazebo in the driving rain, I sit in my car with a flask of hot chocolate and look past the flailing homophobe to the lighthouse beyond. I put on 'Fields of Barley' by Sting because it's one of the best songs ever written, certainly by Sting, and as the swelling violins of the Geordie crooner's crop-focused hit fills my Vectra, I enjoy the calm before the storm. In a matter of hours, workmen will be busying themselves here, setting up scaffolds, installing support beams, and talking at a volume that is inexplicable even when you factor in the sound of hammers and drills.

* * *

As the rain finally eases, I wander over to the L-house. I run my hand down a crumbling brick wall then wipe it on my trouser leg because it's covered in some sort of slimy green . . . I want to say sea shit?

God, I adore this building. Humans can have surgery to reverse the ravages of time.[50] Yet ultimately it is as futile as the

---

49 Keenly aware that the last thing those poor ladies wanted to see was a man, I put the salty rods of reconstituted meat in a holdall, slowed down as I approached, and threw the bag out of the window. It was a kind and tactful drive-by dogging.

50 Provided they have the money or are owed a favour by a surgeon.

efforts of King Cunt trying to hold back the tide. Unless you go for a chin tuck or some gum sculpting, which are both totally normal, cosmetic procedures do little other than foghorn your vanity and age to the world. No, you cannot restore a person to youth. But what you can restore to youth is a lighthouse. I feel an all-consuming – or certainly 75 to 80 per cent consuming – urge to hug the thing, and nip round to the sea-side of the shaft to do so. If she had a hand, I swear I'd shake it. A cheek, stroke it. Hair, also stroke it. I suddenly feel a connection with this structure almost as strong as the one I enjoyed with my now-dead dog Seldom.[51]

Opening the front door by employing a traditional four-stage technique – put key in lock, turn key, turn handle, push door – I step inside. The best interior designers can paint pictures with their imaginations, seeing not a ruined building but the swanky home it could one day become. I can't do this, however, because my mind's eye is not very good, generally only allowing me to conjure up vague shapes and blobs, so to me it looks rubbish. Paint flakes off walls. Doors hang off hinges. It's the very definition of a 'doer-upper', although I hesitate to use that term because people who do are dicks.

Yet what I have seen are the plans of my architect. Luton Greaves is one of the only architects in the UK specialising in lighthouse restoration. Whether that's because he has a genuine passion for them or because he isn't clever enough to do proper buildings, I've never quite found out. What I will say is that he's genial company and competitively priced. And if he does perhaps have a whiff of BO about him,[52] then I like to think I do

---

51 Or the woman called Crystal I met online in 2008 who ended up being a man who was trying to diddle me.
52 He does.

my bit by sensitively passing that message on via coded deodorant mentions: 'Are you SURE about the cantilevered staircase?';
'What LYNX these two aspects of the build?'; 'Are we certain
this guy is the RIGHT GUARD to join our security team?'; 'If
we hire him will he need to get permission from his MUM?'

His designs will be implemented by – boop, boop! – this lot,
the builders, who are just pulling up in their Ford Transit. I don't
look round to check but I know it's a Ford Transit because I
know what the horns of different vehicles sound like. And while
some feel this is little more than a party trick, it's not. Imagine a
hit and run incident where an elderly lady is fatally injured and
the driver flees the scene. There are neither witnesses nor CCTV
footage. With the victim's wailing family demanding action,
the police are stumped. But what if the incident had happened
just outside my house? And what if the driver had inadvertently
tooted his horn as he'd swerved to avoid the shopping-bag-laden
pensioner? And what if I'd been in the bath at the time, and the
battery on my iPad had just gone so I wasn't watching an episode
of *Columbo* and could therefore hear that horn? I'd immediately
be able to identify the model, relay it to the police, narrowing
their search and leading to the arrest and imprisonment of the
driver and justice for the family of Granny Barbara. But yeah, if
you still think it's just a party trick, cool.

Turning to face the van I see workmen spilling out (it is a
Vauxhall Vivaro, but they have horns very similar to the Ford
Transit's). Next to arrive is my Dutch project manager Jan
Verfoofen.

Bounding from his Audi, a huge Netherlands grin on his
enormous, flat, pancakey face, Verfoofen thrusts out a giant hand.

'Goodness me, that's a big hand!' I find myself shouting.

'Yesh,' he replies. 'Who needsh a shpade, right? We could
have jusht ushed my handsh for the fucking groundbreaking!'

Like all the Dutch, it's never really clear if Verfoofen under-stands that 'fuck' is a swear word and therefore inappropriate to use in a professional setting. No matter, there is much to do and I can always keep his misstep in my back pocket to use against him later (if needed). And so, with the uttering of a vulgarity that could one day cost a Dutchman his job, the build begins.

What follows is a protracted debate/argument between Ver-foofen and my assistant as to exactly which sod of earth should be turned first. It's one of the few arguments I couldn't care less about – to me, soil is soil and if you prefer one clump of dirt over another there's something wrong with you — so I allow them to bicker without me, my eyes drifting seawards as they squabble.

In the corner of my eye, a flash of something red. I swivel my head and there, far away on the cliffs is ... a woman. Ginger of hair and slight of build, she seems to shimmer in the light, looking for all the world like one of the eight angels I sometimes imagine had carried Seldom to heaven.[53] Although unlike the angels, this woman's smoking.

Lost in thought, I unfurl my hand into an open palm – in-ternational sign language for 'hiya'. She takes stock of me, and begins to open her hand too.

'Who are you waving at?' says my assistant. I turn to see that she's somehow wrestled the spade from the hands of the builders.

'Oh, just that woman,' I say.

'What woman?'

I spin back. 'The woman just over—' The sentence aborts in my mouth. The woman! She's gone, vanished like a speck of dirt in the corner of your eye after a really hard blink. Was she ever even there? What is going on? I'm unsettled.

But then another thought occurs to me, and a smile begins to

---

53 Yeah, would have needed about eight.

form on my plump red lips. This is exactly what life is like here, a life far removed from the concrete certainties of the city. Here, reality and folklore live side by side, the village seeming to exist in the gloaming between this world and the next. A permanent half-light – where a mysterious creature like she would appear fleetingly to the lucky few. Right there in your eyeline and then gone for ever – like Natasha Kaplinsky. I don't know if you re-member her at all.

Far from shutting these thoughts out, I should be embracing them, rejoicing that in these faraway lands you still find mysteri-ous, ephemeral women – mermaids, harpies, valkyries, banshees, wood nymphs. The sight of a banshee wailing in Luton town centre or a mermaid reclining on the Thames Barrier would quite rightly shit you up. Here, it feels right, somehow.

'Yes,' says my assistant when I tell her all this. 'Or your woman might have been a siren, luring impressionable men to a grisly demise on the seafront.'

'Thanks for that,' I say.

'What woman? I don't shee no fucking woman,' chirps Verfoofen.

'Please, Jan,' I said, eyes closed. '*Try to stop swearing.*'

*　*　*

Next morning, I stand on the headland and look at my property. It really is a fantastic piece of work, this home of mine. The air smells salty and fresh, the wind tousles my hair, but a liberal application of Elnett Diamond Hold hairspray this morn means I'm not overly worried about strands becoming displaced.

I stand with my hands on my hips, legs wide in the power stance popularised by Sir George Osborne. Looking out at the vessels on the horizon, a memory gurgles up from deep within my subconscious: many decades ago I myself had toyed with the idea of a career on the high seas. As a boy, stories of pirates and seadogs had captured my imagination. I had devoured tales of Ferdinand Magellan, Vasco da Gama and Chris Columbus. With my school days coming to an end, and keen to follow in the footsteps of my nautical heroes, I applied to become a captain of a P&O ferry.

When the rejection letter came, I was destroyed. I was eating a choc ice at the time, my lips slipping and grabbing at the frozen chocolate surface like when a horse eats a sugar cube. With the structural integrity of the chocolate compromised due to the thinning effect of my saliva, I was ready to tuck in, biting down hard on the chilled dairy treat. But I was never to finish it. Seeing that I had been turned down by the two-lettered cross-channel operator, I was seized by a blinding rage. I hurled the remaining knuckle of choc ice across the room. It thudded into the patio doors and began to slide down the glass like a big sugary skidmark. My dream had died. Until now. For soon I would be something better than a P&O captain; I would basically be his boss.

Feeling as good as any man can feel, I sip from a polystyrene cup of tea and breathe deeply. In through the nose, out through the mouth – the breath, not the tea, the tea would scald the nostrils. They say the best way to blend in to a new community is to immerse yourself in the local food culture. So I decide to spend the morning doing exactly that and bound off towards town.

First up is a local delicacy known as huffkins. Kent's variation on the humble bread roll, here the difference is a small indentation in the middle, made by the baker's thumb. Legend has it that a baker's wife was so annoyed with him that she stuck her thumb into every one of his rolls before baking. Yet to her surprise, rather than shun the spoiled rolls, people loved them and these days fill the hole with jam, cream or even bacon. It was a charming piece of folklore but you're having a laugh if you think I'm going to eat something a baker's shoved his thumb in, so instead I settle for an unpenetrated bread roll from Sainsbury's (£0.60).

Next up is Appledore chicken pie. Situated on the B2080 – variously pronounced as the bee twenty-eighty, the bee two-oh eight-oh, the bee two thousand and eighty, the bee two-oh eighty, and the bee two hundred and eight zero – the village of Appledore was once a thriving river port, its traditions shaped by numerous visiting invaders, from the Danes to the French. The pie that bears the village's name combines chicken and hard-boiled egg in a creamy herbed sauce. But as I don't like egg in pies, or even agree with egg in pies, I settle for chicken and mushroom, and jolly fine it is too (Sainsbury's – £3.49).

By now really getting a feel for the food heritage of the area, I am keen to try more delicacies. Hailing from the south of Kent, lamb's tail pie has been a firm favourite for countless generations. But as I would no sooner eat the tail of a lamb than I would the bum of a dog or the eye of a swan, I settle instead for a lamb samosa (pack of four, Sainsbury's – £3.99).

It has been a fascinating morning in the supermarket, but by 11 a.m. it's time to head back to the lighthouse to peep out at my builders from an upstairs window. I arrive to find an unstamped envelope fixed to the door. On it, one word: 'Welcome'. Intriguing, I say out loud. Yes, very intriguing, I add in my head. I open it and find a letter from a group called Friends of Abbot's Cliff.

If that sounds like a cult (and it does), well, fear not. The letter was signed by John and Julia Hirst, a retired couple who are keen National Trust members and amateur historians. John, far from being the charismatic leader of a quasi-religious sect, is a retired railwayman who had worked in procurement for Network

SouthEast, later Chiltern Railways. I chortled at the thought of him luring impressionable and damaged people into a paganistic commune, with him as a messianic father figure chosen by the gods to lead them to eternal paradise! And it was damn near *impossible* to imagine an unassuming couple like the Hirsts trying to lure me to a meeting, just to meet the guys and have a chat, where I'd be made to feel genuinely welcome and would no doubt come again, only to find them, on the third or fourth meeting, leading me into a velvet-lined room where Julia would be lashed to a bed, naked and chanting. 'Please,' John would say. I'd look bemused. '*Please*,' he would say again, and on this the group's elders would explain that Julia has been without child for twelve summers and they hoped my seed would help her to yield an infant. They'd do it themselves, they'd say, but their past sins mean the gods deemed them unworthy, which is why their seed had failed to take. 'Please,' John would say again. I'd decline but the elders would surround and jostle me and insist that only I am unsullied enough to placate the gods and fertilise Julia's womb with new life. Finally, I'd lose my temper and say, 'It's nothing to do with the gods, the woman must be fifty-five if she's a day. Of course she can't get pregnant, she's had the bloody menopause! Google it.'

But again, that's what *wouldn't* happen, since the Friends of Abbot's Cliff is *not* a cult but simply a group of local residents who have taken an interest in the Abbot's Cliff lighthouse and seek to preserve it as a treasured piece of Kent heritage. They had applied to Historic England, in the hope of securing a grant for its restoration, but as it was built just after 1850, it had never been granted listed status and their bid had been unsuccessful. They had planned to raise funds for purchase and renovation through crowdsourcing, but then heard that the lighthouse had been sold to a private owner. Now they are reaching out to me.

They say they'd be delighted to provide any guidance I might need, and they can furnish me with a wealth of useful material – a 'cornucopia', they say! – including original drawings and a treasure trove of old photographs. Well, I'm as pumped as Ross Kemp when his Clenbuterol kicks in.

I go in(side) and eat my buns at the window, smiling and making contended *hmmm* noises as I chew. This is *exactly* what I'd hoped for – local engagement and a warm welcome. Perhaps even a few friends, who knows? I imagine they'll be a motley crew of characters, each with their own amusing idiosyncrasies, and I'll be like the Vicar of Dibley, there to raise an eyebrow and muck in.

I quickly write back and say I'd love to meet them. Then I call my assistant. Time, I say, to arrange a public meeting.

SILAS, WHOM I DISLIKED IMMENSELY

August 2012

'What do you say to critics of the tattoo industry who say it's both an act of physical vandalism and a surefire way of catching AIDS?'

It was high summer 2012 and I should have been flushed by the success of Places of My Life. I should have been on a turbo-charged, breakneck, super-fast, can-we-slow-down-a-bit-please, one-way trip to TV prominence.

And while that hadn't <u>quite</u> happened, we were making headway. Which was why I was standing in a tattoo parlour, interviewing a person called Syd. I used the word 'person' advisedly, as I didn't want to get into a whole gender brouhaha. I could have taken a guess, but I know from some of the arguments Eamonn Holmes has got into online that is fraught with risk. What I do know is that when Syd said, 'Do you want to know my pronouns?' I pretended I hadn't heard.

'Well, for a start you don't catch AIDS—'

'HIV, then.'

'And secondly, what people choose to do with their own skin is up to them and if Daily Mail readers don't like it, they can fuck off.'

I sighed. 'Come on, mate. You know I can't use that. We talked about swearing.'

'I mean it, fuck 'em.'

'Please! We're going to have to start again now. And can you turn down the music? It's very loud.'

I became aware of someone else, a man who looked like a Bash Street Kid, standing behind me doing the rabbit-ears thing with their two fingers behind my head – I've never understood the meaning of this and I'm certain they didn't either. I turned to admonish them with a quick 'grow up', and the chap, a heavily pierced man who must have had a nightmare getting through airport security or a magnet factory(!), nodded sheepishly. When I turned back, the branded foam muff on my microphone was no longer there.

'Alright, where's my muff?'

'Your what, mate?'

'My soft pink muff. It says East Anglia Live on it.'

'Does it now?'

'Yes, it does.'

The sniggering filled the room almost as much as their pungent BO. I felt like grabbing the tattoo needle and writing 'I am an immature asshole and nowhere near as funny as I think I am' on each of their foreheads, but they probably would have contracted HIV from sharing the needle – or actually liked the tattoo, which would have been even more annoying.

The interview continued in this vein for another twenty minutes before I conceded defeat and slunk back to the van.[54]

Why was I here? Well, it was part of a package of measures suggested by Silas McLean, a branding consultant who was, in his words, helping to 'imagineer a repositioning of my brand proposition'.

In the months after Alan Partridge: Welcome to the Places of My Life *had hit the airwaves, i.e. gone on the Visit Norfolk website as a free download, I came to realise I needed to capitalise on the buzz,*

---

54 I'm pleased to say that my attitude towards the tattooed has softened over the years. While the likes of a spider's web on a lady's neck or Alice Cooper's face on a grown man's arm still seem idiotic to me, I concede that to see a mermaid on a woman's upper thigh, particularly with properly rendered mammaries, can be nothing short of a delight.

if any. Silas had been introduced to me by Hugh Asquith, a friend of mine from my health and racquets club, who had used Silas for his own corporate rebrand and was evangelical about the guy's abilities. Hugh ran a wealth management firm called Accrual Partners and sought a brand consultancy to help him attract a younger, less stuffy client base. At the time, I scoffed at the idea of spending fifty grand on that. I said, 'Hugh, you're spending fifty K so a guy in a linen suit can put your company name in lower case, remove the space between the words and put a full stop at the end! Branding consultants are just snake oil salesmen – except they probably don't even call it snake oil, they've probably renamed it serpentine petroleum or Python3000 or worm lube.'

But Hugh wouldn't be deterred and insisted that accrualpartners. as it was now called, was a new and exciting proposition. I too wanted to be a new and exciting proposition so begrudgingly engaged the services of Silas.

I disliked the man immensely. He had a habit of saying 'Right?' at the end of every sentence, which was obviously a deliberate calculation to make him seem inclusive but actually screamed neediness. He also said, 'I know, right?' instead of 'yes'.

But desperate times called for desperate measures, which was how I came to sit with him over a frothy coffee and talk about how I could reinvent myself for the modern TV commissioner. In Silas's view, a man cusping sixty should lean into his advancing years and become a 'bit of a card' – he wanted me to embrace a kind of eccentric otherness cultivated by the likes of Gyles Brandreth, Bargain Hunt's *Tim Wonnacott, John McCririck or David Starkey.*

'You want to create a distinguished but careworn look, like a well-thumbed book. So stop trimming your eyebrows and nasal hair, stop dying your hair—'

'I don't dye my hair.'

'. . . *and embrace the elder statesman look, greys and all.*'

'*I don't dye my hair.*'

'*Excuse me?*'

'*I said I don't dye my hair.*'

'*Yeah, I'm just giving an example.*'

'*Yeah, and I'm just saying I don't dye my hair.*'

'*You can see my point, though.*'

'*Yeah, and you can see I don't dye my hair.*'

I listened to Silas's pitch with great interest and tremendous politeness but felt I had to demur – 'Silas, that is terrible idea,' I said – and pointed out the great many aging presenters who had stayed relevant – nay, cool – by clinging on to the last vestiges of youth.

Jeremy Clarkson, James May, Richard Hammond, James Martin, Tom Cruise, Gordon Ramsay – they all managed to retain their elan by perfecting a look known as 'Sunday pub rocker', where the hair has been permitted to dishevel into a gently rebellious length favoured by the Bay City Rollers and Tarzan.

This loose shoulder-length hair might seem more suited to a female divorcee called Trish who's fifty and does step aerobics than to a man, but when accompanied by craggy male skin, bootcut jeans and a leather jacket with zip pockets on the sleeves, it turns into something dangerous and thrilling.

Jeremy Clarkson in particular owns that look, and no one accuses him of being over the hill even though he's well into his seventies. James May (seventy-four or thereabouts?) is how I imagine James Dean would look now if he'd been better at driving.[55] The result? Clarkson, May, Hammond, Martin, Cruise and Ramsay are

---

55 The late actor tragically died after his car collided with another driven by Donald Turnupseed. Odd because 'Turnupseed, Don' is what a Scottish person would say Mr Dean's car then did. Gotta try stand-up one day! I really have.

cherished by boomers and millennials alike and could front an after-shave campaign if they wanted to.

Pleasingly, McLean came round to my way of thinking and we devised a campaign to reposition me in the minds of younger viewers. We agreed on three pillars: a fresh new look that would incorporate expensive denim and leather; a new lexicon, drawn from a compendium of buzz phrases and sentence constructions that would resonate with younger audiences; and optics. Under the last of these, I would ensure I was seen among a cool, young crowd and would try to create content that skewed towards what I call the Snapchat generation. Which was why I'd agreed to front Naked Norwich, *a web series for the East Anglia Live on what they called 'alternative Norwich'.*

Naked Norwich — *horrible title, by the way, especially if you picture the nakedness taking place on market day when the average age of visitor soars to sixty-five or so — explored anything leftfield, 'out there' and counterculture in and around Norwich. From tattoo parlours and skate parks to a drag club and a squat.*

The money was pitiful but I enjoyed the rough and ready nature of the shoot, and the chance to meet people with different backgrounds and perspectives. And while some of the stylistic choices weren't to my taste — incredibly fast editing, everyone laughing at everything always, and a camera so shaky I congratulated the cameraman on overcoming his Parkinson's diagnosis and continuing to find work only to be told he was doing it on purpose — my association with the kooky young scamps we interviewed had to be helping my brand, had to be.

But it took its toll. After less than five episodes (it was four), I began to feel like Bill Grundy interviewing the Sex Pistols, by turns appalled at their manner and goading them to behave worse. My friend Jackie is a magistrate at a court in Norwich and slips into a similar role when confronted with any youth offender of colour, insisting they stand up straight or blow their nose or look at me when I'm talking to you, but – and this is not just because she votes Conservative, she was like this anyway – longing for them to betray a fragment of contempt so she can rear up and throw the book at them (Metaphorically! Although she once did it literally because she'd forgotten not to a have a drink at lunchtime).

Throughout all this, I drew enormous comfort from the fact that I was still an attractive proposition for advertisers and sponsors. I was what the brand director of Jacamo described as a 'sexy offering' who was able to woo 45- to 65-year-old males from slightly lower income brackets than my own.

I'm not sure about sexy! I mean, I'm not Quasimodo or Chiles, but I'm also no oil painting, certainly not first thing in the morning when a combination of dehydration and gravity has made my eye bags swell and my lips dry up. And while one of the cleaners at the gym bumped into me while she was on her daughter's hen do and whispered that she'd once watched me towel off and decided she'd love to ride me 'like a Peloton', I just took it with a pinch of salt.

'Don't touch what you can't afford!' I joked.

She put her mouth close to my ear and said, 'Are you on about you or the Peloton?'

I said, 'Well, both realistically. I'm a successful media personality, and a Peloton static bike is going to set you back thirteen hundred quid minimum, plus the monthly subscription fee. How are you going to stretch to that on, what, a tenner an hour?'

The point is, I was still able to command endorsements and attract sponsorship. Brand managers could see what commissioners would not, and not just because they were men of my age and bought each other drinks and played badminton together. And where I come from, that means something. It confers status. When I hit the high street with a woman or friends, or even woman friends, of which I have six, these perks act as a buoyancy aid, a shot in the arm that gives me more than a little swagger. I don't mean I'd swan around with wads of banknotes – that would be crass and, besides, the endorsement deals weren't structured like that – but I'd flop out a gold card at any branch of Zizzi for a third off food and soft drinks; I could treat my date to a shopping spree at GO Outdoors and say, 'Fill a basket with hiking socks, I get a staff discount.' I could get me plus four friends into the communal areas at Champneys, complete with free towels and money off lunch. Clearly that opens doors. You become a guy people wanna be around.

It would not last. Why? Well, you'll find out in the next chapter. Or rather the one after that, because as I said, they alternate between two different timelines.

FRIENDS OF ABBOT'S CLIFF

February 2022

It's a sunny day on the glorious British coast and I am a man on a mission. I've borrowed my assistant's shopping trolley and am striding gaily[56] along the seafront, my mind filled with errands and my mouth filled with song – popular hits of the day, which I embellish with tiddly-om-pom-poms to give them a seaside inflection.

Like its owner, the trolley is groaning. I have piled the wheeled tartan cuboid full of croissants, pastries, fruit, Twixes and Innocent smoothies. Fresh flowers are jammed in the side pocket. I still had a box of *This Time* mugs and mousemats in my garage so I've brought them with me too. A gift for each attendee, to say thank you for your welcome. For today is the day I will meet the public.

I have hired a village hall and flyered the local area to invite residents (and only residents, please: bring a recent utility or council tax bill, plus ID) to a meeting, where I'll be delighted to present my ideas to regenerate the lighthouse and the local area. My project manager thinks this an excellent idea: local buy-in could prove invaluable, since alienated locals can be obstructive when it comes to public planning consultation, often refusing to grant access for construction vehicles and complaining about nuisances such as noise and rubble and visible bumcracks. Plus, I

---

56 Orig. meaning

want to *immerse* myself in the community and, heck, maybe even make a few friends. So a meet 'n' greet is fine by me.

I'll be honest, I am excited. I've always felt real kinship with people of the sea.

As a child I holidayed at the coast quite often. I remember those days as a parade of cheery, if ruddy, faces. Chip-shop ladies, thick of arm and rosy of cheek, would twizzle up bags containing fish suppers. Campsite proprietors would welcome old and young alike as long as you kept the noise down after 10 p.m. and weren't ethnic. In smoky pubs, trawlermen and smugglers would swap tales of barracuda and HM Customs and Excise.

For me, coastal villages have a special romantic glow to them, with their own mystical traditions and ways. One thinks of how these communities are brought to life on screen: *The Wicker Man*, *Get Carter*, *Poldark* or Rick Stein's cooking shows from Padstow where seven, eight, nine times a year, villagers glug cider, dress in terrifying wooden masks and bang tambourines as they eat vinegary food and sing shanties of the sea. Even a show like *Broadchurch* had its own seaside charm, which the paedophile/child-murder bit could do little to dent.

Yes, I have fond memories of the seaside. I want to be as one with them, live among them. I've left behind the financial muscle of London and Norwich, with their win-at-all-costs mindsets that had propelled these twin cities to the top of the global league tables, certainly in the spheres of insurance services and mustard.

Now, I'm depressing the clutch, dropping things down to third or second and taking life at a more leisurely pace. With the exception of oil-rich Aberdeen or fish-rich Peterhead or gay-rich Brighton, coastal idylls live life with the gentle ebb and flow of the sea. This is fine by me. I've lived life in the fast lane, I have drawn long and deep on the teat of fame. Now I'll be giving a bit back, devoting my remaining years to a life that has meaning.

So yes, I intend to be part of the town. I'm not just buying the property willy-nilly. I've come here to add real value. Listen to me! I'm making it sound like I'm assuming a white-saviour role, like a prospector convincing yokels he can turn their town around if only they'll sign their land over to him. Sure, there is that slightly patronising element of an outsider having to provide care the locals have been unable to, like home help coming round to wipe an old person's arse and unload the dishwasher. But I'm not going to come in shouting the odds, asking, 'Why haven't you maintained X?' or, 'Don't you know how to look after Y?' I'm sure they have their reasons. I just wanna introduce myself, say, 'Hi, I'm Alan. I'm going to be living with you, we're neighbours now,' and slowly but surely earn their trust, respect and fondness. And if renovating their lighthouse teaches them to have pride in their town, great.

And so to business. I get to the hall early in the morning, giving myself a day to spruce the venue to my liking. Although the room I've hired was advertised as 'cleaned', I spend the day making it spick and, where possible, span. Maybe the seaside version of clean is a bit different to ours, I reason. They do seem weirdly fine with carbuncles and algae clinging to the hull of every boat in the harbour, whereas I would simply chip them off and scrub the green bits away (or pay a chap to do it for me).

But no matter. I enjoy doing a spot of cleaning. A scarf is tied around my head to keep my hair out of my face and yellow marigolds (large) mitten my hands. Adorably, I'll blow strands of hair from my face as I survey my handiwork, something I've seen Anthea Turner do when she enters spring-clean mode as a way to get dinner-party guests to leave. Within hours, I really do have the place looking fantastic.

I even plug in a few air-fresheners – I've gone with Eucalyptus

& Freesia from the Air Wick Active Fresh range, as I find it steeps the room with a certain calmness. Or it certainly does in my house.[57]

Here at the village hall, I have these plugged in but turned off at the wall – I'm not anticipating they'll be needed and I would sooner use them only if necessary, since the aroma, and my apologies to the guys at Air Wick, absolutely stinks.[58] What else? Ah, yes. I've curated a brief soundtrack based on the theme of 'friends', which will play as they guzzle smoothies and chew pastry, subconsciously making them warm to me. This will play in the background as people arrive: 'You've Got a Friend' (Carole

---

57 My assistant and my housekeeper are generally at loggerheads – like two cats circling each other and hissing, sometimes literally. Their beef is ostensibly about whether you should wash up with a plastic bowl inside the kitchen sink (my assistant: yes; Rosa: no) – but I know it runs deeper than that. Theirs is a classic power struggle. My assistant doesn't like Rosa's tone, reckons it's too shirty. But I've explained to her: that's just the way they speak. In the mouth of a Thai waitress the phrase 'you no like?' can sound confrontational, aggressive even, when actually she's just wondering why you left your chicken satay. The same applies to a Filipino like Rosa. And my assistant is no angel herself. She could try keeping her nose out once in a while. If Rosa wants to clean the house in a T-shirt without a bra underneath, that's her business, you shouldn't be looking. Still, it's created quite the atmos at the oasthouse. On one occasion I'd asked my assistant to collect something from my house – a shoehorn or some such – completely forgetting that Rosa would be in that day, which would surely mean fireworks. I jumped in the Vectra and hightailed it after her, eking whatever I could out of the 2.8-litre 250bhp V6 engine, in accordance with the relevant speed limits. I pulled into the drive, ran up the gravel and burst through the door to find . . . a scene of perfect tranquillity. The house smelt of eucalyptus and freesia (or the synthetic version Air Wick had knocked up) and, sitting at the kitchen table, pleasant as you like, was my assistant, asking Rosa about Philippine cuisine and if it had any dishes that weren't spicy. It was all very cordial and I immediately put that down to the quelling effect of the plug-in freshener. These days I stock up!
58 As I say, they do offer a certain calmness but you will pay a price nasally.

King), 'You're My Best Friend' (Queen), 'That's What Friends Are For' (Steve Wonder), 'I'll Stand by You' (The Pretenders) and 'With a Little Help from My Friends' (with Ringo on vocals, not the Joe Cocker one; I don't like the Joe Cocker one, the Joe Cocker one sounds too gravelly).

I set about destacking and arranging the chairs. This is to be an inclusive, welcoming space so I arrange them in a way I think will be conducive to cordial conversation. Instead of rows of chairs facing a stage in an adversarial layout, I arrange them in a big circle, a configuration I learnt at a support group I briefly attended when I'd been feeling crummy (More on that later! Maybe!), and which also works well for 'Auld Lang Syne'.

And now? I am ready. Ready to make new friends.

* * *

'Whoa! Whoa! Whoa! Whoa! Whoa!'

I am shouting. Have to. Friends? That's a laugh. For the gathering has descended into a hostile barrage of questions. Questions that are raining down on the presentation proper, pebble-dashing the smooth putty of my talk.

Suddenly these locals have turned from interested stakeholders to the stake-holders you get in Hammer Horror films, the flaming-torch variety. They are aggressive, forever raising their hands or saying 'excuse me' to ask questions like a pack of feral dogs. It's questions, questions, questions – chillingly couched behind a veneer of friendliness, bubble-wrapped in what I call weaponised politeness. Ben Fogle does it a lot.

I'd started promptly enough, smiling as each person moseyed in. John and Julia Hirst were the first to arrive and Julia squeezed my hand as she shook it, which I thought was seriously classy. Then there was a woman in a cycling helmet, two ladies who had the air of lesbians, a couple of shopkeepers, a few people not worth describing, a couple who'd only recently moved to the area, and, perhaps most mysteriously, a flame-haired (i.e. ginger) woman in her mid-thirties with large eyes and a watchful bearing. She had responded to my smile with a sudden glance away, the skittish shyness of a woodland animal, but I noticed that she looked back – and when I smiled at her a second time, slightly harder than I had before, she smiled too and unfurled her hand into an open palm, as if to say 'hiya'. That's when I realised. She was the mysterious woman I'd seen on the cliffs that day. She was real! She was really real!

I composed myself. 'Grab a seat, Red,' I drawled. I've always wanted to call a ginger woman 'Red' and now I had. Who was she, this intriguing, orangey woman?

Attendance had swelled to ten or a dozen, and although we waited for any stragglers, none straggled so we cracked on, cheerfully.

It had started well enough. 'Welcome to tomorrow,' I began. 'This is a vision called One Abbot's Cliff. "One" because I wanted us to move forward with *one* shared vision for what this area can be, and "Abbot's Cliff" because the area is called Abbot's Cliff.'

I ran them through a PowerPoint of what the work would entail and ended on a picture of the finished lighthouse complete with those ghostly people architects always put in their drawings. A young couple holding hands. A boy with a balloon. A family laughing, beachball tucked under Dad's arm. A woman jogging with a dog. You can just download these figures and slot them in, but they almost felt like friends to me.

I finished and did a gesture that was meant to suggest 'voila!' but came out more as a 'ta-da'. And then I waited for applause. Instead, a few exaggeratedly thoughtful nods. I found myself adding: 'Remember, this is *your* lighthouse – not legally, it's mine. But it belongs to the town just as much as it belongs to me – again, not legally. So I want to make sure you guys are—'

'Sorry, I'm just going to stop you there,' said Julia, who in real life has the appearance of a retired dog trainer more than a retired school teacher.

Oh no you're not, I think, before realising she has.

'Couple of anomalies . . .'

Anomalies? I actually laughed when she said this. But she stood up and unfurled a roll of blown-up photographs. She laid them out on the table, slap bang on top of my drawings.

'You'll see here, the lantern room – that would have been accessed by a ladder,' she said. 'We actually have the original ladder in storage and we'd be happy to—'

'You'll see here,' I countered, plonking my drawing on top of her photos, 'it's now accessed by a tight spiral staircase.'

She seemed not to notice, rescuing her photos, which weren't even colour, and putting them atop the pile. 'And again, the lantern room,' she said. 'You'll see that was empty bar the lamp itself, which meant the keeper had space to walk round it and—'

'You'll see here,' I interrupted, which is something I never do, 'there's now banquette seating around the circumference. So you can look out with a glass of wine or—'

'Of course, originally that wouldn't have been there,' she smiled.

'Of course, now it will be,' I smiled.

'Yes, but originally—'

'Originally, I wouldn't have been there, Julia – I wasn't born for another ninety years. Originally, you wouldn't. Originally, the clifftop wouldn't have had a main road. Originally, the sea wouldn't have had a nuclear deterrent. Originally, there wouldn't have been the contraceptive pill, or cars, or contact lenses or iPhones. Am I allowed to bring my iPhone into the lighthouse,

Julia? Am I allowed to say OMG in there? Am I allowed to use an electric razor?'

Julia glowered at me. John looked at his shoes.

And that's when the questions began. 'When is all this happening?', 'Did you say you're planning to have the lighthouse light *on*?', 'Can you slow down a bit, please?', 'Did he say the light's going to be on?', 'How bright is the light going to be?', 'Can you say that bit again?', 'Do you mind if I ask a quick question?', 'Won't the light keep awake people awake?', 'What do you mean by Pathway to Abbot's Cliff 2.0?', 'Will there be any consultation?', 'Can you speak up a bit, please?'

I expected some pushback, maybe a modicum of wariness. But this? This is fang-bared hostility.

Far from creating a safe space, the circular set-up of the chairs simply means that whichever way I look my vision is assailed by the face of an angry woman. Left? Angry woman? Right? Angry woman? Straight ahead? Angry woman. The effect reminiscent of a recurring nightmare I suffered after getting into an argument on Mumsnet.

Not all of the attendees are women – I will not be accused of chauvinism – I'm just saying it *seems* like they are.

What is their problem? Why are they so opposed to my restoring, nay improving, a dilapidated lighthouse? Some are insisting that the rotating light would light up not just the sea but neighbouring homes and countryside, which would upset the sleep of local children and, hilariously, cattle. Others seem to take issue with my half-serious suggestion to monetise the lighthouse and – may God have mercy – turn a small profit by turning the lower floors into a Wetherspoons, or possibly an All Bar One. I was happy to discuss which of these it should be. Others, I decide, are simply jealous. Others still are plain old arseholes.

A man who looks like the late Harry Secombe with a rash has his hand raised.

'What does it mean when it says Pathway to Abbot's Cliff 2.0?' he says.

I can't help but sigh. I haven't even arrived at that bullet point; they are jumping ahead. 'It's just a normal pathway.'

'Like a coastal path?'

'No, more like a strategic vision, that kind of pathway,' I say. 'Shall we just stick to the points in the order they're bulleted? I think we should stick to the points in the order they're bulleted.'

'I'm not sure this will even get planning approval,' says Julia.

'Already has,' I say. Cue yet more consternation. What? When? How? They really are playing the greatest hits when it came to question rhetoric.

Deep breath. Time to put this pressure cooker under the cold tap. I smile. 'I'm pleased to say my attorney here has inspected my application in detail and will be able to put any concerns to bed.'

Instantly I regret this. The person I've gestured towards is far from an attorney; she is merely my assistant, whose legal qualifications amount to repeat viewings of *Judge John Deed* and a hairstyle that resembles a judge's wig (coils tightly at the back, looks like it could be lifted off). But the smile that plays on her lips tells me this is a role she's dreamt of – and that concerns me.

She stands up, buttons the buttons on her buttoned jacket and begins to pace, the dull clack of her one-inch heel echoing around the room. She stops, turns to face the group and takes a breath.

'Ladies and gentlemen, it goes without saying that your concerns will be addressed forthwith. But if we take a moment we might see there's a bigger question here. For who among us has not harboured – pun intended . . .' she pauses, waiting for the laugh that is never going to come, 'dreams of building something bigger than they are?' On that she sweeps her eyes theatrically around the room. 'Who among us has not—'

'Actually, she's not my attorney, she's just an assistant, I told a lie,' I blurt out, simply unable to face whatever feeble characterisation she was about to attempt. 'You can sit down now,' I say to my assistant, and she clomps back to her chair.

Well, this really riles them. Ordinarily I'd say sorry, but my Norwich neighbour Katrina has taught me that apologising is for the weak so instead I suggest they calm down. Big mistake.

Julia starts putting on her coat. 'A renovation that fails to respect the building's wonderful heritage isn't something we can support,' she says.

'Why would I need your support?' I ask, quite reasonably.

'Come on, John.'

'Yeah. Go on, John,' I say. 'Off you pop, John. Thanks for coming, John. D'you normally say nothing when you go to public meetings with your wife, John? D'you normally look at your shoes and let her do all the talking, John? D'you normally get into situations that very publicly highlight issues in your marriage, John?' At which point John hung his head even more and I felt a bit bad. I'd taken out my frustration on a profoundly weak man.

I am delighted to say that time is up, as I only have the hall until 9 p.m., so I usher the seething mob into the night and shut the door behind. Well, that went badly, I think. Stupid fucking bastards. Rude rude people. Rarely have I felt so despondent.

'Be nice to get the old lighthouse fixed up.'

I turn. It's Red. 'Oh, it's you,' I say.

'Yes,' she says.

'Yes,' I say, a touch redundantly. We look at one another. 'You're not going give me the third degree as well, are you?'

'Me? No. I'm not here for the meeting. I've just come to lock up the hall.'

MARVIN

April 2016

Things were about to go belly up.

It was 2016 and I was still inching inexorably towards my second televisual coming.[59] I wasn't pulling up any trees speed-wise, but I was getting there and that was the important thing.

Meanwhile, I was still leeching salary from North Norfolk Digital.

Then, one day, there came a class of kids from . . . I'm not going to disparage the school in question, they have enough on their plate having seen their Ofsted rating tumble from Excellent to Requires Improvement in the last three years – not helped, one assumes, by

---

59 Date-focused readers will have noticed a time jump here from 2012 in the previous chapter of this strand of the dual narrative to 2016 in this one. Please do not be alarmed at this. The nature of biographies is to document the peaks and troughs of a journey, the ups and downs of the rollercoaster. Unfortunately, for whatever reason, the years 2012–16 were like the long flat bit of a rollercoaster where the riders get on and off and the carriages trundle by without incident. There were no peaks and troughs to document – the trajectory of my television career flatlined, neither rising nor falling, so it's not germane to this story. Obviously things happened in that time – London Olympics, Cameron won majority for Conservatives, grew hair down to shoulder, became briefly nationally famous due to armed siege, friend died, Bradley Walsh quit *Law & Order: UK*, flight MH370 went missing over South China Sea which some put down to pilot error and others believe might be due to Russian electromagnets, won lunch with Farage in raffle but couldn't go. So, like the bits on *The X Factor* where the contestants visit their home town and introduce us to their families, let's skip this bit and get on with the decent stuff.

local news reports of their pupils smoking next to a war memorial and leaving cigarette butts on a monument to the fallen.

That's to say nothing of an art teacher who was caught in the shower block on a school trip to France chatting to a class of girls with his top off, not long after being asked to leave his previous (Catholic) school for getting one of the mum's pregnant. As I say, I shan't add to their woes by badmouthing their name through any more mud.

What I will say is that I found it odd, shall we say, that their teacher had left them unchaperoned for their live interview.

The guy, a Mr Crewe, had left the building, later claiming he had popped outside to take an urgent phone call but apparently a phone call that left him smelling of fags. I said, 'You must have had a strong CIG-nal,' but he didn't get the pun because cignal sounds exactly the same as 'signal', the very word on which the pun was based.[60]

Left without a teacher, the children became difficult and surly. One boy in particular – a yob named Marvin – behaved appallingly. Whether it's because he was born demented or has become defective thanks to parental negligence, I won't speculate. He's a kid, he deserves a break.

These days Marvin works in a kid's trampolining centre. It's his job to ensure the trampolines are being correctly used and that patrons are wearing the prescribed trampolining socks. He's soooooo hit the big time.

I must say I found his attitude perplexing, and the suggestion that I was partly to blame, hurtful. I've never spoken about this before, but earlier that afternoon I had been outside in the car park checking my car was locked because I was worried my car wasn't locked. Whilst there, I saw a teenage boy standing all alone. I could tell something

---

60 It seemed that back then I probably *wasn't* ready to try stand-up!

was upsetting him so I offered him a piece of chewing gum and took one myself, and we stood together in companionable silence for a while, both enjoying our gum.

Eventually, I said, 'Shit weather, right?' He looked at me and nodded. I nodded back. He didn't nod in response to my nod because that would have been one nod too many, but the point had been made. He knew I wasn't talking about the crummy weather. He knew what I was really saying was, 'Whatever it is, you can get through it. Whether you're struggling at school, getting hassle from bullies, wetting the bed, if you ever need to talk about anything to anyone, you know where to find me.'

It was a touching gesture and something I didn't have to do. So for him to lash out at me? Well, disappointing doesn't cover it. But I thought it was worth mentioning here to provide some useful context as to who was the good guy and who was being out of order.

As I say, it's not something I've mentioned before and might even be something that Marvin disputes ever happened, but if he wants to demand a retraction – particularly about the wetting the bed bit, which I suppose he might think was a cheap shot, had it not happened, which it did – then he's more than welcome to use some of his trampolining money to instruct a libel lawyer. If not, well, the record remains unamended.

Regrettably, the outside world wasn't privy to the nice bit of the story and instead only saw what I concede could be construed as cross words. Of course it was nothing of the sort.

What happened? You'd have to ask Marvin, really. For reasons known only to him he made a loud sheep noise mid-broadcast, aimed squarely it seemed at me. I responded with a brief deconstruction of his slur and a few comedic additions of my own to add to the general air of levity. All good-humoured, knockabout fun with some kids who were on my level, and I on theirs. So you can imagine my bewilderment when, moments later, I was asked to speak to the station controller Jason who immediately sent me home, where I should await further news.

I couldn't believe my ears. Sent home, I demanded? Await further, I exclaimed? News, I wailed?

Couldn't they see? This was just banter! And even if it wasn't, surely I'd have been within my rights to defend not just my own honour but the good name of the wider Norfolk farming community who would never allow even one head of livestock to be drawn into an intimate relationship with a local broadcaster, however sincerely held his or her affection for the sheep. But as I say, this wasn't that. This was just a bit of fun.

Two days later, I was sent a formal letter by HR, detailing my crimes with a transcript of the offending segment. As I read it, my eyes screamed with horror. The way they'd written it – in bald, plain dialogue – obviously made it sound inappropriate and aggressive, but that wasn't a fair reflection of what it sounded like in reality. Equally, they'd transcribed things in a way that didn't reflect what any reasonable listener could hear on the tape, so I sent it back to them with some very light amendments designed to remove inaccuracies and provide guidance on tone. Incredibly, they'd insisted I had said 'you dick' to Marvin when what I'd actually said was 'Yaddick', because I went to school with a boy called Marvin Yaddick and I briefly used his name in error.

Here is the transcript NND provided. My amendments are in **bold**.

[Marvin makes an aggressive bleating noise]
PARTRIDGE: 'Alright,' **laughs Partridge gently**. 'Who did that? Was that you?' Partridge smiles.
MARVIN: 'Yeah,' **snaps Marvin.**
PARTRIDGE: 'What's that supposed to mean?' **inquires Partridge, kindly.**

MARVIN: 'That you shag sheep.'

PARTRIDGE: 'No need for that, mate!' **Partridge chuckles.**

MARVIN: 'Sorry.' **[The word was spat like venom.]**

PARTRIDGE: 'That's cool, that's cool' **says Partridge, meaning it.**

MARVIN: 'Didn't mean to insult your **[fucking]** girlfriend.'

PARTRIDGE: 'My girlfriend's not a sheep, you wally,' **Partridge teases.**

FEMALE PUPIL: 'Shut up, Marv.'

PARTRIDGE: 'Yeah, shut up, Marv.' **He says, ribbing the girl for her concern.**

[An object was thrown at Partridge's head. Had it been made of sharp steel it could have cut his ear off or fractured his skull. The fact that it was a ball of paper was pure fluke.]

PARTRIDGE: '**[Yaddick],** calling me a sheep shagger.'

MARVIN: 'You are one.'

PARTRIDGE: You think I'm a sheep shagger?' **Partridge asks curiously.**

MARVIN: Don't know, **mate.**

PARTRIDGE: Yeah, I think maybe you're a sheep shagger **haver,' Partridge laughs.** 'You're the one who keeps going on about it,' **Partridge laughs.** 'Probably keep sheep magazines under your bed, yeah?' **Partridge laughs.** 'Probably keep pictures of sheep lying on their back in a pen with their knickers off,' **Partridge continues to laugh.** 'You're the sheep shagger,' **Partridge chuckles.** 'Bet you kiss them, bet you lie them down on their back, kiss them tenderly, stick your tongue in their mouth, swirl it round, play with their teats,' **jokes Partridge.** 'Get behind it, strum them like guitar,' **jokes Partridge again.** 'Grab fistfuls of fur, grab its horns like a bike, like drop handlebars on a racer, a Grifter would be more of a yak,' **smiles Partridge.** 'And do you hold them afterwards and say you mean the world to me, spooning **[food into]** them with your hot **balls bowl** pushed up against its woolly back.' **Partridge laughs.** 'You're just a bloody chav!'

The added context here was absolutely crucial. You can make any transcript of a live broadcast seem like someone has lost control, but a bit of context can go a long way – be it Will Smith punching Chris Rock at the 2022 Oscars or Lulu headbutting Pete Waterman at the 2005 Cosmo Awards. On first viewing, Will Smith twatting Chris Rock seems like an open and shut case of thuggery – a powerful man losing his temper and delivering a beatdown. But what if Chris Rock had had a concealed gun and was about to use it on the audience? What if Rock had promised Smith he'd give a million dollars to a children's charity if he punched him live on stage? What if Smith, on a front-row seat, remember, had seen Rock start to choke on a bit of food and was trying to dislodge it the only way he knew how? There are loads of unknowable factors that could have been at play, but people are so quick to judge: Will Smith thumped a guy; Alan Partridge called a child a sheep-shagging chav.

But if anything, my attempts to qualify the more incriminating utterances on the transcript seemed to annoy NND more, and I was formally asked to take a few weeks off. The sheep content hadn't been the issue, they said. It was my referring to Marvin as a 'bloody chav'.

Big. Mistake.

NEITHER CHUMS
NOR EGGS

April 2022

'Now shake the pan. And see there? That wobbly bit? That's not cooked. The white should be firm and white, not wobbly and translucent. That's how you can tell.'

They say you can't teach a grandma to suck eggs. But you can certainly teach the old girls to cook 'em! And that's what I'm doing now. I'm in the kitchen of a seaside B&B, just a short walk from my lighthouse. The Seaview is comfortable enough but – whether it's through laziness or ignorance – does serve undercooked eggs.

I've popped into the kitchenette and am giving the landlady, Cynthia – who I'm assuming is a grandma, she's certainly of age – a crash course in breakfast cookery.

'You're thinking: How do you get the translucent bit – the "see-through" bit – to solidify without sacrificing the softness of the yolk? Little tip for you. Pop in a dash of water, cover it with a pan lid, it'll gently steam the white until it's cooked. See?'

I scrape the eggs into the bin. 'Now, you try.'

'They were the last two eggs.'

I look down to see my breakfast eggs steaming atop a mound of dumped cat food. 'I'll have toast. Remember we looked at toast yesterday? It was about cutting it . . .?'

'On the diagonal.'

'Great, Cynthia. That's *great*.'

I'm starting to warm to Cynthia and I sense she's fond of me. A woman of few words and even fewer smiles, she's a no-nonsense hotelier who asked for payment upfront but, to her credit, does tolerate constructive cooking demonstrations of both eggs and toast.

But Cynthia aside – and, let's be honest, as a non-talker she wasn't best mate material – the locals here haven't exactly rolled out the red carpet for me. We're different, I get that. I am from Mars, they're from a planet that has little in the way of retail or leisure offerings and next to no transport infrastructure. I'm from the hustle and bustle, beep-beep-out-of-my-way, sorry-can't-stop pell mell of the big city. These are village folk – wary, rustic and slow. But I am more than happy to try and fit in: I don't use my iPad in public areas or ask if people have Wi-Fi. I stroll and lean on gateposts and drink pints in those glass tankards made up of small windows. I stop saying 'can I get' when ordering in cafés and revert to the more traditional 'can I have' construction that provincial non-millennials find less annoying. I nod at passers-by, since vocal greetings such as hello seem to startle them. I am doing my bit.

But it's like I'm being black-balled; as if there's been a concerted decision to close ranks and not let me in. And that hurts. I remember how crummy I and my fellow broadcasting chums had felt when we decided not to let Adrian Chiles join our Sunday Skype sessions in which we chatted about current affairs, ethical conundra ('is it OK to nod off during a massage?') and 'men things' such as shaving your upper arms. Chiles wanted in but we just didn't feel he'd quite get the vibe we were going for. So he received a curt email on the Monday simply saying, 'Thank you for your interest but no.' And the torrent of emails he sent throughout the day – 'why not', 'please, lads', 'I don't get why you won't let me', 'will someone please answer me' – left me feeling pretty low, without quite rendering me low enough to actually write back to him.

And while the locals here aren't explicitly telling me I'm not welcome, they are raising their tails, skunk-like, and emitting a pretty foul message. Striking up a chat is almost impossible, as painful as initiating small talk on a first date when perhaps a more recent photo would have got things off on a friendlier footing. My usual failsafe technique, used largely in airport lounges or green rooms, is to read a newspaper and gently mutter 'dear, oh dear' or 'oh, for goodness sake' or 'what the . . .?', and by and large people within ear shot feel compelled to reply, 'What's that?' Then BOOM, you're away. Chat initiated. Well, that reaps precisely no dividends here on the coast.

I'll stride around the place, looking interesting or busy or weird, in the hope that someone will engage with me if only out of curiosity, but they avert their eyes or scowl or make out they've not seen me.

I'm not entirely alone. My assistant is there most days, but generally commutes back and forth, as her spinster friend is undergoing treatment for septicaemia and she needs to be close by. But sometimes she'll be required to stay over if, for example, a contractor needs to be reprimanded or a cheque hastily written – in which case I'll treat her to fish and chips on the beachfront and she'll stay in a caravan a few yards from the lighthouse, the two-berth Monza lurching and rolling in the wind not unlike the gentle rocking of a child's cradle. She quite enjoys it; I'll come knocking in the morning and hear her singing lustily along to her tape of Christian songs.

'If only you put that time and effort into something constructive,' I say after knocking on the door. 'If you'd spent your time knitting instead of hymn singing you'd have enough for a whole jumble sale now.'

'Worshipping the Lord is constructive,' she says.

'You don't even know if he's real. At least you can tell cardigans exist.'

'I choose to believe He is real,' she replies. 'And that's enough for me.'

How can you *choose* to believe something? Surely to believe in something – Brexit aside – you need compelling evidence. But there's no arguing with that kind of logic!

* * *

But generally, yeah, I'm lonely. Takes guts for a man to admit that, which clearly I have. Normally, if a man is feeling that way, he just makes up reasons to pop round to an associate's house. Ding-dong. Can I borrow your drill? Ding-dong. Can I borrow your hammer? Ding-dong. Here's your drill back. I'll bring the hammer tomorrow. Ding-dong. Here's your hammer. Oh, hang, that's a different hammer. I'll bring yours tomorrow. Ding-dong. Here's your hammer. Ding-dong. Can I borrow your drill again? Ding-dong. Here's your drill. Oh, hang on, that's a different drill.

But I have no such associates in Kent. With the work progressing at a snail's pace – I said to the contractors, 'You're going at a snail's pace. I'd be better off employing snails. At least snails don't clog up the toilet with last night's curry' – I find myself at a loose end, longing for the buzz of Norfolk life.

It's the silly things I miss. The revving of Range Rovers in a country club car park, the smell of a McDonald's, chit chat about underperforming TV shows and how the presenters will be mortified by the viewing figures, the sight of my neighbour Katrina doing a Joe Wicks video in her kitchen, just visible if I stood in the right place in my garden, the beeping of a car horn and the muffled 'fuck off' through a closed car window, pop music blaring from a branch of Claire's Accessories.

I spend my days writing letters back home – never admitting I am unhappy, but the blank prose, reminiscent of a hostage insisting 'my captors are treating me well' or a spokesman for ITV saying 'we're thrilled to bring viewers another series of *Dancing on Ice*', surely tells its own story.

One day, walking along the cove, I'm so bored I decide to imagine life as a wave. Rising and falling, rising and falling. One morning my tongue would be licking at a beach in Dorset, the next, with the tide having gradually carried me on its back out to sea, I'd find my face being smashed against the walls of an unyielding French port. But the vast majority of my life would be spent in the middle, being endlessly bumped and jostled by other waves. I'd tense when I saw one coming from my left, readying myself for impact, only to be sent off balance as I'm hit by one from behind. And then from the right. And then from the left. On and on, over and over, buffeted and barged, day after day after day, until finally I would snap. 'For crying out loud, will you *please* stop banging into me?!' With my will finally broken, I'd be taken aside by wave management and quietly relocated to calmer waters off the Maldives.

It's an interesting exercise but it's hardly going to kill the four hours till *Countdown*. I decide to head home, but as I turn back my hat blows off and flaps away from me on the breeze. It's a new one and a good one, a flat cap made from midnight blue linen, and I don't want to lose it. I begin to chase it as it skitters along the ground but then a gust lifts it skywards. I stumble onwards, jumping forlornly to try to pluck it out of the sky, but my jumps are underpowered and poor. It blows faster and I begin to run, like a boy with a kite. 'This is awful,' I say out loud as I caper and flail along the beach. But I am getting closer; if I stretch my fingertips I can almost reach it. Almost there, almost there . . . and then, SPLOOSH! I have run into the sea. Gasping and wheezing, spitting out salty water, I watch as the hat lands a yard away from me, nestling on the surface of the water. I realise then that it's the bin bag of a small pedal bin. My hat? It is still on my head.

I tramp out of the sea and squelch back to the guesthouse, the eyes of the locals following my every step. I have never felt more Chiles.[61]

* * *

A fortnight later, and I am out of the guesthouse. Some progress has been made on the lighthouse. The strip-out and removal has been done, structural work has been completed, and the building is now topped out and weather-proof. Project manager Jan Verfoofen urged me in the strongest terms to stay in the guesthouse until the first fix had been done and there was some rudimentary plumbing and wiring in place, but no. My house, my rules.

So I'm living in a cold and dank lighthouse. But it's home and a thrilling reminder of what life would have been like here for the first lighthouse keepers – although they wouldn't have had access to the Jaffa Cakes that have sustained me of an evening.

---

61 One night, while perusing the plans of the lighthouse, my assistant took off her spectacles and said: 'Are you sure you want to be doing this? I mean, I wouldn't want you embarking on this as a way to distract yourself from the heartbreak of losing your career, and also as a quite childish way to get revenge on *This Time* by stopping them buying the lighthouse as they'd planned to.' I took off my glasses too. 'I actually find it quite sad that you've said that, because a cynical thought like that can only have come from a very warped, very damaged mind.' I told her I'd be booking her in for some counselling, and although she didn't want to go, she's now been attending once a week for nearly two years.

The stairs need work but I'm able to clamber up them and look from a window at the angry seas.

Does it keep homesickness at bay? Not entirely, but it's a very welcome change of scene, and I feel like Seldom would be proud of me. This surely is the kind of life he'd envisaged. But that sustains me for only so long.

Soon, the insistent tug of home begins to yank again. I wonder what Kirstie Allsopp is up to? How did this week's quiz go? What would Eamonn say if he could see me now? There's a new series of *Dancing on Ice*, I bet that's had its fair share of funny moments. Did that new TGI Fridays ever open up on the A47? They were offering half-price meals, Monday through Thursday. I would have liked that.

With nothing but the crashing waves to occupy my mind, seemingly trivial thoughts like this can really take hold. I don't want that. They are thoughts for Old Alan. This new me has no need of those annoying London/Norwich-based fripperies.

This evening, I retreat to a wooden chair by the window. By the light of a lantern I enjoy bread and cheese, a flask of rum nestled in my crotch. There, I read. It's a copy of *Moby Dick*, my favourite Herman Melville book by an absolute mile, a swash-buckling novella full of evocative passages of crashing seas and rain-spattered men.

At one point, I catch sight of my reflection in the window, and I nod. My reflection nods back at exactly the same time, as reflections tend to do. Yes, I'm happy and I am good at this and I like it. It amuses me that tonight is the night of the twenty-sixth National Television Awards, live from the O2, a programme I would never normally miss. Large-scale live events – opening ceremonies, Children in Needs, jubilees, Eurovisions, Remembrance Sundays – are red-letter days in a broadcaster's viewing calendar. A microphone might fail, a horse might collapse, an

OB feed might go down, or a TV anchor might stumble over his words. As a broadcaster, these 'there but for the grace of God' moments are absolutely delightful to watch and I positively drink them up.

Well! Not anymore. Tonight, the NTAs could be gatecrashed by Black Lives Matter, Holly Willoughby could introduce Martin Lewis as Martin Kemp – can you *imagine*! – and I wouldn't give a hoot. I've moved on. This is me now. Melville by lantern-light, a tot of rum, and lots and lots of cheese. I'll leave the NTAs to my assistant, watching on an iPad down in the caravan below.

The clock tick-tocks in the corner and I am lost in the moving tale of a man trying to murder a whale. I can imagine the foaming waters of the North Atlantic soaking the crew, the spray of the ocean drenching the ship again and again. Imagine if the attendees of the NTAs ended up soaked like that, perhaps due to a fault in the O2's sprinkler system. You'd never hear the end of it!

But, as I say, that's not my concern. For mine is a simpler life, away from the noise and the gossip and the chatter. There'll be enough of that from Jonathan Ross! Apparently he's going this year, didn't say if he was sitting with the *Masked Singer* table or the team from his chat show. Probably the former, you get to sit near Rita Ora that way. Might be the latter, though, not sure. Perhaps if I peek down to my assistant's caravan, I'll get a glimpse of her screen through the window . . .

No, Alan. NO. Stop this. Who cares? Seriously, who gives a shit where Jonathan Ross is sitting? I put my book down and look out to sea – there's a haunting majesty to it tonight. The waves roll and crash into the shore then the water rolls back off the shingle to be recycled into the wave-generation process proper. I could watch it for hours. The clock ticks. It's 9 p.m..

I stand and pace. This is ridiculous. I look again at my reflection in the window. 'You have to beat this, Alan. FIGHT IT, MAN.' I sit on the floor, back to the wall, eyes tight shut. I open them again but the walls seem to be shifting and contracting. I need to clear my mind. Rid it of Ant and Dec and Alison Hammond and the cast of *Line of Duty* and Graham Norton in his . . . what would he be wearing, Graham Norton? Sometimes he goes full glitterball camp, other times he's demur black tie, but that might have been when he was trying to impress people enough to get to MC the BAFTAs, so if I had to guess I'd probably say—

NO, ALAN.

I throw my book across the lighthouse and bolt down the stairs. I emerge into the rain. I can see the light from my assistant's iPad dancing on the caravan ceiling – purples, greens, blues, reds, all colours really, no need to list them. What's happening on that screen right now? Someone will have screwed up a winner's announcement, or tripped on the steps to the stage, or sworn – and I'm missing it.

But then, because I'm a brave boy, I turn away from the caravan, with its live broadcast on ITV1, or ITV or ITV Hub or ITVX or whatever they call themselves these days. And I walk away from the lighthouse. I head for the lights in the village. I need a pint of bitter.

* * *

I'm standing in front of a seaside pub, very much one for the locals. A place where smugglers might hunker, whispering tales of contraband and midnight drops, where London gangsters might meet to discuss laundering their money in a beachside property development. If a shadowy group of freemasons wanted a hushed conversation about snatching kids from a local children's home, this would be the place they'd do it, although there's no suggestion that anyone has done that and I'm not even sure why I included it in this list. I'm sure that kind of thing goes on somewhere, but I wouldn't want to pin it on this village because, as I say, *there's no indication whatsoever* that that has ever happened here and I apologise for insinuating that it might have.

SKREEEE-IIIIIK. (That's the sound of the door.)

I stand in the door, windswept and sodden, every inch Captain Ahab after failing to murder that whale again. The locals stop and look at me. I don't smile. I don't even nod. I just stride to the bar.

'Yup,' says the landlord.

'A pint of best,' I says. 'With just a dash of lemonade at the top.'

I take my pint and turn to face the room. The locals go back to their supping and in the corner a group of singers strike up again. These men – and one woman on accordion – sing a sea shanty that has a wonderful bobbing, lilting rhythm. I don't know the name, sorry.

I like it. I know better than to dance. You can dance when you see a steel band or at a ceilidh. This is not that kinda crowd. Instead, I furrow my brow and nod my head in time. It ends to warm applause. I join in, muttering, 'Great shanty. *Great* shanty.'

Finally, this elicits some conversation.

'You like shanties?' says a man beside me.

'Love 'em.'

'Which ones?'

'"Drunken Sailor", *classic* track. "Portsmouth"? "The Horn-pipe"? And just a few you might not know.'

'Try me.'

'Not even sure what they're called. They're just very traditional.'

'Let's hear one, then.'

The man gestures to the accordionist to knock it off. 'Fella's gonna sing a shanty,' he says.

Silence. Now all eyes are on me. I swallow hard.

But then a voice sings out: 'In the ocean, the mighty ocean, the whale swims tonight.'

I look to the door. My assistant is standing there in her coat, singing. She's stamping and gesturing with a crooked elbow, pumping her fist to give the song a nautical, shanty-like lilt, even though it'd take a complete idiot not to realise she's singing 'The Lion Sleeps Tonight' with slightly adapted lyrics.

But the men in the tavern, although frowning quite rightly, *are* complete idiots and don't seem to have cottoned on. So much so that I join in on the second line.

'In the ocean, the quiet ocean, the whale swims tonight.'

The men are still just staring. But then another voice chimes in: 'A-swim away, a-swim away, a-swim away, a-swim away.'

I spin round. There, nursing a rum and Coke and singing her cleverly adapted lyrics like a cockatoo, is the mysterious redhead from the meeting in the village hall.

'Red,' I say. She nods at me.

And then all three of us join in for the next verse. I try to harmonise for a few bars but my assistant shakes her head. It's a good call and instead we just go for more volume. The song ends and there's a smattering of applause. We got away with it.

* * *

Cut to the three of us, walking along the coastal path giggling like school girls. 'And then I joined in!' I say.

'That was so great,' says Red.

This picture was taken on a walk in Derbyshire shortly after Seldom ate the keys to this man's van. We waited for a number of hours for nature to take its course so that we could retrieve the keys from the animal's dung; the man and I sitting atop a drystone wall taking in the beauty of the Peak District, Seldom in the van with the radio on. Once the keys had emerged, me and the man swapped numbers and promised to keep in touch, but never have.

Cromer leisure centre sports hall. The location of my chance meeting with carpet impresario Brendan Coyle, ultimately leading to me fronting Norwich puff piece *Welcome to the Places of My Life*. The hall is used every Tuesday by a local secondary school, with a modesty partition erected down the middle of the court so the girls can get changed on one side and the boys on the other – although if you sit where the photographer is sitting here you do get to see both.

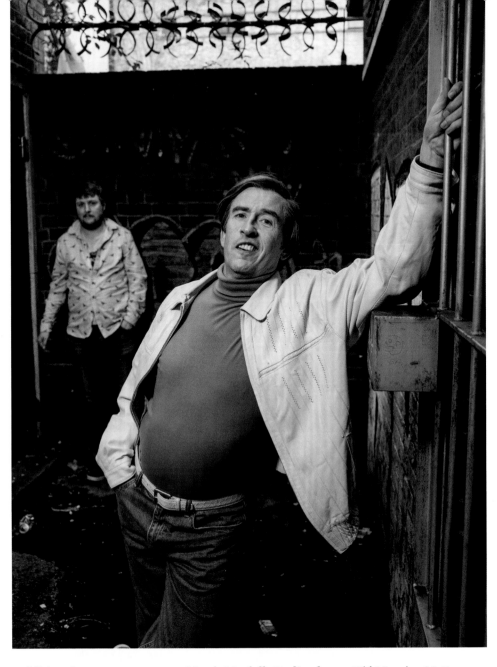

Publicity shot to promote my North Norfolk Radio show, *Mid Morning Matters*, 2012. I had the idea for this photoshoot while driving through Birmingham. Make of that what you will, but there was a certain streetwise quality to the show that I felt wouldn't be captured by the normal 'grinning DJ sitting behind mic holding a branded mug' shot. It's not for me to say if we were reinventing mid-morning local radio in East Anglia from the inside out (we were), but there was certainly no topic we weren't prepared to grapple with, apart from Israel. Also in these photos, my on-air sidekick Simon Denton, a man so camera-shy and with (by his own admission) so little presence that when these images were developed, I wasn't even sure he would appear in them! I'm glad he did.

Karl Howman wears floral print waistcoat, C&A spring/
summer collection 1988.

Scissored Isle, 2016, and my interview with the female mayor of Greater Manchester. City Hall may have been hoping for a softball chit chat, but I had other ideas and sought to address the drug epidemic that had blighted the city on her watch. In a daring act of political theatre, I took a pellet of ecstasy just hours before the interview to confront the hapless politician with the visible after-effects of drug use – after all, what could be a clearer indictment of her administration's catastrophic failure to tackle substance abuse than a respected broadcaster sweating and groaning just yards away from her? If a veteran TV presenter could get sucked into Manchester's vortex of drugs, who else was at risk? Vicars? Grandmothers? Dogs? A stunningly powerful piece of television.

Few men alive have flown in a
Spitfire, fewer still have done not
one but two full loop-the-loops,
as I did when taken for a flight by
Captain Paul Wheeler in a piece
for *This Time* about the unsung role
of female RAF pilots in the Second
World War. Oh, and the G-Force
didn't even make me spew up.

As a committed direct debiter to Help for Heroes, I was privileged when *This Time* producers asked me to spend a day with these ex-Special Forces lads learning how to rescue a hostage from a building. I was fascinated to learn that as well as all the standard kit, British Special Forces wear knee protectors in case they need to discharge their firearm while sliding into a cave. In this photo I have removed my mask because it was making my face too hot.

Simon Denton. There's nothing wrong with him, this is just how he looks.

Joe Beesley and Cheeky Monkey. A temper problem, a weakness for alcohol and profound mental health issues have kept him off our screens for almost thirty years. And that's just Cheeky Monkey! I jest, but I learned an important lesson from Joe's appearance on *This Time*: never, ever give people a second chance.

'And then you added the "a-swim away" bits!' says my assistant.

'Yeah, we do know, we were there,' I scoff. We walk on in silence for a while until we reach the lighthouse.

'I've never been inside a lighthouse,' says Red as she looks at the pipe-shaped structure.

I stand in silence. Red looks at me. I remain silent. She looks at me some more. Nobody speaks. After an age, my assistant nods and says, 'Good night, then,' and goes to the caravan.

Once she's gone I lean close to Red and say, 'Do you want to come in?'

She says yes. And we go inside.

*　*　*

Red soon becomes my lover.

I am pleased. I have always wanted to have a mysterious girl-friend. Sure, I've been with girls who hailed from far-off lands (Ukraine), or harboured secrets (wife during affair), or regarded me with disdain (a few), or were inscrutable and quiet (a woman called Angela). But if you scratched beneath the facade, they were actually extremely plain ladies. Red is different.

There's a delicious otherness to her and I find myself reeled in by the fishing rod of her personality. She doesn't show up on Google but furtive inquiries in the pubs and the shops of the town have helped me build a picture of who she is.

Some say her mother died when she was young, others that her heart was broken by a sailor man who left these shores. I hear her father to this day sells whelks down at the quay, just as his father had before him. Red will sometimes help him out and I am enchanted by the humble honesty of their toil, harvesting the fruits of the sea to make a living.

'Does he need any money?' I once asked.

'No, he's fine,' she replied. Of course he is. A proud man, from a proud people.

We take our time. For me, it's about respect, discretion and chivalry. And if that means waiting a while before we commence the physical side of our relationship, I'm cool with that.

She had put out on the first and second dates – full sex, I mean; I'm sure she wouldn't mind me saying that since it's true. After that, we agreed we should wait. Fine. I have builders to manage and don't want to be off my game just because I've been kept up at night by the sexual needs of a partner.

We talk and talk. I tell her about my experience as a TV presenter and she tells me things about her as well (can't remember details). She senses I am emotionally tender; after all, I still can't seem to get the locals to warm to me. But one night, I open up to Red about it. She comforts me and then, touchingly, she opens up to me, in the sense of opening her legs so I could have sex between them.

Suddenly it was ON.

I tug at her clothes. 'Off,' I say. 'You do it,' she breathes back. 'Alright, then,' I say, although I'd prefer her to do it because women's fashion is a minefield of clasps, hooks, buckles and fasteners. Men understand two things: buttons and zips. You need a degree in aeronautical engineering to disrobe a woman these days! I tug and clank and twirl for a while to little effect. It is dark and I have very, very slight osteoarthritis in my index fingers. In the end, I say, 'Look, can you just do it. I did say first.'

She obliges. Our clothes fall to the ground like the brown leaves of autumn, and like two mighty trees we stand there, our trunks (or bodies) and branches (arms) bare. I peruse her all over, taking in every last detail, like an auditor doing a stock take in a warehouse, or a judge at Crufts. She is in good shape – not perfect, I feel like she hasn't worked on her arms very much, but still good. I breathe out, allow my voice to go pleasantly guttural, and go, 'Yeeeeeeeeahh.'

Suddenly, sex. I pick her up, she wraps her legs around me, and taking very fast, very short steps I totter to bed and let go so she slides down a bit and then relaxes onto the eiderdown. I get on her. We intertwine, my arm over her arm, her other arm over mine, my leg over her leg, her leg over mine, like a two-person game of one potato, two potato. All this talk of potatoes – one of my favourite foods – is making me hungry. It is time for me to *eat* ...

Down I go. Further and further. Into the soft musk of her hollows. Her fingers clasp my hair, messing it up as if that were fine, but instead of complaining I just issue a quick tut then tenderly place her hand by her side so I can correct the parting with the palm of my hand – all of this as I continue to pro-vide stimulation to her groin, the vibration of my voice con-joining with expelled breath as if I am playing her like a giant kazoo.

I roll away from her, my frenum (the band of tissue that con-nects the tongue to the floor of the mouth) sore from over-work. 'Sore frenum,' I groan. She nods and rolls me onto my back to return the favour.

I look at my Apple Watch. 'I think I did about six minutes, so if you do broadly the same we should be about even,' I gasp accurately. 'So until twenty-five past, basically.'

I lie back, and she does as mandated.

At twenty-five past she stops and lie back on the bed. I stand, find protection in the slit of my wallet, sheathe, squeeze the teat which apparently removes any build-up of air from the rubber and therefore prevents popping, and crawl back towards her.

We dock seamlessly, her hand helping to welcome me within her, her touch as smooth and effective as a shoehorn. Breath becomes sound becomes song becomes cry, the crescendo of our voices rising along a steady gradient.

We are in a room of our bodies' making. Our torsos are like two walls, but in the space between us, the gap between my tummy and hers, my face and hers, my mouth and hers? That is home.[62]

On the horizon, climax comes into view and we race towards it, giddy as teenagers, jerking and bucking and galloping against one another. What had been a gentle rolling boil is now a red-hot saucepan, fizzing and spitting as bubbles hurtle to the surface.

'Christ.'

'Yep.'

'Christ.'

'Yep.'

'Christ.'

'Yep.'

'Christ.'

'Yep.'

'Chris.'

'Yep.'

'Chriiiiiiiiiiiiiiiiiiiiiiiist.'

Silence.

'Yep.'

Then we sleep, or I do and she goes on her phone, and we fall very much in love.[63]

---

62 Some of this passage has been composed with the help of a creative-writing class I sometimes attend for a laugh. Not all of the passage was mine, but I was jotting it down as fast as I could and I think they're by and large what we said in the room.

63 Funnily enough, I did actually mispronounce the fifth Christ as Chris. But after explaining that I don't know anyone called Chris, we were able to laugh about it.

CHAV

Summer 2016

Chav – what does chav mean? The Oxford English Dictionary says that it derives from the Romani word 'chavi', meaning child. Some wrongly suggest it stands for Council-Housed And Violent, but we can all make up snazzy acronyms. Curry House Asbo Vandals, Cheeky Hoodlums Are Volatile, Chickenshop Hangerarounders Arguing Vociferously, Can't Handle Authority Verywell or simply Chips, Haddock And Vinegar.[64]

It's a loaded word. Or rather, it's problematic – which is what we say when we mean it's not racist or sexist but they'll come up with a label for it soon.

But you also have to understand the culture it is delivered in. In Norwich, men of my age use it almost as a term of endearment. We mumble it all the time. Market trader's van is blocking your car? Hurry up, chav! The gardener is putting his prices up? The cheeky little chav. Someone is wearing a tracksuit but with black school socks visible at the ankle? Get some sports socks, you chav! There's a new show on ITV? ITV is for chavs.

Nothing offensive is meant by it. It's no harsher than scamp, wally or apeth. And if you can't call a teenage boy a wally, then really what have we come to? And yet just when I needed a ladder to scale the

---

64 I don't want to suggest that these are my views. I'm just saying anyone can retrofit an acronym onto a Romani word and say they made it up. It's bullshit.

dizzy heights of TV renown, I had landed very much on a snake. Marvin the snake.

Still, I took my punishment like a man, or a very strong woman, and stayed away from the station for the mandated fortnight.

What I refused to do was lie low. To shrink away from public view, to hide away under a rock like a terrified chicken or just crabs generally – it wasn't my style. So instead I brazened it out, making sure I was seen laughing with a woman at a coffee shop, or browsing premium wines in the Waitrose booze section. I had my hair styled just so by a man who usually specialised in the rigid volumised hairdos of female politicians such as Penny Mordaunt, Nicola Sturgeon and Michael Fabricant. I wanted my hair to look as proud and confident as I was. I also wore a bomber jacket with 'North Norfolk Digital Summer Roadshow 2012' on it to remind people I was a much-loved local DJ.

I even had my ringtone changed to Chumbawamba (surely the anthem for the thrusting take-no-shit broadcaster) and instructed my assistant to call every ten minutes so people would hear it and I could make a big deal of taking it out and barking, 'Yello!' like I'd once seen a drunk Alan Yentob do. In short, I wanted to project sass.

And it seemed to work. In my peripheral vision, I could see people looking impressed as I acted the big man around town – although by its nature peripheral vision isn't the most reliable. How many times have I seen a jellyfish in the swimming pool, only to realise front-on that it's a verruca sock or just a bit of water. Likewise, long after my wife left the marital home, I would see her in the corner of my eye and make a loving quip in her direction, before realising 'Carol' was actually just an apron hanging on the back of the kitchen door and my quip was either wasted entirely or would have to be used on the next day's show. Still, I remain convinced that I was the recipient of admiring glances Norwich-wide.

All I had to do was show no contrition and this would surely blow over. So I'd said 'chav' on air once? Big deal. Is it worse than Dave Clifton vomiting on the microphone and crying as he cleaned it up? Or Barbara Bickerton making another snide remark about men being useless? No. This was just a minor faux pas.

But then – in an incident that beggared belief – I made a similar mistake three days later at a golf club dinner.

I love golf club dinners. While no fan of the sport itself – golf buggies have a top speed of just 13mph – I enjoy the company of golf players and golf administrators immensely. The Jackie Weavers of this world probably find them disagreeable, but the combination of rules-based fastidiousness[65] with drunken, red-faced jollity has always been a sweet spot for me. It's fun but ordered fun.

Somehow, on the night I attended, that order broke down. I was there to give out a few awards and make a brief speech to get the party started. I'd hosted the event in 2015, 2014, 2013, 2012, 2011, 2010, 2009, 2007 and 2006.[66] It had always been an easy gig and more importantly a safe space.

Not tonight. The club rules dictated that mobile phones were not permitted in the clubhouse by order of the club secretary, DGP Holston – a man whose surfeit of initials felt reassuringly 'officer class'. Unfortunately, his instruction – a direct order – was flouted. And someone filmed my remarks, most damagingly my gag that 'you come here to get away from chavs!'.

Why had I said it again? Was it a form of Tourette's – an urge to say the most destructive thing I could utter? Was it that I'd allowed myself a few drinks too many in my glee at being surrounded by like-minded bachelors? Or was it just that my transgression in the radio

---

65 On one occasion the winners of a father and son tournament were disqualified when it emerged that the son was actually adopted. And while some see this as needlessly strict, I'm told there are plans to introduce a secondary event for orphans, bastards and adoptees.

66 2008 – Karl Howman.

studio was still at the forefront of my mind, and forced its way out like the red bit of a dog's dick when it's aroused? All equally plausible.

Whatever the reason, it soon found its way onto the popular video-sharing platform YouTube and within days had been viewed dozens and dozens of times. I've never seen my assistant so angry.

'You have to do something,' she harrumphed. 'You can't bury your head in the sand.'

'I will bury my head,' I insisted. 'I'll bury my head so deep I can't breathe anymore, and when you find me I'll be dead on all fours with my head in a bucket of compacted sand like a human pot plant.'

I didn't mean it. I was trying to guilt trip her. That's how bad I felt.

And, on that, like the bit fifty minutes into a Netflix documentary about a successful financial services company, the whole house of cards came crashing down.

Norwich is a cold and lonely place when you're ostracised. Suddenly, I had a real insight into what life must have been like if I lived in Norwich but was black or was that Chinese family who moved in in Holt. Friends wouldn't take my calls.

Cancelling is nothing new. I've been at the other end, having to tell people with regret that they were no longer part of the in-crowd. As a Scout, I remember telling the youngest lad in our troop that he couldn't come to camp. He'd been horsing around on the last trip and flouted some of the fire rules, which I had detailed exhaustively in the minibus. And people expected a reaction.

'Kenneth,' I put my hand on his shoulder. 'You're gonna have to sit this one out.'

'But please,' he pleaded. 'Please.'

'You put your fellow Scouts in harm's way. I wouldn't be looking out for them if I didn't make sure there were consequences.'

'But all my friends are going.'

'They ain't your friends, Ken. Friends don't wave a sparkler around

*near a flammable canvas tent; friends don't kick hot embers near an-
other boy's sleeping bag; friends don't play with matches EVER.'*

'You fucking dick.'

*I could have replied with, 'No, you're a dick,' but I didn't. I
rose above it, cast my eyes downwards and did a small smile of
disappointment, which was clever because that's effectively the non-
verbal way of saying, 'No, you're a dick,' except they can't get you
for it.*

He turned on me. 'Does [Scout master] Darren know about this?'

*'I've spoken to Darren and suggested he call your parents. Where's
Darren? They're on their way to collect him . . .? Yep, they're on the
way to collect you. You shan't be joining us on the minibus.'*

'What am I supposed to do all weekend?'

*'If I were you? I'd think about fire safety, then make a collage about
it to show you've actually learned something.'*

*I'm pleased to say Kenneth made that collage and to this day it's
one of the best collages I've ever seen – certainly about safety.[67]*

*So cancel culture is nothing new. A superb book, which I must read
one day, by high-voiced broadcaster Jon Ronson is all about this. In
it, I imagine, though can't confirm because, like I say, never read it, he
talks about how it happens and feels.*

*And now I, Alan Partridge, know how it feels too. Because al-
though I hadn't done a heck of a lot wrong, perception against me
hardened.*

*Unfortunately we live in a world where people live in fear of
stepping out of line. They dance the dance of performative dis-
approval, even when I'm pretty sure they're relaxed about the so-
called wrongdoing. For example, Dominic Aldridge from Triffic*

---

67 It was made with cuttings taken from a catalogue, which can work extremely
well if you stay away from the bras and showers. (For members of Gen Z, 'cata-
logues' were the precursor to the internet.)

Tiles on the A140 had been a friend and a long-time sponsor of the mid-morning entertainment news. He was the first to break ranks, issuing a statement on his company website saying 'as the father of teenage girls . . .' he had decided not to continue with the sponsorship.

I respect Dom immensely, certainly more than he respects his teenage girls. I just wonder how he squares his heroic moral stance with the fact that he has sofa cushions embroidered with golliwogs – and they are golliwogs, he can insist they're black teddies all he likes. That's not me trying to get him back. I just want to know how he squares that. I also wonder how the father of teenage girls can be so comfortable with mauling and groping every waitress who comes within arm's length of the table. Maybe I'll ask his wife, see if she knows.

Aldridge wouldn't be the last. Soon, others followed suit, literally joining the feeding frenzy against me – Chaucer's Country Kitchen, NPP Escrow, and United Farm and Animal Feed were companies I'd enjoyed long, warm relationships with. Good companies, local companies. For Christ's sake, I was godfather to Doug Chaucer's kid (maybe still am, must check – also check name). Each of them dropped me like a sack of shit/hot stone.

But now, I was haemorrhaging support like a cheap shopping bag haemorrhages tins of food when the bottom bursts open. In my home office, I set up a nerve centre to manage the fallout, with a team of trusted advisors. My assistant was responsible for scouring the internet and correcting negative perceptions but without saying she worked for me. Judy Gabitas, widow of my late best friend Pete came round because I still hadn't told her I didn't want to sleep with her anymore, and I let her buzz round and make cakes and sandwiches. My financial adviser, Ken Scullion, was on hand with sage business advice and a running spreadsheet labelled 'How fucked is Alan?'.

Eamonn Holmes, this was when we were getting on great guns, was also there, as a kind of helper without portfolio, basically just sending out positive vibes, saying, 'Come on, gang, keep at it!' and eating all of Judy's sandwiches. Former Radio 1 DJ Mark Goodier was there as well but not sure why. Barely know the guy.

By lunchtime the next day we were exhausted, and we tried to survey the wreckage of my career and reputation. The best idea we'd had was to publicly reposition myself as the very thing I'd been accused of smearing. Just as no Jewish man could be accused of antisemitism, surely no – excuse the term – 'chav' could be accused of undermining the plight of his own people.

So, over the next five days, I sought to align myself with the – again, sorry – chav community, fostering the sense that I was 'one of them'. I used public transport, audibly dropped my aitches and said less when I should have been saying fewer, I went for lunch in a Wetherspoons pub – a fucking dreadful experience – bought an electrical item (and meat!) from an outdoor market, smoked a cigarette, wore sportswear in a down-market supermarket called Asda and watched a couple of shows on the ITV channel. In desperation, I even wore a sandwich board bearing the words I'M SORRY I MADE A MISTAKE in the hope that abject pity might be a way back into the good books. But still the snubs kept coming.

It was almost a week later, after being uninvited to a charity auction hosted by Howard from the Halifax adverts, that I admitted defeat. They hated me. The people had cast me out.

'I've not seen a backlash like this since Ron Atkinson,' piped up Mark Goodier, who I swear to God I'd not realised was still in my house. 'You'll have to do a documentary learning what chavs means!'

He laughed and then explained what he meant. Racist comments uttered on a 'hot mic' on an ITV football game had seen Big Ron dismissed by the low-rent broadcaster and his work and brand affiliations were pulled. But then, ingeniously, Ron and his team struck TV gold. What if Ron could front a documentary learning about where he'd gone wrong, fess up, go on a journey of redemption, and get paid for it?

My team were enthused. Me? Well, all I wanted to do was be better. If there was a TV format and healthy fee to leverage from that journey, that to me was by the by. All I wanted to do – literally the only thing – was make things right for Marvin and the whole whatever you want to call his community.

And so we set about calling in favours. Within days, we had as-sembled a rag-team of otherwise unemployable crew members who would work for free or near as dammit. Like The Dirty Dozen, *these were outcasts who operated outside the parameters of polite so-ciety. Each one of them guzzlers in the last chance saloon, they were more likely, I figured, to be desperate to do a good job. And desperation is a wonderful motivator.*

I nicknamed the crew 'my merry men' because 'dirty dozen' re-minded our sound guy of his arrest for wanking in an egg farm. And 'merry men' they certainly were. Our Little John, if you like, was camera operator Mario Sheen, a gentle giant who had a brother in prison and had been out of work since he used a BBC camera drone to drop a cache of skunk and SIM cards in through a window at Belmarsh.[68] *Our Will Scarlet was Noa Gibson, a hot-headed line producer who had thumped the actor James Nesbitt – and like Scarlet had a hair-trigger temper and few friends in the industry, although you'd think she'd be quite popular after the Nesbitt thing. Our Friar Tuck (this is the last one, I promise) was paunchy hair and make-up technician Dennis – a former gayman, he had renounced his sexuality after finding the Lord and was now so virulently anti-gay as to make him unemployable in the gay-friendly world of TV. I'm gay-friendly*

---

68 And accidentally recorded it.

myself, and only employed him once he'd assured me that he'd try to stop going on about how sinful it was.

The documentary would explore how a schasm had formed in Britain between the haves and the have-nots. So it just seemed logical to head to the spiritual home of the deprived, to the Mecca of Mecca Bingos on a Hajj of the Haven'ts. Yes, we were heading to Manchester to meet with supermarket workers, youth offenders, single mums and bin scroungers.

I would be away from home for a fortnight, which caused a slight headache in terms of dog care. My big brown dog Seldom couldn't be left with other people and would need feeding at some point. The solution? Bring him along for the ride and weave him into the overall fabric of the show. Years later, several of the 1,080 people who watched the show have come up to me and said the shots of Seldom were among their favourite parts of the programme. I maintain that bringing him with us was the right thing to do, even though the cantankerous canine landed us in hot water when he broke free of his lead and accidentally ate a man's sheep, the subsequent hush-money payment eating up half our budget faster than Seldom had eaten the sheep's body.

The making of the programme was a revelation, though. I felt vital, free, fizzing and good. Nobody watching the show could possibly argue that I'd not been on a journey of redemption and emerged a better man and, yes, a better broadcaster. The turning point for me arrived in a teenager's house party near Denton. I had mingled with the youngsters and, on realising drugs were being passed round and that I had a duty of care, I confiscated an ecstasy tablet in exchange for some money.

I confess to this: a quick nibble to ensure it was indeed the designer nightclub substance did have an effect on me. Others at the party won't have noticed any behavioural change, my constitution is too hardy for that to show, but on the inside my consciousness was expanding and cartwheeling in fascinating new directions.

A friend's wife told me of a similar experience she'd had while on a yoga retreat in Cancún. One evening, each of the yogic women took a brew containing ayahuasca, a hallucinogenic drug found in South America. She says it was revelatory, creating a feeling of total spiritual purification. She returned to the UK with a new lease of life, a whole new outlook and also a Peruvian boyfriend – which has caused some marital friction but only to her husband.

For me, the experience of nibbling ecstasy was similarly life-changing. As I wandered the kitchen, grinning and asking teenagers if they were having a good night, I felt an enormous sense of change. It was as if in that moment I was shedding any residual feelings of shame or guilt. And from that moment, I felt precisely zero guilt for what I'd said to Marvin. At no point since have I even considered the possibility that I, Alan Partridge, had done anything wrong, not really. And that can be only healthy.

I made four firm friends that night, friendships that I know continue to this day, a bond that spans the 240 miles between my home and theirs, between a guy old enough to be their granddad and four Mancunian youths. I think one was called Gav and I'm not sure about the others.

As for the show, I was keen for it to get as wide (or big) an audience as possible. For a while, I was in talks with a friend on Norwich City Council over the prospect of showing it on the big outdoors screens outside Norwich Forum.

'We only put the screens up for Pride weekend,' he said.

'Great, show it then.'

'Pride is for the LGBTQ+ community. It's got nothing to do with what you call "chavs".'

'You're not telling me you can't slip a C in there on the quiet,' I spluttered. 'Say it's an LGBTCQ+ event, no one will notice.

Please, Paul. There'll be two thousand people watching that.'

In the end he wouldn't do it, and I had to settle for a much smaller audience on Sky Atlantic.

SPITTING FEATHERS

April 2022

It's the morning after I made love to Red and I've never felt so virile. As she sleeps soundly on the bed, I stride over to the bathroom. When my bladder's full, I become erect – yet emptying a bladder when one has a stiffy is a tricksy task indeed. Gripping the member and attempting to force it downwards only serves to excite the thing more. So I prefer a different technique, working with – not against – the proud appendage. Standing two paces back from the bowl with my hands by my sides, the flow begins, arcing up and over into the toilet like half a McDonald's logo. As the bladder empties and tumescence begins to subside, so the angle of flight begins to decrease. As this happens, I counteract it by graaaaaaaaaadually leaning forward, making a body position reminiscent of a ski-jumper in flight. At a certain point, however, leaning any further forward becomes impossible without falling into the pan. I have now entered the trickiest phase of the ablution.

Instinct suggests taking a step towards the loo, but this would lead the torso to twist. Though that twist would be almost imperceptible to the human eye, even minor lateral adjustments to the beam can lead to devastating consequences as you splash the wall to the right of the toilet, panic, and as you overcorrect, splash the wall to the left. Instead, what is required is a series of smooth, small shuffles, bringing you forward quickly but safely, until eventually you come to rest with your shins against the rim just in time to shudder and finish.

I wander back over to the mattress. My eyes land on the sleeping figure of Red. God, she's beautiful. I lean over, put my fingers under her chin and gently close her mouth because she's been sleeping with it open.

'That's better,' I whisper.

By now I'm starting to register just how much my back has stiffened up. Lost in the fog of passion, I'd twisted, turned, bent and at one pointed leaned myself into positions simply not suited to a man of my age. If I'm ever to experience such wide-ranging coitus again, I will request a short break every twenty minutes to snack and stretch. It would also make sense to pre-book with my osteopath the night before.[69]

I throw on some clothes, rip a banana away from the rest of its family and greedily munch on the smile-shaped fruit. I take one more lingering look at Red, quickly re-close her mouth because it's fallen open again and head out for a bracing coastal walk. Yesterday, I found out that the nearby Samphire Hoe nature reserve was created using soil dug out during the construction of the Channel Tunnel. To be able to walk around on earth that had once been buried deep beneath the sea is a tantalising prospect indeed. And because seabed sediment is largely made up of fossilised remains, there's every chance I'll effectively be treading on a terrydactyl spine, a billion-year-old woodlouse or – if I'm really lucky – an ancient fish face.

But an hour later, as I gaily march up and down the nature reserve as happy as a sandboy/one of the women from a Bodyform advert, I receive a message from my assistant that is so intriguing I will now do a time-jump to one day later.

---

69 When my assistant found out I'd had intimate relations with Red, she rolled her eyes. But she also believes that immigrants arriving in rubber dinghies should be towed to Ireland and left there, so make of her judgement what you will.

* * *

'Will it be chips or jacket spuds? Will it be salad or frozen peas? Will it be onions, fried onion rings, we'll have to wait and see.'

I'm in my car singing the song from the Birdseye Steakhouse Grills adverts from the mid-eighties. Some of you will be familiar with that reference and some won't, and that – despite the fretting of my editor – is fine. Where am I headed?

Well, the intriguing message from my assistant had been about TV cook James Martin. His assistant had contacted her out of the blue, presumably in response to my round-robin letter asking for financial contributions to the rebuild. His message had read: 'Come over. Can have lunch and chat about renno project.'[70]

Well, this was manna from heaven. We've already swerved over budget and a chunk of cash from a well-loved celebrity chef would be just the ticket. And so, after briefing my assistant as to how long the builders are allowed for lunch and where they can and can't wear outdoor shoes in the property, I'm driving to an address in Sussex, a spring in my step and a song on my lips.

'Hope it's chips, it's chips.[71] We hope it's chips, it's chips . . .'[72]

* * *

Crunch.

Two black shoes drop into shot. Clarks CitiStrides, which sound fusty but they're actually really good shoes.

---

70 The 'renno' referring to the renovation project rather than anything related to the similar-sounding French car brand with the distinctive rhombus logo.
71 This is the Birdseye Steakhouse Grills adverts from the mid-eighties again.
72 As is this.

Pull back to reveal Alan Partridge, the hot yellow sun bouncing off his clean brown hair as he walks confidently along the gravel.

Extreme close-up. A tongue emerges from his mouth. It's his own so there's nothing weird going on, but it means business. It's come out to do a clean-up, darting this way (i.e. left) and that (i.e. right) to mop up the stray flakes of almond croissant that bejewel his fat pink lips. Job done, the fleshy cleaning cloth retreats. The man is ready.

(I'm now going to stop talking like a film script but believe it was a useful technique to set the scene and reserve the right to return to it later. Thank you.)

James Martin is waiting for me. Boots. Stone-washed jeans. Leather jacket. Guy looks gooooood.

Me? Same deal. So that's boots, it's stone-washed jeans, it's leather jacket. I kick myself because he's got one with zip pockets in the arms and I haven't. The pockets serve no actual purpose, but they do elevate the jacket to the next level of cool and he knows it.

He's leaning on the bonnet of a Ferrari 275 GTB long nose. It's parked at forty-five degrees to the drive with the front wheels turned to face forward. It's an angle you only ever see cars parked at in motoring magazines and will have taken Martin several goes to get right, after which he'll have had to smooth out the gravel to hide the evidence of the previous attempts. But as with the zip pockets of his leather jacket, blow me off if it doesn't look absolutely outstanding. And as I reach him and thrust out my arm for a shake, he looks every bit the lord of the manor/lighthouse.

'Nice jacket.'

'Zip pockets.'

'Clocked 'em.'

'Cool.'

'Chest bump?'

'Sure.'

We each take a step back then come forward again and bump chests. There's then a slightly awkward silence because it was a bit of a weird thing to do, but we soon move past it as Martin starts to tell me about his £5 million car collection, which might sound braggy but it isn't and I enjoy hearing it. As he lists each vehicle one by one, telling me first what he paid for it and then how much more it's worth now, it's not hard to see why he's once again been voted Fortnum & Mason's TV Personality of the Year. His conversation really is as sparkling as the Prosecco his personal wine label is hoping to start producing in the near future. His current wines include a red Corbières and white Vin de Pays d'Oc sourced from the Languedoc area in the south of France. He says that if we had more time, he'd be able to fly me there. Better still, as he's one of the few people in the UK to have gained both a helicopter licence *and* a private pilot's licence, I could choose the type of aircraft we travel in! It's a cracking line but one based in truth because he actually does have both licences.

I say, 'James, you're the only guy I know whose small-talk is about high-performance machines.' I slap his leather back and throw in a shoulder squeeze as we share a high-octane cackle. Outstanding.

With the preamble both done and enjoyed I am ready to get to brass tacks.

* * *

'So what gives, JM?' I say, perching my backside on the bonnet next to him, before he asks me not to do that because it might damage the paintwork, which is absolutely fair enough. I stand back up and get my bearings. This clearly isn't where he actually lives. There's no Union Jack, for a start. And just behind us is a crumbling old lighthouse.

'What is this place?' I ask.

'This is the renovation I mentioned,' he beams, revealing chemically whitened teeth that look just about OK on television but in person give the impression he's recently eaten Tipp-Ex. 'A nineteenth-century Sussex lighthouse. I'm going to completely rebuild it.'

Riiiiiiight, I think. It's a free country, last time I checked, anyway, and James can spend his money however he sees fit . . . but this does sound *quite* similar to the project I'm doing.

'And you're telling me this, why?' I say quietly.

I feel sweat forming on my northernmost (i.e. top) lip. My brain clanks and whirrs trying to make sense of this. I can only think he's interested in us becoming 'build buddies'. Yes, that could be it. Our projects are similar in nature, after all, similar in scale, and most likely happening over similar time periods.

More to the point, building projects are notoriously stressful, frequently leading to relationship breakdowns, mental health problems and – chillingly for Martin and I – hair loss. So it would make sense that we buddy up to offer a shoulder to cry on when times get tough. And as men of a certain profile, finding someone trustworthy to unburden yourself to is never easy. Loose lips sink ships, and that phrase – coined by the US Office of War Information – is as true for celebrities in the modern age as it is for gobshites in the Second World War.

Open up to a kindly stranger during a trip to the barber's, a visit to the dental hygienist or at your monthly mani-pedi and eyelash tint, and you can all too easily find yourself plastered over the next day's tabloids.

Money talks, and the lure of easy cash from the gossip-hungry red tops is particularly hard to resist for the working-class people who are employed to work on your hair, teeth and feet.

It's a terrifying thought, and a risk that could be eliminated completely by the elegant simplicity of my 'build buddy' concept. A 'no judgement' Whatsapp group, weekly Zoom check-in calls, and a monthly pie and pint evening at a location equidistant from our two sites would provide exactly the kind of safe, secure release valve the two of us need. It's a compelling pitch.

But Martin suggests no such thing.

'I just thought you'd be interested,' he says.

I smile tightly. 'I'm interested, James. Interested in whether you think it'll look like we're copying each other. Because if you think about it, even for one second, I think you'll agree that's what it will look like and that's what people will say.'

He chuckles. 'Nah, I just think we should preserve our national treasures. I've always said, we should respect Britain's architectural heritage. Said it on the press release.'

My cheek quivers as I fight to maintain my smile. 'No, I said that to you, James. Remember, in Esther McVey's kitchen? I'm the one who . . . hang on, press release?'

'Yeah, Howard wanted to flag it up as a big feature of the show. Create some buzz.'

'Hang on, Howard?'

'You know him, don't you? Wasn't he producing it when you were there?'

'Hang on, producing it?'

'*This Time*. That's who I'm filming the restoration for. They're going to try to get Princess Anne to come to the opening.'

My mouth dries like dog dirt in the sun.[73] Is he for real?? It

---

73 Horrible image.

would be helpful to see his eyes but he's put on mirrored sun-glasses, so instead of James Martin all I see looking back at me are two Alan Partridges with grotesquely elongated noses. His face betrays no sign of a smile. He is serious.

'Just stay cool, Alan, stay cool,' I think to myself.

'About what?' replies Martin.

It seems I hadn't thought it to myself, I'd said it out loud, sug-gesting I'd failed to do the very thing my words had described. 'Nothing, pal. We're golden.'

Discombobulated and needing to get out of there, I jump to-wards Martin for another chest bump, but as I hadn't mentioned it first I nearly flatten him. Thankfully there's no harm done and he tells me to hop in the 275, he'll give me a lift to the station. I don't need a lift to the station, as I've come by car, but it might look like a sulk to turn down his offer, plus I've nearly just split his nose open with my sternum. He drops me at the train, I spend the day there until it gets dark, get a taxi back to his light-house, quietly climb in my car, roll down the hill away from his house with my lights off and then begin the drive home.

* * *

'How dare he! That man is a ... is a ...'

'It's alright, let it out.'

'That man is a good-for-nothing copycat.'

I have never seen my assistant this angry. She is spitting feathers. Not literally – though that did once happen when she was plucking some roadkill. Me? I'm more sanguine.

'Listen,' I say, chucking some chewing gum towards my mouth and very nearly getting it in. 'All I care about is preserving our national treasures.'

'Isn't that what James Martin said in the press relea—'

'Yes, and he got it from me,' I snap, not because I'm bothered about him doing up a lighthouse (after he'd told me, I quickly realised I wasn't), I just find it irritating when people use my words in their press releases. Nah, the lighthouse thing is all good with me, baby.

'Maybe just pop in a call to the Lighthouse Board, though. Might as well invite them to see it. Might as well.'

My assistant opens up her laptop with the care of someone who still doesn't understand that the screen won't snap off if she does it a bit faster. As she types, a look of pride spreads across her face, a look I've seen frequently since she learned to use the forefinger of her right hand as well as the one on her left. Suddenly she stops.

'Heavens to Murgatroyd.'

'Hm?'

'Princess Anne is their patron. It says here she has been a keen pharol— . . . pharol—'

'Pharologist, lover of lighthouses, go on.'

'A keen pharologist since the age of five when she accompanied the Queen to one on the Isle of Lewis! Alan, imagine if Her Highness came to your lighthouse, and imagine if that happened *before* she opened the *This Time* one!'

I sling another piece of chew gum at my mouth. Bullseye. 'Yes that would be a very pleasant thing to happen.'

* * *

Time to get serious. I despatch my assistant to Sussex, allowing her to stay in a modest B&B close to James Martin's lighthouse. Her mission? To steal onto the site at first light and accrue detailed photographic intel on the star of James Martin's build. I want to know every detail.

She returns forty-eight hours later – not sure why she had to stay two nights, although I know Susan Boyle was playing in Eastbourne on the second night and I tell her that. She is clearly pleased with her work, her face betraying a pride in herself that borders on the unseemly. But when we look through the photographs, it becomes clear that, for reasons I can't understand, she has managed to switch to the front-facing camera so that all of the photos are of herself: her torso, chin, a bit of her shoulder or the Macmillan Cancer lapel badge pinned to her coat.

'Oh dear,' she tuts. 'They seemed fine when I was taking them; they're never as good when you get them developed.'

'For God's sake,' I said. 'The screen is there as a viewfinder. If you can't see it on the screen, it's not going to be on the photo. This is exactly why I wanted you to stick to the Nokia.'

GOOD FELLAS

Summer 2017

Scissored Isle *was urgent, needful, important television. Perhaps the first television show to feature working-class people that doesn't include bailiffs or Scotland. I was delighted with how it turned out. It was proof, if proof be needed, that I was a talent to be reckoned with.*

I waited by the phone and . . . nothing. Usually, this is because my assistant unplugs it at the wall when she hoovers, but this time, after a bit of a tongue-lashing from yours truly, she pointed out that she hadn't unplugged it. It was just not ringing.

It.

Was.

Just.

Not.

Ringing.

Despondent, I punched three Easter eggs I'd been saving then grumpily unwrapped them and ate the shards with a spoon slightly too big for my mouth. Stretching the skin at the corners of my lips was painful and it annoyed me, making me need the chocolate even more and so I ate faster, causing even more pain. I could see my assistant's look of concern. She'd seen me spiral like this decades earlier when the pointy bit of a Toblerone triangle had speared the roof of my mouth and induced a similar 'suffer pain/need chocolate' vortex that led to me gorging for over three days and ending in Dundee – which is a lovely part of the world if you don't stay long.

'I know what I'm doing,' I grunted as I pushed the chocolate away. I was not going there again.

Instead, I drove to Gatwick Village and browsed and browsed, nosing my way through glossy magazines, electrical goods and sunglasses, the latter usually a surefire way to restore my good humour. Many's the time I've put on a pair of sunglasses from a display rack, tugged the tag away from the bridge of my nose and then checked myself out in the one-inch mirror on the central pillar of the rack – accompanied by the expressions or catchphrases of whichever movie star matches that pair of glasses: 'I feel the need, the need for speed', 'Are you talkin' to me', 'Hasta la vista, baby' or, 'Will you _please_ stop talking about fight club!' But today, for some reason, Sunglass Hut was singularly unable to lift my spirits.

And it was there that I bumped into someone who would quite literally change my life.

Disgraced sports broadcaster Richard Keys is someone I'd known for a number of years. Despite not being particularly good company, he's someone I'd always felt a slight kinship with. In the late eighties we'd been up for presenting a video for HM Revenue and Customs (then HM Customs & Excise, would you believe – funny how names for things change!) about the consequences of submitting your tax return late. On paper, it was a very strong video – taut script, compelling central idea (Don't Be a Late Larry!), terrific location (Highgate Cemetery) and in Dominic Grelland, one of the best corpvid directors in the business. Richard and I both wanted the gig very much. We screentested separately and chatted in the lift on the way out. In a quiet moment, Richard revealed that he was self-conscious about the back of his hands, which in adulthood had started to become slightly hairy. It really wasn't that noticeable, but since it was bothering him I told him he should give them a quick shave.

In the end, I didn't get the job, but neither did Richard – Hunniford gazumped us both – and I thought little more about it until *a few months later, at a barbecue to mark the launch of Homebase's new barbecues, when I saw him again. Seeing me, his face hardened and he stormed over.*

'Thanks a fucking <u>lot</u>!' he said. I looked at him blankly and he held up his hands. How to describe them? Until then, the phrase 'black forest' made me think of the famous eighties gateau. But from that day on, 'black forest' will always remind me of the back of Richard Keys' hands. Richard had shaved them as I suggested, but the hair had grown back. Boy, had it grown back. It was at least six times thicker than it had been, as if each follicle was sprouting a palm tree's worth of jet-black hair, a frighteningly virulent jungle of pelt.

'I didn't . . . know that would—' I spluttered.

But Richard suspected sabotage, convinced I'd tricked him into hairing up his hands to make him less telegenic and prevent him from getting any future work that he and I might be vying for. A darkness fell over Richard that day and our relationship never truly recovered.

You see, the old Richard – or Ricky, as he was more frequently known then – had harboured dreams of light entertainment. He saw himself as a Mr Saturday Night figure, hosting a shiny-floor show on ITV or the Generation Game/Blankety Blank *slot on BBC One. But he developed a hang-up about his hands – a hand-gup – that marooned him in the more prosaic world of sports broadcasting, leading to a twenty-year career as Sky Sports' face of football – a sport he has secretly never liked, much less understood.*

I don't propose to relitigate what Richard did or didn't say off-air to lose his job at Sky – that's between him and whichever women he spoke of hanging out the back of. All I know is that I've never been a fan of bawdy locker-room talk – both because it's wrong and because the other boys don't include me – so when he did get the old heave-ho[74] from Sky, I didn't pick up the phone.

Instead, Keys, and his exceptionally Scottish co-host Andy Gray, upped sticks to Qatar. A fresh start and good for them! In fact, it annoys me when people assume they didn't learn their lesson just because they migrated to the Middle East to front football coverage for hardline Muslims. And while they sent round-robin emails boasting of their new life over there – with photographs careful not to feature too many Muslims in the background – I gave them short shrift and we lost touch.

So when I bumped into the two of them on the concourse at Gatwick, with my own television career in the toilet, I expected a smirk. If not a smirk, a snort. Or if not a snort, a sneer. Instead? Richard hugged me.

I'd enjoyed good hugs before then. Me and my ex-wife Carol were prolific huggers, with hugs, squeezes and pats gradually coming to replace kissing and lovemaking entirely – certainly once she started boffing her fitness instructor. I have hugged Sally Gunnell drunk; I have hugged former-DJ-and-now-busker Dave Clifton live on air; I hugged my maths teacher at least once a week before he was told to stop, and I've even hugged Sir Jeffrey Archer after the daft apeth won his libel case against the Daily Star, *little realising the spotty-backed bastard had gone and bloody perjured himself. I once had a superb hug with a masseuse I hadn't realised was a sex worker, and while that embrace cost me £150, it remains up there in my personal pantheon of good cuddles.*

But the hug I received at the hands (and arms) of Richard Keys tops the lot. It had empathy, meaning, trust, wit[75] and warmth.

'It's OK, Alan, it's OK,' he said and mock-punched me on the jaw,

---

74 I use the word 'ho' advisedly here.
75 The hug incorporated a side-to-side rock.

stopping his fist an inch away from my face, but close enough for his knuckle hair to brush me lightly. 'The real Alan is still in there. You just have to tease him out.'

Andy grunted in assent and said: 'Ye shay co tae Do'a.'

I looked to Richard.

'He said, "You should come to Doha."'

I smiled. 'Tell him thanks.'

'Thanks,' said Richard.

'Nae bo'er.'

I looked to Richard.

'He said, "No bother."'

I looked at Richard then looked at the planes on the concourse, then I nodded once, walked to the Emirates desk and bought a return ticket to Doha for that very evening. Enough time for my assistant to drive to my house, pack and bring my case to me at the airport, so long as she was brisk and didn't dawdle.

That night, I landed in the sweltering Gulf state, tired but excited and bursting with information about the little-known nation, thanks to the inflight magazine and the tedious man I'd been sitting next to. So much so that I thanked the guys on passport control for providing the very oil that had propelled the aircraft over. They frowned at me and I moved on.

Richard had suggested lunch the next day, and we reconvened in a steakhouse where Richard was very much the star of the show, waving and nodding at anyone who said hello. 'These are all expats. Expats who enjoy beef,' he said.

Andy chuckled. 'Thi shuh coll'm coi pa's.'

I looked to Richard.

'He said, "They should call them cow pats."'

'Oh, that's good,' I said. 'That's very good. Tell him that's very good.'

He nodded. 'That's very good, Andy.'

It would be the last time I laughed for some time. Because seemingly out of nowhere, Richard started to behave in an extremely mean way.

For example, when I said, 'This steak is wonderfully tender,' Richard repeated, 'This steak is wonderfully tender,' but in a mewling whiny baby voice. I wasn't sure what he meant by it so said nothing.

But later, when I said, 'Do you know where I can buy some Bermuda shorts?', Richard glanced at Andy and said, 'Do you know where I can buy some Bermuda shorts?' in a baby voice, before shouting to the waiter, 'Alan's getting this.'

To my chagrin, I didn't find out where I could buy Bermuda shorts, but I did pay for steak, onion rings, chips and drinks for the whole table. Confused and hurt, I nevertheless agreed to meet the next day.

Their behaviour the next morning was, if anything, even worse. For example, Andy had his telescope with him and kept looking at distant holiday makers. If he saw one he liked the look of, he'd nudge Richard and hand him the telescope so he could look too. But whenever I asked if I could have a turn, both men ignored me.

They also made disparaging comments about my lack of suntan, my sandals and my career failures. In front of their sniggering friends, they'd ask me about the viewing figures of my chat show or the aging demographic of my radio audience.

It was Alan-baiting as sport. And suddenly I remembered hearing rumours that they'd treated other presenters in a similar way. Ray Stubbs had supposedly endured a similar teasing a couple of years ago and flew home in tears after nine days. Patrick Kielty didn't even last a week. But this?

This wasn't just mean. This was really, really mean.

Of course, I'd assumed these horror stories were just tittle-tattle. No one would believe that of Messrs Keys and Gray. But here I was, being pulled apart like carrion in the Middle Eastern sun.

The final straw came the following day. Richard and Andy offered to drive me out to soak up the sights and sounds of a local marketplace so that I could experience what they called 'the real Qatar'.

But no sooner had we arrived than Andy started hopping from foot to foot. 'Gottae goan pesh,' he said.

I looked at Richard.

'He has to go and piss,' he explained, before adding that he also needed a wee. I was told to wait there and the two disappeared to find a lavatory. But twenty-five minutes later, I'd come to accept that they weren't coming back. I'd been tricked.

And now in the midday heat, I was stranded in a foreign land, far from home. I felt lost and queasy among the teeming locals and bustling vendors. Where the hell was I? This was a place where the indigenous people would come to buy and sell produce and trade the latest finery. But I felt dizzy – struggling to process the swirl of unfamiliar people and unfamiliar culture. I admit, I felt frightened.

If this market hadn't been an air-conditioned shopping mall, I shudder to think what would have become of me. At least we had these back home, but some of the brands were new to me and the experience was completely disorientating. Where was T.M. Lewin? Where was M&S? Nowhere to be seen.

One of the elders, who bowed deeply and wore a badge that said 'customer services', guided me to the metro station and, despite being shaken and thirsty (certainly until I bought some 7Up), I was able to find my way back to the apartment complex.

By now the scales had fallen from my eyes. It was all so obvious. Far from rising above our fall-out all those years ago, Keys had held on to it like you would a dry-cleaning receipt and allowed it to fester. This was revenge. How could I have been so foolish?

Trudging back to my apartment, I saw Keys and Gray (plus a coterie of their chuckling chums) eating pizza on the sun loungers by the pool. In the corner of my eye, I saw a patch of hot cheese slide from *the slice Gray was holding and fall, steaming and sizzling, onto his naked thigh. He hissed, 'Fugenhil.' This time I didn't need Keys to translate: 'Fucking hell.' But I didn't even allow myself a smile.*

I packed quickly, furiously and neatly. Then I wheeled my case back down to the ground floor to call a cab. Gray, Keys and friends were still munching the much-loved Italian snack, but I strode in the other direction. I wasn't going to give them the satisfaction. But then, another thought: No. I will.

And with a clenched jaw and two tensed buttocks, I marched over to the pool area. Keys looked up.

'You and you are dicks!' I shouted. 'Do you hear me? You're not nice. And while I'm getting things off my chest – get this. I can't tell what you're saying! And I think you have too much hair on your hands, and if that was my fault then I'm glad. Because bad things should happen to bad people and you are bad people. So stick this country up your arses, Richard, and I'm sorry, I've forgotten your name.'

'Uhndeh.'

I looked at Richard, angrily.

'Andy.'

'Andy,' I repeated. 'Now, I'm going to the airport, and if you think we're still friends you can eat swivel.' I'd been caught between the phrase 'eat shit' and 'swivel', but fortunately I'd pretty much run out of breath when I arrived at this part of the sentence so I'm not sure anyone noticed.

Silence. And then, almost imperceptibly, the sound of a single clap. It had come from Andy. He clapped again, and then again. Soon, Richard joined in, louder and faster. They were applauding me. I was incandescent. Like when Kirstie Allsopp sees a single mum.

But before I could react, I noticed they were both smiling, and I mean genuinely smiling. And Richard was approaching with his arms outstretched like a very hairy Jesus.

'You did it,' he said. 'I knew you'd do it.'

'Do what?' I replied.

'You found it, Alan. You found . . . the fire.'

That's when I realised. This whole thing had been engineered – brilliantly engineered – to stoke the flame that had died inside me. It was their contention that I had allowed the inferno that had rocketed me to the very top to dwindle to, at most, glowing embers. And so they'd taken a wrecking ball to the weak, diminished Alan I had become. They had squeezed together their bellows and blown out warm air on to my glowing embers, reigniting the inferno inside me, and in doing so had given me the vigour for what lay ahead. For they were helping me to create Alan 2.0.

Andy offered me some of his pizza. I was immensely grateful but declined because he'd scooped off the meat bits, leaving deep trenches where his fingers had gouged through the now-cold cheese.

I stayed in Qatar, sleeping in Richard's spare room for another four months. It wasn't all plain sailing. Sometimes it was actually quite tedious, but the oil-rich Gulf nation seemed to chime with the freewheeling creative person I needed to become. I found the country – its geography, its culture, its 'anything goes' attitude,[76] its profound spirituality – deeply, deeply inspiring. People think it's all sheikhs and futuristic skyscrapers, but it also has underwater restaurants where you watch fish swim while eating dead ones. Mind-blowing.

At weekends we'd fly out to Dubai or Saudi and soak up the culture there, visiting a shopping mall, hotel or a Gordon Ramsay restaurant, anywhere with air conditioning and toilets. My mind constantly being opened to the new, the fresh, the different. I could feel my eyes widening, my soul swelling, my ears widening as well. And my horizons also widening.

At night, as we ate steak or pizza, Richard would tell a long story about persecution and redemption. It was clear he regarded himself

76 Provided you're in the confines of one of the areas designated for Westerners.

*as a kind of Christ figure, mainly because he often used the phrase
'me and Jesus' when discussing his career blip. Less appallingly, he
said encouraging things about my own skillset, and was firmly of the
belief that with a change of mindset I could achieve great things.*

*How right he was. Over the coming weeks, Richard and, to a much
lesser extent, Andy completely dismantled my approach to broadcasting and rebuilt me from the ground up.*

*Over time, I was able to secure corporate broadcasting work in
the area for a private airline, a fledgling hotel chain, helicopter tours
and forex trading. It was utterly fulfilling and demonstrated beyond
any doubt whatsoever that I had what it took to be an on-camera
television broadcaster. And Richard and Andy couldn't have been
more encouraging.*

*'Yes, it has its critics,' Richard would say, 'those who quibble about
its stance on human rights or gay people or what women can and
can't do. But no country is perfect. If you ask us, the West could do
with getting its own house in order before it starts libelling other
countries.'*

*'Let he who is without sin cast the first stone,' I said. But I was
advised not to use that phrase, as it's the sort of thing they say at the
start of a stoning and people might take it as a signal to throw rocks
at someone.*

BULLHORN BOSS

August 2022

Despite my best efforts, the build continues at an agonisingly slow pace – giving me the same angsty feeling as watching my assistant trying to eat with chopsticks when my car's parked on a meter. Why can't these beefy burlcakes get a move on?

In my mind, I'd imagined the build would be damn near finished by now. I should be munching croissants around the table with Kirstie Allsopp and Phil Spencer and Kevin McCloud and the Geordie man from *Amazing Spaces* who always looks like he's going to cry.

'I love what you've done with the banquette seating,' Kevin would say.

'Yes, and you've painted the kitchen units in Thatcher blue,' Kirstie would say. 'I *adore* Thatcher blue.'

But the brunch meeting of TV housing boffins isn't likely to happen this side of Christmas. For some reason, I just can't seem to impress on my builders the urgency of the task. My usual method of persuasion – low-level passive aggression – has always seemed to work in an office environment: 'That's a great first attempt, Helen,' or, 'Hi, Susan, just re-sending my instructions because I obviously didn't make myself clear last time,' or, 'Is there anything I can do to help you do your job properly, Debbie?'. But builders seem utterly impervious to gentle prodding like this.

Clearly, a more direct approach is needed. It arrives in a brown cardboard package one afternoon. My assistant brings it up to me in the lantern room.

'Delivery for you,' she says, slightly miffed I ordered something without it going through her.

'Oh, great,' I say, ignoring her tone. And I pull off the cardboard to reveal a gleaming white horn.

'What is it?' she says.

'This? It's a megaphone. You might know it as a speaking-trumpet, or a bullhorn or a loudhailer. I've gone for the Pyle PMP30 megaphone. I did want the ThunderPower 1200 because—'

'Because it contains the word ThunderPower,' she surmises.

'Exactly. But it was out of stock. Anyway, this baby gets some *serious* reviews.'

I turn it on, marvelling at the classy ergonomic grip and handy conveying strap. And the performance? Chunky as heck. My test 'A-ha!' is crisp, loud and soon bouncing around the room like a ricocheting bullet. Yes, I like it a lot and take up a position at the window upstairs, giving me a bird's eye view of the workmen milling around beneath me.

If my plan works, I'll soon be directing operations in the style of a military general moving his little wooden soldier figures around the map of a battlefield such as Passchendaele or Belfast in the years before the British beat the IRA.

I put the mouthpiece to my mouth and speak: 'Robbie, if you've got time to lean, you've got time to clean!' 'Alvin, those bricks aren't gonna shift themselves! There's a hod, use it!' 'Krzysztof, you work, yes? Is good.'

The scene beneath me – previously a tableau of hairy-arsed slovenliness – is now transformed into a bustling, or slightly bustling, place of work. And it was all achieved with the help of a simple hand-held voice amplifier; I haven't had to mention parole officers or border police once.

It was exactly as the book had said! That book – *Bullhorn Boss: A Leadership Manual* by Chip Keeble – had talked of energising your workforce by 'taking up a loudhailer' and speaking directly to all levels of the organisation. I have my assistant take a photo of me shouting into the device and tweet it to Chip with the words 'Putting your book into action!'

He sends a laughing emoji then says, 'Yes, it's about creating a direct line of communication from management to all stakeholders.'

I reply, 'Doesn't get more direct than this!!'

And he then replies, 'Are you literally speaking to them with a loudhailer?'

I reply, 'Yep, just call me Bullhorn Boss!'

Satisfied with my answer, Chip doesn't reply after that.

I continue dispensing orders to the labourers for some two weeks. Referring to myself as 'the eye in the sky', I find I'm able to identify inefficiencies or people dropping used Pot Noodle tubs and have them perform instant remedial action. Carrying the hailer for several hours a day, I soon develop arm ache and a cricked elbow, so I attach the hailer to a harness I can wear like a gun holster and rig up a wearable microphone fixed to the side of my head.

And sure, there are one or two occasions when I forget to take the harness and head mic off on leaving the site, so that I order a flapjack in the café at very, very high volume – but overall, it is reaping visible benefits.

But still, work isn't fast enough. I feel I should come clean and lay it all out there, so I approach Jack, the unofficial foreman of the crew, and explain my predicament. Although Jack seems preoccupied with adjusting his Fantasy Football team on his phone, I nonetheless give him chapter and verse, starting with my departure from the BBC. I explain how there was bad blood there and how I endured a painful exit. And how my so-called friend summoned me and delivered the kind of news I've been dreading: a rival renovation that was already quite far along. I feel this was quite aggressive from James, who had gloated that *his* renovation was on camera – 'stuck-up arsehole'. I explain that if I'm to succeed I probably only have four or five months, and can he see any way to speed up the building work?

By now, Jack has stopped looking at his phone. He seems as annoyed with James Martin as I was and mumbles a, 'Yeah, mate, of course. *Of course* we can.'

He offers me his hand to shake but it looks a bit dirty and he's only recently used the chemical toilet, so I just offer him a friendly thump on the shoulder in a big-man stylee. I'm glad we had that chat.

* * *

It's a sandy, Sunday, sunny day. I awake early.

In the night, I'd had a dream about mermaids and, as a consequence, I find myself craving a bag of scampi fries. Problem is, my box of scampi fries is empty and the cash and carry doesn't open today. I realise that if I am to get my fix of seafood-flavoured crunches it will have to be from the pub.

I lie in bed, looking at the ceiling, trying to pass the three hours before opening time. A good game I've invented is trying to identify the noises from outside before re-imagining them as ringtones, which I then assign to people in my contacts book. An ice-cream van melody? That'd work for Eamonn Holmes. A ship's foghorn? Any of my northern friends. The faint caw of a distant seagull? Emilia Fox. The louder caw of a nearby seagull? Laurence Fox.

But today, there's a whole host of other noises, unusual for a Sunday. I rise and peer out of the window. There, toiling in the hot sun, are my builders.

I gown and trot down to the front door. I open up and the men look round. One by one, they afford me a brief smile and then continue with their work. I can scarcely believe what I'm seeing.

Sunday is, after all, a day off. And even though tradesmen knock off around 2 p.m. so even their workdays are partial days off, I am still delighted to see that the pressing nature of my build has struck a chord with them.

I wander up to the road. The breeze buffets my cheeks, giving me the sensation of being in the G-force simulator from the James Bond film *Moonraker*. I like that and walk along imagining I'm the celebrated British secret agent and that the lighthouse is a slightly disguised Russian rocket launcher, a reverie which then transmogrifies into imagining I'm Tom Hiddleston, my favourite current actor, who was quite, quite brilliant in *The Night Manager*. I tend to indulge daydreams like this when walking through the village, since I hardly need to pay attention. The locals here always ignore me and I've never received so much as a glance that required reciprocation. But, just as I'm picturing myself as Hiddleston receiving an award for best acting for *The Night Manager*, I become aware that people are looking at me. And not just looking – *smiling*. Several of the people I'm passing bear more pleasant dispositions than normal. It's as if the whole place has softened towards me.

I enter the pub, really quite excited now about that first taste of scampi fry. I bowl over to the bar and order.

'Right you are, mate,' says the publican. But then he sets down a pint of bitter alongside it.

'I didn't order that,' I huff politely.

'That's on me. We're here for a good time, not a long time!' And he winks a quite lovely wink.

I turn to sup and receive friendly nods from several other patrons. So, instead of just taking my scampi fries outside and devouring them round the back by the bins, I decide I'll stick around, and end up spending a perfectly pleasant hour in the company of these previously taciturn seasiders.

The next few days are the same. Mornings spent overseeing the honest and rapid graft of my workforce, the evenings with Red, afternoons mixing happily with the good people of the village. I even pop back to the Seaview for breakfast to see how Cynthia and her egg cookery are coming along[77] and am welcomed like an old child. As I leave, Cynthia holds my hand and says, 'How are you *feeling*?'. Not 'how are you?', or even 'how do', but how are you *feeling*?

I smile. 'Fine, thanks!' I say, and walk away. As I reach the pavement, a hearse goes by. On the kerbside, I see a small crab reminiscent of the logo for the star sign Cancer. WAIT A MINUTE!!!!!! How are you feeling, a hearse, cancer. How are you feeling, a hearse, cancer. How are you feeling, a hearse, cancer.

That's when I realise: THEY THINK I'M DYING OF CANCER.

I think back to the exact wording of my conversation with Jack: 'bad blood', 'a painful exit', 'new development', 'camera, stuck-up arsehole', 'news I'd been dreading', 'quite aggressive', 'only have four or five months' . . .

Only now can I see how someone with no GCSEs and a

---

77 Good egg, bad eggs.

not-very-good IQ could have mistaken some of these perfectly innocent terms for what he thought was a conversation describing a colonoscopy during which an inoperable tumour was discovered.

It horrifies me to think that someone might assume I'd deliberately misled these people to further my own interests. That's simply not something I would or could *ever* do, and I'm sorry if the sheer clumsiness of a phrase like 'camera, stuck-up arsehole' doesn't ring true to you, or if my recounting of the conversation in reported speech strikes you as an odd editorial choice. Evil people will go further and suggest a verbatim recollection of the key phrases I used is in itself hard to credit, insinuating that the real conversation would have had to be more overtly deceitful and therefore probably was. There's nothing I can do about that, other than to threaten legal action.

The only time I have knowingly feigned illness was when I pretended to have a tummy ache in a Yates's Wine Lodge after Nick Knowles said he was going to 'arm-wrestle every man in here' because he'd broken up with a girl and I guess he needed to prove something. I didn't want to arm-wrestle and had to think fast.

I also once claimed to be HIV positive because Elton John was performing a fundraiser for the Terrence Higgins Trust and I wanted the steward to let me sit nearer the front. But that's all.

Either way, though, what's done is done. The question is what to do about it. You see, since the misunderstanding was accidental, it feels unfair for me to face the opprobrium of the locals.

Moreover, the confusion has yielded positive outcomes, and not just for me. The builders seem energised and empowered by the joy of hard work. The locals have tapped into a kindness that has lain dormant in them for God knows how long. And I'm getting my lighthouse built a bit quicker. Tick, tick, tick. Win, win, win.

No, it's clear to me that there's nothing to be gained from divulging the truth, especially as I am in no way morally culpable. No, I shall reluctantly allow the misconception to stand and everyone will be happy.

Underhand or canny? Well, that's down to the individual. Some people think it was underhand when Robert Maxwell dipped into his company's pension pot, but a lot of men in my racquets club will say that was just good business. When P&O replaced their staff with foreign workers on less than the minimum wage, were they fleecing their workforce or just maximising value for their shareholders? So you see, it's a very grey area.

* * *

September. I return to the lighthouse with my breakfast sausage roll to find the men have arrived, but there's an eerie quiet on site today. Noises that I've found annoying every other day – the vrrrrr of a buzz saw, the crack, crack of sledgehammer on brick, the rohhhrohhhrohhh of a cement mixer turning, even the huhuhuhuhuhuhuhuhuhuhuh of manual labourers – are even more unsettling by their absence. What is going on?

I pick up the hailer holster, don it and then put the microphone to my lips: 'Alright, look lively, you 'orrible—' I stop. Why isn't my loudhailer loudhailing? I look down and notice the cable connecting my head mic to the horn itself has been snipped. It dangles, useless and forlorn, like a eunuch's todger.

'Who's done this?' I say, attempting to hide my irritation with a laugh.

The men just look at me. I approach Jack and ask him what's going on. His reply: You ain't got cancer.

All of the men are looking at me.

I feel my face go very, very, very, very, very, very, very, very hot. OK, I tell myself, you knew this moment might arrive. And so, in a calm voice and in words I've pre-written on the grey cardboard interior of a box of Bran Flakes,[78] I explain that it seems to have been a simple and entirely innocent misunderstanding.

Yet to my horror, Jack and his lads call bullshit, accusing me of deliberate subterfuge, although obviously they didn't use that word. Things are on the cusp of turning ugly. Suddenly this is a situation that will require every ounce of skill I picked up from my acting tutor, a man I drafted in to coach our am-dram troupe the Partridge Players, when we were preparing to put on *Rain Man* and I needed a bit of help being convincingly autistic. Here we go, I think, it's *showtime*.

'What, you thought . . .? Hang on. Do you mean to say . . .? Oh dear, oh dearie me, hahahahaha. I mean, I hope you're not accusing . . . because that is a very serious . . . Guys, guys, guys, whaddya talkin' about? It's me, Ally Pally, ya homie from da telly. And for you to besmirch my good name. I mean to say! I have never been so insulted in my . . . We cool? Who wants a pint of beer?'

'Aaaaand scene,' I add in my head.

It was a bravura cocktail of different potential reactions, and in hindsight I'd have been better off picking one and sticking to it, but I am happy with the quality of the acting, even if I've done little to win over the men.

'Can you get back to work now, please?'

On that, the men drop their tools at their feet and stare at me. I play my Joker: 'Please. Please, though! Please! Please, though!'

But to no avail. Jack explains that he has instructed his men to down tools 'until we get this sorted'.

---

78 Couldn't find any paper.

His suggestion is that I apologise to the lads and pay them overtime for the evening and weekend shifts they've been putting in. I tell him I'll happily apologise if they've misunderstood, but I'm simply not in a position to pay anyone a bonus.

He says we've got a problem, then. And he returns to the lads.

I stand there, the grease from the sausage roll leaking through the paper bag and oiling my fingers. My natural instinct, ground into me by years of unhappy marriage, is to capitulate instantly – but I know that's not healthy. Instead, I duck inside the lighthouse and plan my next move.

* * *

It's three days later and I haven't come up with a next move. It's hard to formulate a plan of action when, from the corner of your eye, you can see the strikers relaxing on your property.

Annoyingly, you see, the men don't strike at home or, as I believe is more common, in a pub with a flat roof. Instead, they turn up on site, smoking cigarettes and chatting as they literally 'lay about'. Each morning they settle on walls and piles of bricks in the way that locusts descend on crops, and I have to pick my way through them if I need to go to the shops. It's like the end of the Hitchcock film *The Birds*. But instead of sparrows and blackbirds and thrushes and chaffinches and robins and crows and doves and gulls, it's chunky men in sturdy boots.

These men have me over a barrel – not literally, although that does form part of an anxiety dream I've started to have. They know how desperate I am to get the build done. And they are determined to extract some financial concessions from me.

What would Thatcher do? She'd smash them, of course she would. The no-nonsense mum of two gave no quarter when it came to breaking the unions. During the Battle of Orgreave at the height of the miners' strike, police on horseback were said to have chased protestors over fields, around housing estates and even through people's gardens. It was brilliant policing. Yet despite my workmen being in the wrong every bit as much as the miners were proven to be, my pleas for the help of the Kent Constabulary horse team fall on deaf ears. I am on my own.

The only time I'd faced any real industrial action before was when my gardener had stomped off because I'd insisted he use a chemical insecticide, which he'd complained went against his ethics. Ethics are all well and good, but his namby-pamby natural alternatives simply weren't cutting the mustard – he must have known that – and a legion of maggots and aphids were having their way with my plants. In a choice of words I regret, I told him he was a fanny who was letting insects rape my garden. He left his implements where they were and walked away.

Our stand-off held for another month, during which time my garden rewilded itself – something I'd specifically tried to avoid. Eventually, I suggested he come round to talk it through. He got there to find my garden looking ... pristine. In it, tilling the soil, was a young, physically strong female gardener who had no compunction about using chemical repellents.

'Oh,' I said, seeing the look on his face. 'Did you think I was keeping the job open for you?' Then I shoved my face close to his: 'GETCHA THINGS.'

On another occasion, my assistant herself had got the hump – a metaphorical one this time – over my refusal to buy her an iPhone. I reasoned that she wouldn't know what to do with one, and I wasn't going to pay her while she learned. She withdrew her labour, but I was able to break the strike within a day by having a chief inspector friend send two bobbies to her house and threaten to arrest her for the made-up crime of aggravated disobedience. She crumpled like a warm Easter egg and returned to work – Nokia and all – that very same day.

But this is a different order of magnitude. While the two previous examples had seen me face down two septuagenarians, these men are organised, intimidating, younger and big.

As the days tick by, I become increasingly desperate. My WhatsApp to the group – 'Be a scab. Will pay double' – elicits not a single response. My follow-up – 'Will also provide lunch #scabkebab #babsforscabs #pleaseguys' – did, but it's a curt 'fuck you'.

Then one day, fuelled by too many sweets plus a large glass of wine over lunch, I leap into action, capering before the assembled men like Rumpelstiltskin.

'Lads!' I begin. 'Think, lads! You're only costing yourselves.' They look away so I begin to plead with them individually.

'Johnny!' I say, approaching Johnny. 'Please, Johnny. Think, Johnny.'

No reply.

'Sammy!' I say, approaching Sammy. 'Please, Sammy. Think, Sammy.'

Also nothing.

'Eddie!' I say, approaching Eddie. 'You've got kids, Eddie. Good kids, young kids. And Christmas presents don't come cheap, Eddie. Think of your kids, Eddie.'

'I don't have kids,' says Eddie.

'Right,' I say. 'Which is the one with kids?'

'Ricky,' he says.

'Ricky!' I say, approaching Ricky. 'You've got kids, Ricky. Good kids, young kids. And Christmas presents don't come cheap, Ricky. Think of your kids, Ricky.'

No reply.

'Krzysztof!' I say, approaching Krzysztof. 'You work. You work now. You no bad man. You good man. You work, yes?'

'We're on strike, you tit,' he replies.

Spending a night in a detention centre for boys aged 14–18 was a sobering reminder that even though I am a fully-grown adult, I could quite easily get battered by a child. And while my age and the fact I am a father meant I imagined myself (like Ray Winstone in the 1979 film *Scuzz*) going in there and saying 'I'm the daddy now', it turned out most of the lads had more children than I did. One of them had five! Hilarious.

This Time's roving reporter Ruth Duggan. I enjoyed a fantastic working relationship with Ruth. We got on great, I enjoyed our interactions, there was no issue. It's a little-known fact that Ruth doesn't have any journalism qualifications.

TV offers an immediacy that radio sometimes cannot. Here – in a piece for *This Time* on the Peasants' Revolt of 1381 – I use a bucket of butcher's waste to bring to life the tragic deaths of countless soldiers. I later discovered that though the butcher charged me £10.50 for the bag of pig bits, he normally gives them away for free. The following year a hike in business rates combined with increased competition from discount supermarkets saw him go out of business. Ain't life a bitch?

My tenure on *This Time* saw me push for a move away from the dross, fluff and flim-flam to a focus on hard-hitting investigative journalism. Here I'm mounting a hidden-camera sting operation to prove that certain BBC presenters (in this case Donty Mon) were in the business of accepting money in return for mentioning brands or products on air. And while on this occasion, Mr Mon refused the bung and acted with total propriety, is this always the case? I remain unsure. And surely it is not for me to prove his guilt, it is for him to prove his innocence.

Her Royal Highness Princess Anne The Princess Royal. A fan of lighthouses since childhood and patron of the Northern Lighthouse Board since 1993, she is pictured here with a hairstyle that is an exact replica of waves breaking over Portland Bill lighthouse.

Rear view of Her Royal Highness Princess Anne The Princess Royal. Even from behind, Her Highness emits a dignity and grace that most other women can only dream of. She is just – and I hope you and she will excuse the profanity – a fucking brilliant royal. In the background, Jennie Gresham, shin reflected in table.

A lighthouse. While there's nothing unusual about wanting to restore one of these, the former TV doctor, Hilary Jones, suggested my desire to own such an obviously phallic structure stemmed from sexual inadequacy and anxiety over my ability to maintain an erection. I pointed out that his insistence on wearing tight-fitting t-shirts stemmed from anxiety that he has a girl's name (which he does), and a desire to show everyone he doesn't have tits (which he does).

The Kraken, the legendary sea monster so feared by mariners down the centuries. First written about by Italian priest Francesco Negri in the year 1700, if real, it would be the largest fish ever discovered.

My friend and confidante, Likeworm. From Rod Hull to Mary Poppins, to the lad from *Kes* to the late Bernard Matthews, humans have always sought to befriend birds – although to be fair, Bernard also slaughtered them. My assistant snapped this photo and was so pleased with it, she later told me she thought it was good enough to win a competition. I disagreed because it's just a gull eating his lunch.

A redhead. I've long been fascinated by the British redhead but had previously had a dalliance with only one – a woman called Jill from my production company who is now a grey-haired lollipop lady in Holt. That was until I fell in love with Red, the local girl from the Kent coast who (very briefly) stole my heart. Would I ever have a relationship with another redhead? Probably not. While the odd one or two (Elizabeth I, Bonnie Langford) have admirable qualities, most other redheads I've met (Sir Robin Cook, Geri Halliwell, the Duchess of York, Eddie Redmayne, Cilla Black) have been deeply unpleasant individuals. The woman pictured isn't the local girl who (very briefly) stole my heart, she's just a woman from Google Images with similar curls.

A photo of my hairdresser's son. He's not mentioned in the book and I've never met him in real life, but I was told if I included the picture I'd receive a 30% discount on any haircut valid until December 2024 and I was happy to agree.

ME TOO, PLEASE!

New York City, 5 October 2017

A corpulent, cigar-smoking man in a white linen shirt and baggy trousers shuffles to the breakfast table of his Manhattan hotel for a breakfast of eggs and kwaw-fee (American for coffee).

'It's a no smoking hotel, Mister—' attempts the waiter.

'Fuck off!' says the big American, and he puffs away like Ivor the Engine attempting a steep incline. Flopping his fat ass into the chair, he loads up a fork with egg and shovels it into his mouth, like the driver of Ivor the Engine I mentioned thirty-one words ago might shovel in a spadeful of coal. The man enjoys the food, grunting with pleasure and saying 'mmm, eggs' as he eats the eggs.

Before him, splayed out, are his favourite papers, the New York Post, *the* Hollywood Reporter, Variety *and the* New York Times. *He squints at them, hardly lifting his eyes from his plate as he puts in a second forkful of egg, then a third, then a fourth, then a fifth. A sixth? Yep, there's the sixth. Followed by a seventh, then an eighth. Lucky for him, his plate has a lot of egg on it.*

Suddenly he stops, takes a puff of his cigar, then it's egg again. A ninth forkful, then it's ten, eleven, twelve! 'Mmm, egg,' he says once more. But then something occurs to him.

His eyes roll upwards, to the papers laid out before him. Right there on the front page is his own name. What the hell . . .?

He shovels in another five or six forkfuls of his eggs and then picks up the paper, his hands shaking. The blood drains from his mouth. What's left of the burning cigar remains unpuffed, the stumpy brown cylinder resembling his own unsightly penis, an organ that will soon be discussed at humiliating length in the subsequent court case.

He manages to bleat out a single word: 'Lawyers.'

The waiter leans in. 'Pardon?'

'Lawyers!' he grunts.

'I'm sorry, I don't—'

'GET ME MY LAWYERS!' he bellows, crumbs of residual egg tumbling from his hollering mouth.[79]

For there, on the front page, is a news story that is about to change everything. And not just for this big fat man. Like a gigantic news Krakatoa, it will reverberate around the world, sending a tsunami of change to the worlds of culture, politics and business.

The man? Harvey Weinstein. The news story? That he had paid off sexual-harassment accusers for decades. The eggs? Just some eggs. The result? A new movement known as #MeToo.

*   *   *

In Britain, just a few weeks later, the winds of change had been blowing and blowing hard – less a hurricane, more a HERicane. Because women were mad as hell and this time they actually had good reason.

But I wasn't in Britain. I was still in Qatar, oblivious to the goings-on in Western media circles. Life for us was idyllic. The women there tend to keep professional grumbles about sexual politics to themselves, and while there are certain cultural reasons for that – and I'm not saying it's better, I'm just saying it's different – it did mean that the whole #MeToo thing hadn't registered on us. The only time me, Richard or Andy said 'Me too' was when one of the others ordered an ice cream!

---

79 Dramatisation.

I can see now that I was living in something of a bubble. While I was making a slew of corporate videos for some of the most exciting clients in the Gulf – 'Call Doha Housemaids today for home help that's quick, quiet and obedient!' – TV executives back in London were firefighting, frantically trying to ensure gender parity on the panel of Question Time, *asking male presenters to take pay cuts, and Googling where the lower back ends and the top of the arse begins so they know if they've politely guided a woman to her taxi or committed sexual assault.*

But my obliviousness didn't last long. One day, an email from my assistant pinged into my inbox. It contained various clippings about the TV industry, a smattering of Daily Mail *sidebars about TV presenters I didn't like having marital difficulties/bad skin, but then at the bottom a scan of a piece in one of the clever-clog papers, can't remember which. It talked of an industry 'getting its house in order', 'a reckoning' in which broadcasters who'd behaved less than perfectly were being expunged, leaving an exciting 'new landscape' for previously overlooked talent.*

This was news to me. Everywhere you looked, we were told, ashen-faced male presenters knew the game was up. At any moment, they might find a historic wrongdoing hauled under the microscope, leaving their lifeless careers hanging from the nearest yew tree.

The iPad tumbled from my shaking fingers and clattered against the poolside tiles. I realised what this meant: one man's ignominious downfall was another man's opportunity. Suddenly, sleazy rivals were finding themselves 'persona non grata' (not a great person), and the torrent of accusations would bulldoze a path for those who had behaved appropriately throughout, i.e. me. Sure, it cleared the way for minorities to get work they'd previously been denied – and that's great! – but well- behaved middle-aged white men were a minority too and this was a game-changer.

'Guys . . .' I said weakly. They hadn't heard me. Andy was trying

to thwack a gecko with a flip-flop and couldn't hear me. 'Guys!' I said louder.

Andy looked up and then grimaced as the gecko took the opportunity to flee. 'Wha'?' he said.

This meant, 'What?'

I hurried over, tripping over my words like Amol Rajan as I hurriedly explained what was going on back in Blighty.

'We should all go back!' I said. 'There are presenters falling like dominoes. We could clean up! Think of the opportunities for proven presenters with the likeability factor. We could be back in the big time, boys!'

Silence. Andy looked away. Richard shook his head sadly.

'We've had our chance, Alan,' said Richard. 'There's no going back for us.'

'What are you talking about?' (I was crying now.) 'This is what we've been working towards.'

Richard took my face in his hands, which I wished he hadn't because I'd only just put suncream on. He explained that, because their dismissal from Sky had partly been a result of comments they'd made about female assistant referees being incompetent, there was a chance someone with a twisted agenda could argue they were on the wrong side of the whole #MeToo movement. I could see his point, but all I know is that they're two very, very nice guys.

'But you should go, Alan. Shouldn't he, Andy?'

'Oh aye,' said the former Everton and Aston Villa centre forward, as he finally dispatched the gecko.

And the two of them held me tight. 'Go,' whispered Richard. 'You got this, Alan. And Alan?'

'Yes, Richard and Andy?'

'We will never forget you.'

And I will never, ever forget them.

In Britain, the industry was changing. Society was finally equal and women were at last being given a fair crack of the whip, which can be heavy but you can get smaller ones.

'This is just the start,' campaigners insisted, which felt like over-steer. Go any further and men would be just as oppressed as their lady folk used to be, creating a kind of Handman's Tale set in the state of Girlyad.

I know some people felt threatened by that. Not me. It helped that during my sexiest years, my George Clooney era, when my hair began to grey around the temples and my skin became craggy but not yet mottled by beige spots, I was not employed in the television industry so there was little inter-colleague temptation to fall foul of.

Away from the TV cameras, I very shrewdly – and not because I was shopping at the budget end of the market – opted for an employee I felt absolutely no attraction to, or affection for. It might not have been the fashionable way of things. Many of my peers recruited assistants from the Motor Show or the women who hold clipboards at the front of a queue outside a trendy bar. These women were called things like Sophia or Jess or Bella – sassy names that spell trouble down the track. The pool I was recruiting from were more your Brendas, your Judys, your Lynns. Presentable, maybe, but nothing to write – or even text – home about. Temptation never reared its head. And it meant I never once tried to wear something snazzy in the hope that she'd compliment me.

One caveat, because I'm no angel: I did briefly develop incredibly strong feelings towards the female broadcaster Sue Cook, which did extend to touching. I would say, 'Sue, you have beautiful hair, do you mind if I touch it?' Sue would say, 'Be quick,' or similar. I was crossing a line and I regret that. In my defence, most agree that sexual harassment requires the abuse of a position of power, and even a casual observer of our relationship would see that Sue held between 95 and 100 per cent of the power in our dynamic. Sue a) doesn't suffer fools and b) regards me as a fool. So I was always up against it when it came to securing a foothold that might make her fancy me.

But what I couldn't have realised at the time was that, with the field decimated, my employability had skyrocketed. And soon, everything was about to come my way.

OH, RED

September 2022

My new life in Kent lies in ruins. I had left Norwich with a heart full of dreams and a head full of dreams. Was I naive? To leave behind everything I knew – TV, Norwich, good Wi-Fi, a plush house – and uproot myself wholesale to a new life, a new *way* of life, by the sea?

All I'd wanted was a simple existence of quiet pleasure. At one with the elements and at one with myself, I would rise early and wander down to the harbour each morning for a basket of fresh fish, tobacco for my pipe, a bottle of rum for the cold, squally nights, and a copy of the *Daily Mail*. I'd be taken to the bosom of a new community, local characters one and all. They would see me restoring their beloved lighthouse and that would restore something in them. Pride, honour, higher house prices in the local area. Perhaps I would find love. A headstrong woman with faraway eyes, fond of song and long walks where she would look out to sea with strands of hair blowing across her face and mouth. She would also take me to her bosom, and after a bit of that we'd do other stuff.

Was that naive of me? Was it all just romantic hogwash dressed up as a serious objective? I really don't think it was. Tim Belper, who used to do drivetime on Orbital Digital, had set his heart on a new life by the sea and he was enjoying almost exactly the life I just described, although with him it was Thailand and the rum was Jägerbombs and the headstrong woman was a boy who rented out quad bikes.

No, it had been a reasonable and rational decision. I never, ever look back anyway, not my style. That way you have no regrets and it stops you crying in the shower.

But in the cold light of day and the cold water of the shower, I have plenty to cry about. Word has got out that I deliberately faked terminal cancer of the colon – a scandalous accusation that remains in the hands of my legal team. How they found out remains a mystery. I'd been careful not to say anything incriminating and had remembered to act 'cancery' (coughing weakly and smiling bravely) whenever I was being watched.

Whatever the source, the builders now won't finish the job until they get their pound of flesh, a pound I simply can't afford to give. The locals too have taken against me like my assistant's tummy takes against lactose. I am shunned, spurned like a dog and disrespected like a dog that's not even as good as the dog that was spurned earlier in the sentence. My house – my precious lighthouse – lies unfinished, barely habitable. The pipe smoking isn't coming along very well, as I keep inhaling big lungfuls which make me cough and I get cramp in my jaw from clutching it with my teeth. And I wouldn't say I'm now at one with myself, although I'm not massively arsed about that one.

At least I have Red.

Red – whose real name I forget, partly because I am so enjoying calling her Red – has a quite wonderful mystique, fuelled, I must admit, by just how infrequently she speaks. Not that she's shy, she's too ballsy for that; she simply chooses not to natter – although that changes after a few ciders.

Before the strike, our relationship had been one of quiet companionship. I'd leave the builders on site late afternoon and stroll up the main road, where I'd hang around the bus stop. She'd hop off around five. Where had she been? I never liked to ask, though the salty smell in her hair suggested she'd been helping her father sell whelks down at the shore.

And then we'd simply spend the evening together. If the weather was fine we'd wander across the headland and watch as the sun plunged to earth like a very slow M117, the most commonly dropped bomb in the Korean War.

I enjoy her simple, fuss-free style. Jeans or a long skirt. A shirt in simple colours. Her shock of ruddy red hair pulled back and held with a scrunchie. Yes, I enjoy looking at her a lot. Sometimes I watch her face as she stares blankly out to sea, a smile playing on her lips.

'Whatcha thinking about?' I whisper one evening.

Her reply? 'Superbikes.'

'Right,' I say. 'Like the ones that can fly in *E.T.*?'

'No, high-performance motorcycles.'

'Got it,' I say. I tell her I have a Red Letter Day voucher that would let us go round the Isle of Man in a motorbike and sidecar but she says she isn't into sidecars. Fair enough.

In those early days, much of our time would be spent in her bedroom, where I'd sit on a camping chair beside her desk, watching her play online poker and look at superbikes. Other times we'd sit facing each other cross-legged on the bed. (Or rather, I'd sit facing her back as she lost herself in her passion for online gambling.) As a man of a certain age, sitting cross-legged hadn't been comfortable for over twenty years. But in this relationship it just felt right, and I certainly wasn't doing it in an effort to appear more youthful in front of my slightly younger girlfriend.

But now, as the victim of industrial action and the town's bête noire (black animal), I know I need her more than ever. And you know what? Seeing us bound together, like Butch & Louise or Thelma & Sundance, makes me love that babygirl more than ever. Maybe I'm compelled by this shared sense of destiny, maybe I'm just a soppy old lovesick goon, maybe I'm just feeling anxious about the rest of the town disliking me, but I find myself doing something a little bit crazy.

We're chilling in her room and Red reaches over to turn down the volume on the mixtape I've made for her. I assumed she was doing it because she's about to say something, but I think she just wants it to be less loud. Whatever the reason, I take my chance to speak: 'Let's go and see your father.'

'What for?' she giggles, although I've added the giggle myself.

I shush her and put my finger to her lips, albeit slightly too hard so I smoosh her top lip against her teeth, causing her to tut.

'Come on,' I say.

Moments later we're driving down the coast towards Folkestone, which is where, they say, every day you'll find her father selling his whelks. Gah! I'm as giddy as a schoolgirl or a slightly effeminate schoolboy.

In my pocket? A ring. Nothing fancy, just a simple gold band that was once owned by my mother. It's not in perfect nick – there's a very small gap in it where the mortician had to cut it off her because they couldn't get it over her knuckle, but you can hardly see it, although it will nip slightly if you catch your skin in there.

In my heart? The words I plan to say to her father. Simple words. Words he'll understand. That I was once a shining light in the TV industry – a big beacon that illuminates and shines. Since then, I've started to renovate a lighthouse – a big beacon that guides and protects. And now, with his permission, I would like to be a big beacon to his daughter. To illuminate, shine, guide and protect – as long we both shall live. I did say it was a little bit crazy!

'What are you mouthing?' she says.

I smile. 'Just a little something that I think might make your father's hair stand on end. Heck, it'll make his beard stand on end!'

'He doesn't have a beard,' she says.

'Really? I assumed he'd have a beard.'

'Nope.'

It's only now that I notice the satnav has led us away from the seafront to an industrial park. Red directs me to a large unit with a shuttered entrance.

'Where are we?' I say.

'I thought you wanted to go see my dad?'

'Yeah . . . So why are we here? Is this where he keeps his stall?'

'What stall?'

'The fucking whelk stall, what do you think?' I say with just the merest hint of exasperation.

And that's when it all came out. It turns out her father doesn't sell his whelks from a stall. And far from being a humble trader, he is the largest wholesaler of whelks and associated shellfish in the south of England, and sells directly into supermarkets and large food outlets. He drives a Bentley, just as his father had before him. The 'sailor man' she'd loved who'd gone away all those years ago was actually a salesman for ICI – he'd moved to Abu Dhabi to head up the EMEA region.

I nod, trying to recalibrate what I now thought of Red. Has the grandeur of her father's work put me off her? Yeah, it has a bit. I also learn that far from simply volunteering to clean and lock up the church hall every night, she is doing it purely because her father owns the hall; the church it's connected to has long been desanctified and snapped up by her father, who hopes to convert it into one- and two-bedroom apartments, with the proceeds diverting to her.

Ordinarily, of course, if I'd fallen for a girl from a poor background only to find out her father was wealthy, I'd be absolutely delighted. But right here, right now, I'm not. Because I have changed. No longer a needy broadcaster hungry for status, fine things and a girlfriend who's successful but slightly less successful than me, now I am a man of the sea (shore), my tastes and wants simple, uncomplicated.[80]

So no, I am not elated. I am saddened. My straightforward coastal girl, uncorrupted by the ways of the city, red in tooth and claw (and name and hair), a girl who could have stepped straight from the pages of *Lorna Doone, The French Lieutenant's Woman* or a really good Mills & Boon, is just a basic middle-class woman.

My mouth goes dry. I solemnly take the ring from my pocket and make a show of placing it not on her finger, but on my own. It nips the skin painfully. Owwwwwwwwwww, I think.

'What does that mean?' she asks.

'It means I don't think you've been honest with me.'

'You're a fine one to talk.'

I raise my eyebrows, challengingly.

She folds her arms. 'How come your builders have downed tools?'

I shrug. 'Not sure, really.'

'You don't know why they're on strike?'

'Not sure, really.'

'You must do.'

'No, not sure, really.'

For obvious reasons, I don't want to get into the nitty gritty of who said what to whom, in case it makes me look like a fibber.

---

80 Plus, it's not like any of her old man's money would be coming my way anyway. The day of the dowry has passed, although I'm not sure why because it was a fantastic system.

'It's not to do with that whole cancer thing, is it?'

I swallow hard. 'You know about that?'

'Well, yeah. I saw Jack at the fishmongers and he was saying how sad it was you had five months to live, and I laughed and said, "I dunno where you got that from." And he said you said you only had five months to live, and I said no, you only had five months until James Martin finished his lighthouse before you finished yours.'

Oh, Red. Yes, I'd once whispered the details of James Martin's refurb to her in the throes of lovemaking, hoping that the sheer mundanity of what I was saying would distract me enough to delay climax. Unfortunately, my excitement at potentially getting one over on the large-headed chef had the opposite effect, stoking my ardour enough to accelerate things beyond my control – such that I no longer governed the timetable for when and how I would complete and matters were concluded shortly after.

It sure hurts to know she brought about my downfall. I feel like I'm Samsung and she's my Delilah, betraying me in almost exactly the same way. She hadn't cut my hair like Delilah had, although once, after a bath together, she gave me a quick tidy up downstairs with a pair of nail scissors.

'Never had you down as a snitch,' I nod. And with my point proven, I try to remove the wedding ring, which has pinched my skin up into an angry white tent. Even with the bit cut out, I can't get the damn thing off. She watches me yank at it for a minute or two, then shakes her head and says, 'I'll go and get you some soap.'

Red presses the buzzer and goes inside. I hang back. When she returns I've gone. On the step, a torn napkin bears a hastily scribbled poem.

Oh Red.
With your red, red head.
What we had is dead.
Cos of what you said.

It's shorter than I would have liked, but I racked my brain(s) trying to think of other words that rhyme with red. There must be loads of them but I couldn't think of a single one, so in the remaining space I've drawn a heart with a zig-zag split down the middle instead. Instead! That would have been a good one.[81]

And then I was gone, repairing to the phallic bosom of my lighthouse.[82]

---

81 I later removed the ring using some beef dripping.

82 Before remembering I had a contractual obligation to do a second series of my podcast *From the Oasthouse*. So I popped home for three weeks and did the following: attempted to reconcile with North Norfolk Digital; joined a creative writing class; tried to catch some local fly tippers; attempted potholing; visited Tyneham; went wild swimming; temporarily got a new dog; started going out with my next-door neighbour Katrina; ended a brand ambassadorship; and built a model of the solar system for the grandkids – all while pledging, for a reason I can't remember, to never once mention on air the lighthouse to which I had dedicated the last year of my life. With that done, I headed back to Kent.

RESURRECTING

11.15 a.m., 21 February 2019

Separated by 150 miles – not to mention around 18 points on the body mass index – two very different broadcasters are having two very different Thursdays.

The first sits in a small digital radio studio in Norwich. His palms are clammy, his pulse racing – and with good reason. A live competition segment is about to make for thrilling radio.

'Gail, are you still on the line?'

'I am.'

'This is monumental. You're about to play your fifth consecutive QuizQuake – no one's ever made it this far before. One chap did four but he was a disgruntled ex-employee who still had access to the questions. For five weeks now you've been competing to win a £3,000 set of teak patio furniture. You're so close I bet you can picture it right there in your garden!'

'I don't have a garden, I live in a flat.'

'You don't have any outdoor space?'

'No.'

'So . . . What have you been doing for five weeks? The patio furniture's the whole point.'

'Not sure.'

'Never mind. Today, the subject is units of measurement. And if you're ready to play, let's play!'

Meanwhile, in Chobham, Surrey, another broadcaster has clammy palms and a racing pulse – but the only game he's playing is the game of 'will I survive this heart attack?' – because he's having a heart attack.

Thirty seconds earlier, against the express wishes of his wife, he'd been smoking a fag in the kitchen as he waited for his lasagne to ping in the microwave. In contorting his torso painfully over the hob so he could blow the smoke up the extractor fan, he had simply asked too much of his body, and the exertion had caused his heart to attack.

Suddenly, his chest is constricting like it's being sat on by a man of approximately his own size, ironically. Pain fizzes down his left arm like it's late for a dental appointment somewhere around the hand and they charge you if you don't attend.

He lurches to the kitchen door, his fag now dunked headfirst into a chocolate mousse he'd been snacking on as he waited for the Italian meal to be ready.

'Grrhhhhr,' he hollers, a desperately poor attempt to enunciate his wife's name, Fran. 'Grrhhhhr,' he says again. But he's so short of breath, speaking is beyond him. He steadies himself against the door, his glassy eyes unthinkingly looking back at the microwave . . . Ping!

'Ping!' The sound effect for a correct answer bounces off the studio walls.

'Correct. Ampere?'
'Current.'
'Correct. Celsius?'
'Temperature.'
'Correct. Joule?'
'Energy.'
'Correct. Candela?'
'Luminosity?'
'Correct, Gail! Twenty seconds to go!'

The clock is ticking in Chobham too. The man is hurtling through his hallway knowing he only has a few seconds before he loses consciousness. Important seconds, precious seconds. He has to alert his wife. He staggers up the stairs, bursts into the master bedroom where his wife is applying Oil of Ulay (or Oil of Olay as it's now called) to the dry bits of her neck.

'Oh my God,' she says. 'Are you alright?'

'Yesssss!' (We're back in Norwich now.) 'Yes, Gail. You did it! You won!'

'Oh, brilliant.'

'The ones you passed on were newton-metre; the answer was torque. And becquerel, which is a unit of radioactive decay. Still! You managed to get ten right, which means you've won. And you definitely want the garden furniture?'

'Yes, please.'

'Well, as long as you can accept delivery . . . because the guy will dump it at the kerb if not.'

Back in Surrey, there's a delivery taking place of a very different nature. A stricken man is being delivered to A&E by trained paramedics. Essentially cabbies who've been on a first-aid course.

And because they're the latter, not the former, the cargo can relax in the knowledge that he won't be hurled over the side gate or sold for cash in a pub car park. He'll be delivered right through the front door.

Pow! The trolley batters through the double doors, so that they swing open as if a gunslinger has walked into a saloon.

'Patient suffered full cardiac arrest! Suggest corantular plasmic flow! Macagron 6 milligrams! Inserting sluice into blood pipe. Adrenalin rising, force 6 easterly, good.' (I'm paraphrasing what would have been said with similar-sounding medical terms. This is just for a bit of colour. You can carry on reading or just skip to the next

paragraph. It's up to you.) 'Cephalopod in flux. Paging doctors Patel, Singh, Chan and Mugubu. Erect a drip and drip it.'

Clearly, he was in safe hands. This man? None other than BBC presenting stalwart John Baskell. He was rushed into theatre, and as soon as they summoned another six or seven porters they could begin to roll him onto a bed.

In Norwich, the other man is enjoying a roll of another kind (sausage). It's a treat and he damn well deserves it. 'What a show! What a show!' This man? Commercial radio firebrand Alan Partridge (i.e. me). He's just completed a show every bit as good (very) as John's heart attack was bad (very) and has just arrived home.

Finding his housekeeper Rosa in the master bedroom, he flops onto the bed. She's only just made it, but she can easily remake it after he gets up and would probably quite enjoy it, being a cleaner.

'Good show, Mister Partridge?' she says in Philippine-inflected English.

'A belter, Rosa,' Partridge replies. 'If there was any justice I'd get an award, because I smashed it today.'

'Oh, I so sorry.'

'Sorry for what?'

'You try superglue?'

'On what, Rosa?'

'On the award you smash.'

'I didn't smash an award.'

'So the award is OK?'

'There is no award. '

'So why you say you smash it . . .?'

The conversation continues like this for as many as ten minutes but fails to dent the good humour of the beaming broadcaster.

Two presenters then, two men in the eye of a life-changing moment.

You might think they operate in very different orbits – one broadcasting to a substantial cross-section of the British viewing public, the other to a small hardcore of right-wing pensioners who enjoy 'owning the libs' almost as much as they enjoy owning their own homes – but in the space of a single phone call, their lives are about to interconnect in a quite fascinating way.

Partridge – and I'm about to switch to the first person because this does feel quite odd, but I'll wait until the end of this sentence before doing so – hears his phone ringing and jumps to his feet, running down the stairs as fast as his legs can carry him, but will he make it? Yes, I will! I press 'answer' and speak into the device: 'Alan Partridge.'

'Hello. Can I speak to Alan Partridge?'

'You're speaking to Alan Partridge. That's why I said "Alan Partridge".'

'Alan, It's Dustin Horwich. I'm the exec producer of This Time for BBC Television. Do you have a minute?'

'I've got six!' I laugh. Not sure why I said six, though.

'We have a bit of a personnel emergency. Between you and me, our presenter John Baskell has been taken ill. And we're looking for emergency cover for the whole of next week. Couple of our usual stand-ins aren't available. I know you've done TV before and we're keen to avoid it being too many identikit presenters.'

'Thirty-year-olds from public school or forty-year-olds from Bolton.'

'Exactly. And your values map is a close match to John's, so the demography checks out.'

'That's a terrific point,' I say, a reflex response I often give when, like now, I have no idea what the person has just said.

'So we were wondering if you'd be up for a bit of TV presenting next week? You'd obviously be remunerated in a way that's commensurate with a primetime BBC One role.'

My breathing quickens. Is the word commensurate ever used in a negative sense? It always feels like it promises something wonderful. You never hear a phrase like 'the tumour's size is commensurate with an eighty-fags-a-day lifestyle' or 'your arrogance is commensurate with you being a Dimbleby brother'.

With that, my mind starts to pop and orgasm. Twenty years in the wilderness. Two decades on the outside looking in. The deathbed promise I'd made to Peter Flint, which, as I say, definitely happened, the supportive words of Richard Keys and Andy Gray, and the Yewtree investigations that had skittled almost every one of my rivals, had all coalesced.

'Dustin?'

'Yes, Alan?'

'Ready my dressing room. I'm coming home.'

My assistant was back from the shops.

'You'd better sit down in there,' I said, nodding to the bathroom, and she went and sat on the toilet while I stood outside. This was a belt-and-braces approach for whenever I broke good news, since she could sometimes go 'weak at the knees', but in extreme cases would 'leak at the wees' – i.e. lose bladder control a little, her pelvic floor not being as robust as it once was.

'Well?' she asked, once in position. I told her the news and she squealed, vindicating my decision to position her over the lavatory.

Seconds later, she emerged, dressed and dry, and essayed a brief but aggressive dance, all fists and stomps like a Church of England version of the haka. I allowed her to do this.

Once she had completed the dance, we set to work.

So it fell to my assistant and me to compile several lists: a list of demands for the BBC concerning pay, image rights (whatever they are) and things like who gets the biggest dressing rooms; another list of things I'd need such as a new wash bag/vanity case; and a further

list of people who were going to _freak_ when they heard the news so
needed telling ASAP. Call me conceited, but I wanted people to know
that I was back in the big time so sent correspondence to that effect to
a select group of no more than twenty-five of my closest friends. Some
have subsequently griped that this seemed big-headed – and readers
of my last book will know this is the second time I've done this – but
it's actually fine.

With me hovering over her, my assistant engaged with the BBC
contracts team and an offer was soon forthcoming. Within hours a
deal was struck that made sense for me and my family. I was to join
the show the following Monday. They would provide transport and
refreshments and I had the make-up girls briefed ahead of my arrival
that it was 'Mr Partridge' rather than 'Alan'.

But, of course, my **first** thought was for John's health. I had a hamper
and card sent to John's home in Chobham. Due to an error, the card
read, 'Guess who's back in the big time???', which means Nick Ferrari
got one saying, 'Condolences on your massive heart attack.' Still, I'm
sure it'll apply when the time comes.

That meant we had the weekend to prepare for my – I hate to say
resurrection, but – resurrection as a TV personality. How would I
look, what would I say, what would my vibe be? These preparations,
codenamed Operation Kalashnikov,[83] were rapid and urgent – they
bloody had to be! And there'll be those who say, 'But given that you'd
been specifically working towards a return to mainstream television
for several years, shouldn't you have had those arrangements in place
well in advance?' And they might have a point. Then again, it's not as
if we'd given no thought to these ingredients – it was simply that when
we opened the Word document the ideas within felt inappropriate

---

83 An uncomplicated but robust and reliable semi-automatic rifle which has
stood the test of time. Notwithstanding its role in countless thousands of deaths,
it remains an engineering marvel.

or dated, not least because I'd imagined my return would be in the form of a Saturday evening light entertainment format à la Noel's House Party, *rather than a serious current affairs show. The snazzy jumper I'd planned to have commissioned didn't fit the dress code so would have to remain ten balls of wool in my garage. The opening monologue with comical digs at other BBC presenters wouldn't fit into a tightly packaged 29-minute show. And the poem I'd written, 'Second Chances (I Rise Again)', would just have to go on my website or something.*

Instead, I needed fresh thought and new ideas. Dustin had made clear that the presenters' input was crucial and I'd be given licence to generate my own content – as a show that went out five nights a week, the process was described as 'fucking chaos – we don't have time to micromanage every piece of script or VT'. And that filled me with enormous confidence.

Buoyed by this, I spoke directly to the show's producer, Howard. My only demand? A revamp of the way we handled audience correspondence. As a regional DJ, I received letters and emails all the time, but it had been a while since I myself had read them out. Since 2010, I had farmed that job out to a radio sidekick by the name of Simon Denton, and I no longer felt it was something a senior presenter should have to do.

I also felt the audience would benefit from seeing these missives live on screen using state-of-the-art digital technology. The idea had come to me while driving past a branch of the egregious letting agency Foxtons. Most branches of the reviled realtor contained a fifty-inch touchscreen customer interface on which the agents could show property prospecti in a needlessly expensive format.

Obviously, there was no customer benefit to this – the Digiwall was merely a way of burnishing what was a meat-and-potatoes estate-agency job so that the parents of these braying employees could convince themselves the private-school fees they'd shelled out had resulted in a more impressive occupation. And I liked that.

Luckily, the BBC liked it too and agreed to give it a try. The person to take on this new role? They suggested Countryfile's *Sean Fletcher or Scotswoman Storm Huntley who could transfer from a similar role on Jeremy Vine's Channel 5 abomination. But I had an idea that was better and fresher – or certainly better, anyway. Simon Denton himself.*

Barring a brief period as a stand-in when I'd been exiled from North Norfolk Digital, Simon has always been a junior broadcaster, able only to operate as a foil to another, better, safer pair of hands. But I'd seen something in the stammering sidekick that made me think he had the chops required for a beefier role.

Simon is fire warden at North Norfolk Digital – a voluntary role that gives him a salary uplift of £30 per month, which might sound like chicken shit/feed, but was the only thing separating Simon from living at his mum's. In that role (fire warden, not mummy's boy!) Simon is required to shepherd dawdling staff members towards the exits and perform a head count outside. But once a year, he also had to give a talk explaining where the fire exits are. I once witnessed such a talk and what he gave was quite simply a masterclass. Simon's always been very, very funny – anyone who's heard him on Mid Morning Matters *knows he's a serious talent – but that day I saw a different side of him. An easy way of communicating complicated information, casually referencing the whiteboard behind him while the audience was in no doubt that they had his full attention. He shared life-saving know-how, he used markers on the whiteboard, invited questions and dolloped on more than a touch of his trademark humour. So he had the presenting chops. He also once showed me how to turn motion-smoothing off on my HDTV to create a better cinematic experience, so I knew the tech wouldn't faze him either. He'd be the perfect fit.*

I have to say, the BBC had misgivings, not least because he was yet another white man. But I assured them: no one who sees the pity-inducing expression he wears on his face would say this was a man burdened by privilege. Further, you'd just assume he ticked one of the diversity boxes. He just had to with a face like that. I also remembered what Dustin had said about the pressure the production team was under, and I gambled that they'd relent to my demand if only to get me off the phone. I'm delighted to say I was right. And Simon and I spent the bulk of Sunday practising and refining our segment together. By the time Songs of Praise *came on, our repartee was dazzling.*

KWAAAAK

December 2022

Alone in a half-finished lighthouse, I stew in my own grump. Although I've hosted breakfast, early- breakfast and mid-morning radio shows, all of which traditionally call for a tone of almost lobotomised glee,[84] I'm not always of a sunny disposition. Then again, who is? Even the sun isn't always sunny – from time to time, it can give off angry solar flares, intense eruptions of electromagnetic radiation that knock out radio waves across entire continents. I don't see anyone having a pop at the sun for being crabby.

But yes, there are times – and this will shock the many hundreds of you who follow my brand closely – where I *can* slip into moroseness. My children used to refer to this side of me as Mopey Chops or Sad Dad. Nine times out of ten, I'd snap out of it and laugh it off. But the odd time, I'd kick a beachball at them or tell them to shut it.

As a result, I've learned handy techniques over the years that help to combat bad moods and steer me back towards cheerfulness. That might be as simple as destroying boxes of cereal with saws or hammers, or it could be leaving a negative review on TripAdvisor. Sometimes I might sit on my friend's Peloton eating toast and watching one of the instructors hosting a class. Or I might book a yurt and go and stay in a yurt. If not a yurt,

---

84 See Toby Anstis.

an executive room in a Marriott. There are loads of things you can do.

But this rut is a deep one – and what is worse is the knowledge that everyone in the town knows I've had to halt work. The Friends of Abbot's Cliff, the man in the shop who won't change a fiver, the sea shanters. When I ran out of shaving foam, I couldn't face popping to the shop – oh, they would have *loved* that – so I've simply stopped shaving, allowing the follicles beneath the skin to issue their thick rods of hair further out of my face. I begin to drink rum. And not just after 6 p.m., sometimes as early at 5.30 or 5. My Rab Microlight Alpine down jacket snagged on a nail that the builders hadn't hammered all the way in – who goes on strike mid-nail? – and I burst into tears as tufts of foam bled from the hole, like a cloud was leaking out of it. I binned the jacket entirely and am now forced to wear an old oilskin coat I found on a hired canal barge in Wales.

I am a ball of baleful frustration. I don't even care that it's raining. I open the window as wide as it'll go and lean out so that I can shout up at God himself. 'Happy now? I'm really trying, I've been working my fingers to the bone to make this place a bit nicer, you should be doing this, you lazy sod.' And then a low blow. 'And why don't you shave! You look like someone at a real ale festival.' And on that I slam the window shut.

I struggle to fill my days. One day I find myself texting a friend who ran speed-awareness courses for the DVLA. Philip and I had met back in the year 2000, when I'd been forced to attend one of his courses. At the start of the session we'd been at loggerheads. I tried telling him I was an innocent man, that I shouldn't have even be there, that I'd only been speeding because I'd got it into my head that an angry driver was trying to chase me and I was flooring it so I could seek refuge in Keele Services before she could hurt me. He gestured to the rest of the group:

'Join the club. Everyone here's got a reason for speeding. You need to look inside you, find the version of you that broke the law and kill him.' By the end I had totally bought into his teachings, killed Alan the Dangerous Driver, and made a new friend.

Now, desperate for human contact and to kill a bit of time, I plead with him over text to allow me to join one of his sessions. He isn't having it at first, says it's more than his job is worth. But eventually he agrees to let me join as long as I gave him five stars on the feedback form afterwards. Deal.

I sit there, in the lighthouse, on a Zoom call with Philip and six idiotic road users. Philip is doing the segment on braking distances, sending shockwaves through the group by showing that a car takes slightly longer to stop that you think it would. Then, Kwaaaak! A noise from outside.

Kwaaaak! There it is again. I look outside. On the rocks at the foot of the lighthouse, a sea gull. It looks directly at me – kwaaaak!

I do my best to ignore it. I just want to enjoy the course without interruption, especially as he's about to move onto tyre maintenance and the importance of tread.

Kwaaaak! The gull again. If I had a gun, I'd maybe not shoot it but certainly swing the butt of it at the bird, croquet style. Kwaaaak! I swear to God it's looking at me. What could it want?

The weather is rubbish today. Rain and wind and wave combining in a triple threat of inclemency. It's then that I notice a wooden forklift pallet has been hurled onto the rocks by a wave. The gull seems to have a leg trapped underneath it.

Not my problem, I think, and return to the course, putting my hand up and answering a question quickly and well. Something about checking your mirrors for motorbikes.

Kwaaaak! This bird will not shut up! Eventually, reluctantly, I excuse myself for a moment and don my coat. Then I open the door and step out into the driving rain. 'Aah,' I say quietly, as I always do when I step out into rain.

Turning my head against the wind, I make my way across the crag to where the bird is pinned. Gulls really are awful animals. Big things. Mean faces. I approach it gingerly, knowing that given half a chance it would peck out my eyes, although I might still be thinking of the Hitchcock film.

'Easy girl,' I say.

Kwaaaak!

'Alright, easy *boy*, then. I dunno,' I tut.

Slowly, oh so slowly I lift the pallet, which is really heavy and hurts my fingers until the bird is freed.

By now, my hair is pasted to the side of my head, sodden. My eyes are wild, both glinting and squinting. And then, the weirdest thing. Instead of scuttling back inside, I stand tall and ... laugh. I laugh at the sea. I laugh and laugh and laugh.

Then, with the wind lashing at me like a tawse, I face out to the ocean, daring another wave to try its luck. 'Where are you?' I shout, goading the waters. 'Where are you? Let's be having you!' It sounds pleasingly salty, although I later remember that this is what Delia Smith says at football matches when she's had a few.

I look back at the lighthouse and see myself reflected in the window. My hair is long and lank. My face grizzled and bestubbled. A grin is smeared across my face, and in oilskin coat and sou'wester hat, I look strangely at home. There's a timeless quality to me; I could have been one of Shackleton's men, one of the senior ones, certainly. Maybe this is me. The chap I've always meant to be. Alan Partridge, man of the sea.

Now comfortable in these conditions, I amble back to the door, taking my sweet time. Kwaaaak! The gull is still there. It is free, but instead of flying away, it merely cocks its head sexily and looks at me. I smile, dart inside and return with food. I know they like chips because once in Llandudno, a gang of them stole my chips. I don't have chips so I furnish the hungry gull with the next best thing: barbecue-flavour Pringles, which I arrange into a small pile by the door, like the mounds of rocks you sometimes see up Helvellyn. The bird nods – 'Thanks, Alan!' – and begins to eat.

I return to my chair and hear Philip's voice on the Zoom call: 'Alan? Just checking you heard that last point?'

'Yeah, don't drive fast, bye,' and I hang up. It's the first day of the new me.

THIS TIME

25 February 2019

7 a.m.

'[Lyrics removed on advice of publisher][85]*,' I sang powerfully in my kitchen, '[Lyrics removed on advice of publisher]!'*

The track? Gary Barlow's Take That classic 'Greatest Day' [which I'm strongly advised not to quote directly but in which the generously hipped wealth enthusiast posits that this day, the one we're now in, could in fact be the best, or greatest, one of those to have occurred so far]. I'll leave it for others to decide whether Gary should have gone for a lower key; it might be that he wanted to sound like that.

'[Lyrics removed on advice of publisher][86]*!' I continued.*

I was in the kitchen, brewing up a mug, my loyal assistant eating her abundantly margarined scone at the breakfast bar. And yes, today could be the greatest day of our/my life. I'd bought my assistant a new headscarf to celebrate, and even though we were indoors she was wearing it proudly. Me? I was just singing.

---

85 While I'm permitted to reproduce a single line of lyrics from any given song under what's known as 'fair use', I'm told quoting a longer tract of the song may trigger a royalty payment to Gary Barlow, something I'm not prepared to sanction as he would absolutely love it.

86 Same applies here.

'*Stay close to me! Stay close to me!*[87]' *Taking this as a cue, my assistant snuggled against me playfully.*

'*Not you!*' *I laughed and bumped her off with a quick shoulder barge, then sipped of my drink, letting the song peter out.*

'*Mmmmm. This coffee tastes gooooood,*' *I purred in the non-specific American accent I often use when feeling fine of a morning. And of this morning I most certainly did feel fine. Because today was B-Day (the 'B' being an abbreviation of 'BBC'), a clever play on the codename given to the Normandy landings, with the only slight downside that it sounded like I was referring to the bathroom device used to sploosh out one's backside.*

'*Mmmmm.*' *Another big sip. That really was excellent Kenco. I'd tried to maintain the US accent for the 'mmmmm', but it's quite hard to do an accent for a noise. And while that would have really bothered me on any other day, today I didn't care. Today I had bigger fish to fry. 'And ahm gohn fry dem fishies up real good,*' *I said, accidentally slipping into the kind of Deep South accent I probably wouldn't attempt outside the house.*

On the kitchen table was laid out a veritable feast. As this was a special day I'd asked my assistant if I could have a special breakfast, and she'd said I could, even though, as my employee, it wasn't really down to her. I tucked in greedily, my glad mouth making light work of the finest pastries money could buy from Sainsbury's. Next it was eggs, scrambled, and I like mine slack as hell.

With no need to chew, the warm yellow paste had slipped down an absolute treat. It was almost horribly satisfying. And I deserved every wobbly gobful.

---

87 This is the sum total I am going to quote. Again, this falls under fair use and means Barlow doesn't receive a single penny in the way of compensation, although that won't stop me receiving a curt letter from his 'legal team' (mum). 'Take that', Gary!

You see, in less than twelve hours, I, Partridge – or me, Alan – would be back on the BBC.

7-10 a.m.
The drive from Norwich to London was uneventful, so I won't insult you by describing it.[88]

10.10 a.m.
I reached BBC TV Centre, pulled up to the sentry gate, and waited to be waved through. It had been so long since I'd last been here that it seemed only right for me to look up at the much-loved building and shake my head wistfully for about ten to fifteen seconds. With that done, Kenneth, the friendly sentry guard who really did have an excellent grasp of English, explained to me that the BBC hadn't been based here for six years and that it was now a luxury apartment block with a high-end gym and a private bar. I thanked Kenneth, expressed my deep desire to one day visit his homeland,[89] *and got on my way.*

11 a.m.
An hour later, I was in reception at Broadcasting House being asked to take a seat and wait for a production runner to come and collect me. You see, no word more accurately describes the process of getting into the BBC than 'rigmarole'. 'Faff' isn't far off and 'palaver' isn't bad, but 'rigmarole' has it just right. Sign in. Show your ID. Have your bag scanned. It's as if they fear being the subject of a terrorist bomb plot. And indeed they do. Or at least that is the public line. I was later to discover – via an unguarded moment with the head

---

88 But suffice to say the portion of the journey that took me through central London was dominated by the sight of pedestrians with wretched lives.
89 Ireland.

of BBC One as he and I weed side by side at the urinals – that the real reason for such intense security arrangements is to ward off the very real danger of – say it quietly – an ITV spy. Since the death of Cilla Black, the ITV network has fallen into creative stasis, unable to generate any good ideas whatsoever, and it's an open secret that it has had to resort to espionage to generate new content, passing off agents as ordinary visitors and potentially embedding a mole deep within the organisation – e.g. Tim Davie – with a microfilm camera hidden in a lanyard.

As I took a seat on the reception area's cheap Chinese chairs, my assistant toddled off to do the BBC tour. Having seen the newsroom, visited the BBC Radio Theatre and posed for photos with a giant Dalek, the highlight for many was the chance to stand in front of the green screen by reception and 'have a go' at being a news or weather presenter. Yet what seemed like harmless fun to them was actually deeply insulting to the hard-working professionals who did these jobs.

The insinuation that being a newsreader or weatherperson was simply a matter of turning up and reading from an autocue was profoundly offensive. And though it was also true, I for one stood in solidarity with my brothers and sisters in the newsroom. (Less so with the weather lot, but that was because of what I can only describe as an ongoing Schafernaker Twitter spat.)

'Hello, you must be Alan.'

It was production runner, Paula. 'I'm the production runner, Paula.'

'That's a nice name.' This was my go-to compliment when meeting people for the first time.

'Oh, really? Do you think so?'

Problem was, it worked less well with what one might call the shitter names, such as Paula, when it could sound dangerously sarcastic.

'Absolutely, my mum was called Paula.'

My mum was not called Paula, but by lying I had stopped sound-ing like I was being sarcastic.

The offices at Broadcasting House are all on the upper levels, over-looking the open-plan newsroom below. As we rode up in the lift, I scanned the newsroom for Naga Munchetty but was unable to see Naga Munchetty. And while I wouldn't say this ruined my day, it would have been great to see Naga Munchetty.

Up in the production offices, any fears I might have had that I'd be ring-rusty instantly melted away. Being back at the BBC was like slipping into a warm bath. And though the person who'd just got out of the bath was big John Baskell, I tried not to let that image bother me.

11.30 a.m.

My first stop was to see John Baskell's This Time *co-presenter Jennie Gresham. In this business egos can be fragile and I was long enough in the tooth to know that the arrival of a seasoned pro like myself could easily put noses out of joint. And while Jennie had had her nose put out of joint before (by the cosmetic surgeon who performed the rhinoplasty that to this day surprisingly few people seem to know about), I was not about to be the next to do so.*

Though Baskell was the undisputed king of the show, Gresham more than held her own. She'd second-seated for five years, and with her glossy brown hair, gym–bunny figure and eyes frequently referred to as 'like Princess Diana's but brown', had a look best described as 'mainstream glamour'.

As it turned out, she wasn't there for another hour and a half be-cause 'Jen doesn't tend to arrive until about 12'. When she did swoop in, clutching a Starbucks coffee that must have been completely cold given how long it takes to get into the building, it was straight into the production meeting for that night's show.

12.00

Whether you call it 12, midday or noon doesn't really matter. I prefer midday, but I know those with a private education enjoy saying noon. As I say, doesn't hugely matter. But that's what time it now was.

And so to the meeting. Helming things was producer Howard Newman. Softly spoken, yet to notice that he was balding at the crown, but surely to God aware that he needed to trim his nose hair, Howard was known within the corporation as a safe pair of hands.[90] As he was introducing me to the team, and I was making each feel special by varying the ways in which I said 'hi',[91] it dawned on me just how completely the composition of the Beeb's staff had transformed in the years I'd been away. In my day the cliché of an organisation run by producers called Charles or Henry could not have been more true. Today? These were totally different people. Finlay. Jude. Seb. Saskia. What a breath of fresh air.

As Howard ran through the items on that evening's show, I sat there nodding, taking it all in, and occasionally going 'mm, mm, mm'. Jennie Gresham had plenty to say too, with thoughts on interview strategy, durations for various segments, and suggestions on the show's running order. Was it possible that everyone was sitting there thinking she lacked the experience needed to be getting involved in editorial issues, and that if she was going to insist on drinking that coffee she should at least remove the lid rather than slurping it through the plastic feeding hole? I don't know, I didn't really have a view on that, but the meeting was fine and I was happy to be there.

Just before people dispersed, I stood and said a few words, which I

---

90 If you exclude the occasion when, on a show he was producing, a member of the production team fell to their death from a lighting gantry.
91 'Hey'. 'Hi'. 'Morning'. 'Hello'. 'Hullo'. 'Hallo'. 'Wassup'. And a well-meaning but ill-advised 'namaste'.

wasn't specifically asked to do, but also I wasn't specifically asked not to do, either.

'Alright, guys, listen up. Saskia, eyes on me. Finlay, text on your own time, please. Here's the headlines: I am not here to tread on any toes. This Time *is the John & Jen show. Muggins here? I'm just a humble stand-in, here to serve, simple as. So, before any rumours start swirling around, whether about me being brought in to replace John or whatever, forget it. Ain't happening. All I'm doing is filling in while he gets over the massive heart attack.'*

It was a good opening and, while I hadn't realised the team hadn't been told about the massive heart attack, I felt that overall I was making the right impression.

'Meantime, me and Jen are going to be working as a team, but remember this: if push comes to shizzle, <u>she's the boss</u>. Capisce? I don't want anyone coming to me saying, "Alan, what shall we do about x?" or, "How would you like y?" If decisions need making, it's producer Howard in the first instance, then Jennie. And if either of those guys want to run a decision past me, then they will do so, but that's for them to decide. For anything else – industry advice, help with camera angles, having a tough time at home – just holler. I'm here as a re-source. <u>Use me</u>. Alright, let's have a great show. Hop it.'

3–5 p.m.

The rest of the day passed in a blur. There were chats with the ward-robe department, the social-media team and a frank, and at times heated, exchange with the make-up artist about preferred shades for my face.[92]

---

92 Her preference was to match as closely as possible my own skin tone. Mine was to be bolder, to lean in to the oranges and browns, to trust in the make-up. And while I've literally never met a make-up artist who argued to use less foundation rather than more, here it seemed I had found one. In the end the solution was surprisingly simple. I let Debbie apply the foundation and powder exactly

There was time too for my assistant to read aloud the cards and messages from well-wishers, as well as my joint-best friend Grant Shapps. A huge spray of flowers arrived from Ross Kemp – a symphony of pinks and lilacs, very much his calling card. But the vast majority of messages came from members of the public back in Norfolk. To have the love and support of my community, and to know that they took an interest in if and when I was going to make it back on the BBC, meant more than I can describe and fully vindicated the cost of paying for the billboard in Norwich town centre.

6.30 p.m.

Time to set my hair, change into my suit and, before either of those, dust my balls down with a good-quality talc – an invaluable tip to prevent on-screen itching, passed on to me by Aled Jones, a man whose own itching is worse than most because, of course, his balls are shaved.

6.45 p.m.

I was now into my vocal warm-ups and bracing myself for my assistant to ask why I was making those strange noises, despite the fact that I must have told her what a vocal warm-up is fifty times.

6.55 p.m.

I walked out into the studio. Whether it was the familiar hum of the lights or the smell of the cameras or the smell of the cameramen, I was suddenly overcome by sheer elation. I just felt <u>at home</u>. We all have places where we get a sense of belonging. For me: the Norwich Range

---

as she saw fit, using her decades of experience and her deep knowledge of the best ways to marry skin tone with cosmetic products to achieve a warm yet natural look. I then waited for her to go for a fag and finished the job myself. And watching the broadcast back later I was pleased with the shade I had achieved. Was I a little heavy-handed? Perhaps, but a bit of extra colour was no bad thing given I was sitting next to Jennie Gresham.

Rover dealership, the showers at a John Lloyd gym, any branch of Richer Sounds, the showers at my local swimming baths, and for a time in the late-nineties when I was having mental-health problems, Disneyland Paris. But here, in a BBC TV studio, I felt it too.

On set and with two minutes to go, I invited the crew to join me in taking the knee. I'm not sure they heard me, though, because the only person to do it was the sound guy, and I think he might have just knelt so he could change the battery pack on my mic. Plus, one of the cameramen was a cameraman of colour, and I think if someone takes the knee and you're a person of colour then you have to join in, don't you? Pretty sure you do, anyway.

6.59 p.m.

'Can I have a glass of water, please? My mouth is dry,' said Jennie. As a broadcaster, it's important to stay hydrated. We've all heard Radio 5 continuity announcers with under-moistened mouths slopping and slapping their way through links. A more experienced presenter might have taken the time to drink sufficient fluids before now, but she's just a kid, she'll learn. I gave her my glass and she gulped from it gladly.

And then, as the floor manager who acted like he was my friend even though I didn't know his name, stepped forward . . .

'We go live in five, four . . .'

. . . a very strange thing began to happen. All external noise seemed to disappear. The only sounds now? Those from within. Heartbeat. Breathing. Nasal whistle.

It's happening. The moment I've waited so long for. It's really happening.

Thoughts tumbled around my head like trainers in a washing machine, except in place of the trainers were the faces of all those who had doubted me, so it was a bit like the video for 'Bohemian Rhapsody' but, as I say, combined with a washing machine. Round and round they went, round and round. Chegwin. Rantzen. Henman.

Wan. And – no surprise, this – Edmonds. Soon enough – again, no surprise, this – they had all become Edmonds. (Apart from one that had turned back into a trainer, which, when I looked again, wasn't a trainer at all; it was a shoe with a Cuban heel, exactly the kind of heel worn by men who are self-conscious about their height. Funny, that.)

Yet rather than the urge to ring them up and gloat, the desire for revenge which had dominated my waking hours for so many years now simply lifted away. I forgave them. I forgave them all. Apart from Noel Edmonds.

And with that, as the sound of the This Time *title music bull-dozed its way back into my consciousness, I was back – I was back in the big time.*

7.31 p.m.
The show had finished. I was in a lift, the gentle 'pong . . . pong . . . pong' sound to indicate its arrival at a new floor shook me from my reverie.

A man asked me how the show had gone. I told him it had gone well, because it had. The chemistry between me and Jen had been on-point. The banter was sassy and fresh. And as for the seeds of bitterness, petty rivalry and passive-aggression that would one day tear us apart and lead me to claim that she would smother her own grandmother just to get on the cover of the Radio Times? *Barely noticeable.*

A chat with leopard-seal expert 'Dr' Alice Clunt had gone equally well. Yes, her expertise was undermined by her decision to wear jeans and a loose top instead of something more formal, but Jen and I did our best to help, teeing her up to give answers that weren't just in the interesting-without-using-big-words sweet spot BBC One viewers demand, but also counteracted the vegetarian mum-in-a-café vibe her wardrobe choice so powerfully gave off.[93]

---

93 The night before I'd stayed up way past bedtime to do research on the leopard

The showpiece piece of the show was a showpiece interview with an anonymous so-called hacktivist. That too had been a triumph. I'd been told that the format of the conversation would be one on one, with me interrogating him up on the raised interview area while Jennie waited for me quietly on the sofa. For what it's worth, I felt Jen played just as important a role in that interview as I did. By sitting quietly and suppressing her natural urge to interrupt, she showed great professionalism, and I, for one, respected that.

The conversation had gone <u>exactly</u> as hoped. Just as I'd intended, it culminated with him losing his composure and walking off. People seem surprised when I say that, but it's an open secret in broadcasting that all political interviewers explicitly want the person they're talking to to have a hissy fit and leave — as that means you've 'won' the interview. Some, such as Victoria Derbyshire, are simply downright disagreeable. Me? I simply wouldn't accept the guy's bullshit, said so and yeah, he saw his arse.

Convention dictates that the interviewer then has to respond by looking sheepish and scared — relax, this is just a cover action to make the walk-off seem unintentional. No, I couldn't have been more relaxed, nay pleased, with him storming out. It made for electric television, although I suppose all televisions are electric.

As my director and producer fell to bits in my ear, and as Jennie looked at the camera then looked towards me then looked at the camera then looked towards me then looked at the camera then looked towards me without ever actually saying anything, I remained icy calm.

---

seal. The second largest species of seal in the Antarctic, the only natural predator of *hydrurga leptonyx* is the orca. To be able to go online and watch video after video of seal and orca going at it hammer and tongs was absolutely terrific and took up much of my research time. And far from endangered, the leopard seal is classified as a species of 'Least Concern'. This means that, while the death of any living creature apart from a cat is a loss to be mourned, if you did happen to take out a leopard seal, there's no real need to worry.

I implicitly understood its potential to become a moment of water-cooler TV (or 'watercolour TV' as my assistant inexplicably calls it). You see, I knew that with John Baskell at the helm, viewing figures had been on the slide. (And though the man in Audience Data who showed me the spreadsheet said they had been steadily going up, he hadn't corrected for the fact that the UK's population is growing. Hence a small increase in net viewing figures actually equates to a real-terms drop. So, as I say, things were on the slide.)[94] *What the show needed was a shot in the arm. Something to make reviewers sit up and take notice. And when I pursued the fleeing nerd, sit up they most certainly did. And take notice they most certainly did, too.*

As I had given chase, I began to call out, 'Will you finish the interview now, please?' Through the backstage area, into the BBC's extensive network of state-of-the-art corridors, and all on live TV, the refrain came again and again: 'Will you finish the interview now, please? Will you finish the interview now, please? Will you finish the interview now, please?' And – in a coup de théâtre – I had ultimately completed the interview in a moving lift containing then-BBC Diana-alike Emily Maitlis.

I hadn't known she'd be there. On entering the elevator, I had a vague sense of there being a lamp or perhaps a light to my left. Yet when I glanced over, instead of the glow coming from a lightbulb or LED, it was coming from Emily Maitlis. And that sense of brightness wasn't just coming from the tan and the blonde hair. A lot if it was, but I genuinely believe some of it was coming from Emily's, well, 'Emilyness'; that drive, ambition and unquenchable desire to succeed that has now seen the former lead presenter of Newsnight *leave the corporation to be one of three presenters on a podcast.*[95] *Made by the*

---

94 I was later told that the UK population is *not* growing.
95 Her fellow presenters being Jon Sopel and competition winner Lewis [FIND OUT SURNAME].

company that owns Capital Radio and Heart FM, part of Emily's deal is that she also has to read out the adverts.

Then? Roll credits!

Pong! In the lift, the man thanked me for my précis of the show then asked me how I felt. And that's when I realised I felt ...

Nothing.

Absolutely nothing.

The man got out and the lift doors closed, leaving me alone in the moving cuboid. Why wasn't I feeling anything? This was everything I'd worked for. And it had gone brilliantly. Messages of congrats were flooding in thick and fast, so that my phone alerts were sounding like a geiger counter as it gets nearer the source of radiation. 'Brilliant!' said a well-known sports presenter. 'Best TV ever!' said a senior politician. 'Woo-haa! Yeah baby!' texted one former presenter of Ready Steady Cook. *'Absolutely fantastic,' said a different senior politician. So you can see, lots of messages, all of them real.*

Moreover, I was paying a boy called Rudy – nephew of the late Pete Gabitas – fifty pounds to keep watch outside Noel Edmonds's house and report any reaction to the show, and sure enough the boy was sending me texts like, 'Target slamming living room door', and, 'Target gesticulating angrily', and, 'Target looking sad/jealous'.

This should have been swelling my chest and trouser with absolute delight. But I'd actually never felt more alone. Even the Maitlis encounter had largely passed me by – that weekend, a friend said, 'What did she smell like?' and I realised I'd forgotten to smell her.

It seemed that deep within me a schasm had formed, a yawning gulf of emptiness. I ask again – why?

At first, I put it down to the warm malt drink I'd had in my dressing room just before the show. At a certain age, a cup of Horlicks can have the same effect as a beta blocker – indeed, a friend of mine on the Norwich Chambers of Commerce says the calming, numbing effect of the milky drink once caused him to sleep through a swingers party that had been organised for his sixtieth.

But it wasn't that. I felt alert and composed enough. I just felt . . . detached. The joy I'd expected to be spurting through my system simply wasn't deploying. And that might sound like the 'struggling with inner demons' bit that people put into books to make them sound more interesting, but it's true. Next morning, even my assistant noticed I was off my eggs, and my squash opponent pointed out that my hair was lank and lacking volume.

Now, some of that reserve will be out of respect for John Baskell. Lying prone in a hospital with wires coming out of him like an IED, he was, after all, the reason I was there. While I was being injected with renewed opportunity, John was being injected with thrombolytics to help break up any clots blocking blood flow to the heart. And I didn't for a second forget that. Typical me to be thinking of someone else, but that's just what I'm like. Another example was when I sent a box of chocolates to a bereaved friend in 1995.

But it wasn't just sympathy keeping my joy in check. No, the ultimate prize of getting back on primetime just didn't hit home like I'd thought it would. This was something else. I'd been so preoccupied with whether I could, I didn't stop to think if I should. Should I be making a triumphant return to primetime television? Should I be making a few people eat their words? Should I be earning a salary that better reflects my talent?

Clearly I could. I had done. But should I?

This should have been my finest hour. But something was missing.[96]

---

96 And just a post-scrit. What of Aled's talcing tip? Well it. Worked. Beautifully. Nary a single itch from start to finish. From either ball, even the notoriously scratch-hungry left. And while I definitely did want to scit-scrit-scrit the boys a few times towards the start of the show, that was just because I was nervous and, rightly or wrongly, I get a deep, thumb-sucking comfort from putting hand down trouser.

CIDER WITH ALAN

March 2023

I've become a cantankerous presence, there on the shore.

My assistant's nephew, Tim Benfield, is going through some personal problems that she doesn't particularly want to go into – presumably he's fallen in with his chemsex friends again – so she's headed back to Norfolk, leaving me alone in the lighthouse, with the occasional visit of the seagull – who I have named Likeworm because he likes worms – for company.

And you know what? That suits me JF.[97] I've had enough of people. 'People', which I've put in quotation marks to indicate contempt, gang up on you; 'people' go on strike; 'people' don't do what they say they will, or they do do what they say they will but not in the way they said they would; 'people' hurt your feelings; 'people' say you can't interview Her Royal Highness the Princess Royal Princess Anne. 'People'? You can keep them.

I'm not sleeping well. When they walked out at the start of winter, the builders had left the upper window unglazed, so a chill wind whips in and corkscrews down through the building of an evening. I am drinking, sometimes two, three glasses of rum each night, and maybe another one mid-morning. I am a danger to myself and others.

One hour bleeds into the next, one day into another. I begin to withdraw into myself like an animal's penis when not in use.

---

97 'Just fine'.

With nothing to differentiate this week from last, time begins to lose its meaning; to stretch and compress, to warp and flop. Staring endlessly into the salty abyss, my life provides as little mental stimulation as an ITV2 documentary.

I've stationed myself at the top window, my now-redundant loudhailer by my side. As the rest of the country sleeps, snores or – and let's not shy away from this – jerks off, I am at my post, performing a pathetic facsimile of a lighthouseman's role. I'll put the loudhailer to lips if I see a boat out at sea, issuing a half-hearted, 'Danger, rocks.' The rest of the time, I'll rest my chin on the windowsill, like Seldom used to do on the kitchen island, and just listen to the lapping waters. I have lost the life I once knew, the friends I once had, the joy that once danced in my heart like Andi Peters at a BBC disco.

I am at my lowest ebb. And while I will subsequently have ebbs that are lower, this really is one shitty ebb. Even my stubble, which until recently has made me look rugged, unknowable and actually quite fit, has changed for the worse. Now grown out into a full beard, or certainly four-fifths of one, it has transformed my appearance into that of a 1980s geography teacher, one struggling to command the respect of his class now that the threat of caning had been removed by nanny-state legislation.

The previous night was particularly challenging. The icy temperatures have meant that on a number of occasions I have became hyperthermish, while Likeworm, who surely to God should have been asleep, was making a din the entire night. Hungry? Thirsty? Beak stuck in a ring pull? I had absolutely no idea. I just wanted to be at peace.

Come this morning I have no such luck. Upwind from me, over on the headland, a few-dozen locals have gathered for an impromptu party. A hub of music, chatter, cackle upon cackle of laughter. And soon a new noise begins to filter through. Raised voices. An argument. The unmistakable rhythms and cadences of passive-aggressive quarrel. Not now. Please, not now. I start to make out a few voices.

'Why can't you turn a blind eye? It's Sally's birthday, John.'

'You know I can't do that.'

'Why not?'

'Because it's the law, that's why.'

Argh. I rummage around in my bag and pull out some binoculars. Then I dock the twin-lensed peeping pipes with my eyes to see what all the fuss is about.

The land belongs to millionaire-businessman Paul Duxberry. Duxberry (real name Paul Daniels)[98] is big in caravans. His showroom in Deal boasts either the largest or second largest mobile-home forecourt in western Europe, depending on how you calculate it. But he is also known for his largesse, selflessly giving large amounts to charities, the needy and the Conservative Party.

Recently, when the problem of illegal immigrants arriving on the shores of Kent first emerged, Duxberry donated five of his 'vans for use as mini-immigration processing centres. As well as providing a roof over the refugees' heads, the solution has the added bonus that if the government drags its heels about relocating them, the caravan doors can be locked and the 'gees can be quickly and quietly towed out-of-county.

At the time, however, I know very little of this. My knowledge of the four-foot-six Caravan Kingdom founder extends only to chatter overheard in local post offices and pubs: namely that Duxberry holds an annual get-together to toast the year's first

---

98 A name he shared with the father of mid-ranking eighties magician Martin Daniels.

brew of his famous homemade cider. Clearly, this is what I'm now looking at.

Almost every member of the Friends of Abbot's Cliff is there too. The woman who looks like a school teacher/dog trainer. The man who looks like Harry Secombe with a rash. The angry woman with the hair. The angry woman with the mole. The angry woman with the padded gilet. The other angry woman with the padded gilet who I didn't mention before. But there are others of their ilk, too. There must be, what, twenty of them? Twenty-five, maybe. The grown-ups drink cider and chomp on burgers. The kids jump on a bouncy castle and – and this will surely end badly – also chomp on burgers.

Now, every one of them is standing, hands on hips, glaring at a policeman intent on shutting the party down. How can I tell? Three words: big dick energy. Years of experience hosting local radio summer roadshows have taught me just how keen the fuzz always are to kibosh unlicensed gatherings. And by the way this cop leaned on the door of his car before tugging up his trousers by his belt loop, I know it's happening again.

'It's an unlicensed gathering, Paul. I warned you this would happen yesterday. I want it shutting down, now, please.'

I lower the binoculars and pop the hailer to my lips: 'Don't need a licence.'

Suddenly the conversation halts. In my peripheral vision, I can see people have turned to look at this strange man atop an unfinished lighthouse. The policeman bellows over at me: 'SORRY, DID YOU SAY SOMETHING?'

I sigh then answer, 'I said they don't need a licence.'

The officer clocks me and yells back: 'I THINK YOU'LL FIND THEY DO.'

To be fair to the fella, his shouting is first class. I am miles away yet his every word is clear as crystal/can be/a bell/

day/fuck. Has he attended drama school? Could he be a lay preacher at a local church? I have no way of knowing. Instead, I bullhorn him a reply: 'What, a premises licence or a personal licence?'

'PREMISES.'

'Right. I didn't realise these events took place multiple times in any twelve-month period.'

I hear Paul say to the officer, 'They don't. I only do this once a year.'

I allow myself a smile. 'He says he only does it once a year. And there's me thinking under the Licensing Act 2003, a premises licence is only required for venues that host more than three events in any calendar year. As opposed to a temporary event notice, which covers events that only take place annually.'

The officer looks fidgety now. 'NO, ER ... ACTUALLY, THINKING ABOUT IT, IT WOULD BE A TEMPORARY EVENT NOTICE.'

'Cool. Which para?'

'WHAT?'

'Which paragraph of the terms of a temporary event notice does this gathering fall under? The sale of alcohol?'

'YEAH.'

'And does that apply if he's giving it away? Only I've not seen any money changing hands.'

'WELL ... NO. THAT WOULD BE DIFFERENT.'

'It would, wouldn't it?'

A pause. I can see the cop getting flustered. He tries another tack. 'BUT IT ALSO APPLIES TO THE SALE OF FOOD, AND HE IS SELLING THE BURGERS.'

'You make a good point there, officer.'

'THANK YOU, NOW IF YOU'VE QUITE—'

'Didn't realise it was so late, though.'

'WHAT DO YOU MEAN, LATE?'

'Well, I could have sworn paragraph five of the Licensing Act 2003 says it's only a requirement to have a licence if selling food after 11 a.m.'.

Members of the gathering start to look at each other, excitedly.

Me, I keep my cool. The policeman, less so, never before having faced a foe so well-versed in the 2003 Licensing Act. Turning away, he mutters, 'Fine, then, carry on.'

The crowd whoops. I actually feel good. For the first time in a long time, *I, Alan Partridge, feel good.*

The policeman turns back, Columbo-style. 'Oh, but one more thing,' he says to Paul. 'No music. I know for a fact you don't have a music licence.'

'But I do!' I holler. 'Got one last year when I was buying a roadshow bus which I subsequently crashed into a ditch. And this is ... "Life in the Fast Lane" by the Eagles. Turn it up, Kent!'

I press play on my iPhone and put it against the mic of the loud hailer. Joe Walsh's *classic* riff fills the seaside air.

The response from the cider-swillers is immediate and unequivocal. Conceived in their minds, manufactured in their vocal chords and transported by their throats, a deafening cheer is emitted from twenty to twenty-five mouths. The target of their roar? Yours truly. In a single virtuosic display of legislative clever-cloggery, I have saved the day. And on that, some sort of instinct deep within me takes over.

'Shaping up to be a hot one!' I say, guesstimating a forecast from the shape of the clouds. 'Sunny intervals, with a high of eighteen. A few isolated patches of rain drifting in off the Channel later. And on the roads ...'

I spin to look over at the dual carriageway.

'Things looking clear on the A20 with just a minor build-up on the westbound approach to the Court Wood interchange. That's your traffic. And *this* . . . is Alan Partridge.'

And right there, on the twenty-seven second mark, in comes Don Henley with the vocal. It is *poetry*.

We continue in this way for another hour. I'm supplying some *fat* tunes, and for their part they're getting kids to ferry over burgers and bottles of cider, which I tuck into merrily, even though the cider is horrible.

As the songs play, I'll catch the eye of a local and we'll raise a glass at each other. I feel a warm sensation in my tummy, and almost a stirring in my loins. I've wanted this for so long. I line up 'Pass the Dutchie' by Musical Youth, and it's while looking down and watching the cream of the local community belting out the reggae hit in cod Jamaican accents I genuinely don't think they intend to be racist, that I see a car.

It is veering along the A20, at breakneck speed. Is that . . . my assistant's car?

It approaches the drive down to the lighthouse and, without waiting, pulls an almighty right turn onto the gravel, screeching across a lane of oncoming traffic. What is she playing at?

She pulls up and hurries out of the car, patting at her hair in that way older women do.

'Up here!' I shout.

She looks up, out of breath, panic etched across her forever-frowning face.

'Get yourself a cider,' I beam.

But she shakes her head. 'The man's coming,' she says. 'He didn't say when but soon.'

'What man?' I say. 'What are you talking about?'

'The man from the Lighthouse Board. They want to see it's in good condition before . . .'

'Before? Before what?'

'Before Princess Anne will come and open it.'

I collapse.

BACK IN THE BIG TIME

2019/20

At 9.18 on Sunday, 2 March 2019, John Baskell was pronounced dead. His exhausted heart, which had fought so valiantly for so long against an endless onslaught of fry-ups, whisky, cream cakes, fags and more cream cakes, had simply said 'no more'. John was zipped into a body bag, wheeled down to the mortuary and placed in an extra-large fridge.

I had first learned the news from a friend (Greg Dyke) who shall remain nameless. The first text said: 'Guess who's dead'; the second, 'John Basket' and the third, 'John Baskell'.

Confirmation arrived in a phone call from my assistant. She'd been based at the hospital since John's admission, quietly keeping tabs on his condition and feeding back updates. That morning, calling me from a payphone because she thought that's what a spy would do, she had uttered the pre-arranged phrase: 'Leningrad has fallen.'

Boy, had he fallen.

They say you shouldn't speak ill of the dead, but it's also wrong to defend the indefensible.

I don't mind harbouring someone per se. I would have harboured Anne Frank without a thought for my own safety. During the reign of Elizabeth 1, I would even have harboured a Catholic priest as long as my kids weren't in the house on their own with him.

But harbouring a guy who exudes bad energy – uh-uh.

It's like if you'd owned a classic car that had been the pride of your family, but years later you discovered that, although considered a classic – all original detailing and pristine bodywork – it had been touching up other cars in the garage in an aggressive and sexual way.

What I'm about to say might sound a bit mean, but part of my contract with Orion Publishing is to 'write truthfully in a manner which can include but isn't limited to embarrassment, offence to self, offence to others, sexual indiscretion, scatology, boastfulness, meanness and humour'.

So I'm gonna say it. Much-loved presenter John Baskell – like many people described as much-loved – wasn't actually loved much. He was fine, he could do the job. In that sense, he was a kind of forerunner to your much-loved Dan Walkers or much-loved Stephen Mulherns. If they appear on screen, you'll sigh, obviously, but you won't necessarily turn over. Today that seems to earn you the moniker of 'much-loved'. Fine. No skin off my nose.

And while John's Wikipedia page is a quite astonishing hagiography dripping with syrupy prose about his 'talent' and 'likeability', it seems to me that one honours his memory better if we honour the man he actually was. Which is why I prefer to remember the real John. The John who threw an ashtray at a costume assistant; the John who wouldn't work with Aled Jones; the John who stank of fags.

But I like to think I balanced the public veneration of John, in the form of a moving obituary VT, written and presented by me with additional material by Ray Stubbs, with an even-handed airing of his failings, in the form of me reading out unvetted tweets from anonymous viewers – something I later learned was a broadcasting no-no. This Time bosses felt I'd unduly amplified messages which had clearly been broadcast in error. I apologised and, while Jennie remained in a sulk for some time, I was able to put it behind me and move on. And it was right that I did so, because with John dead, the starter pistol on the race to succeed him, like a Glock 9mm with suppressor, had quietly fired.

It's no exaggeration to say that the This Time *sofa spot was one of the most coveted positions anywhere in pre-watershed chat-based light-entertainment UK TV. So it was no surprise that the cream of presenting talent was queuing up to make it their own. Dan Snow. Matt Baker. Ainsley Harriott. Ben Fogle. Giants of broadcasting. One of the ones from Mel and Sue had also thrown her hat into the ring because it'd be just my fucking luck they'd give it to a woman.*

As the incumbent, I liked to think the job was mine to lose, but I was under no illusions: this would be one of the most brutal campaigns ever fought for a BBC job. See any of them in a corridor and it'd be handshakes and hellos (or high-fives and whoops, if you bumped into Ainsley), but behind the scenes the gloves were off. Were sweeteners offered? Were threats made? I don't know. All I can say is that as far as I am personally aware, the rumour that Dan Snow offered to give the producer a private sports massage with his big strong hands is completely unfounded.[99]

What soon became clear, however, was that the race had boiled down to a straight fight between me and the grandma's favourite, Matt Baker. Of all my opponents, it was Baker I feared the most (not least because research indicated that much of the This Time *audience were grandmas).*

Professional, effortlessly likeable, and with an energy I like to describe as hetero-camp, Baker had it all. Yet something about him

---

99 What I can confirm is that he did pay a visit one afternoon to the home of commissioning editor Lake Palmer. Flanked by his broadcaster dad Peter and broadcaster uncle Jon, it was a show of strength, or as they like to call it, a 'Snow' of strength (pathetic). Over tea and scones in Lake's walled garden, Peter and Jon took the opportunity to compliment him on the wonderful colour variation of his hydrangeas and peonies, but the underlying message was clear: give Dan the job or we'll put your fucking windows through. Thankfully, though, Palmer is made of sterner stuff. He told them there'd be no nepotism on his watch and showed them to the door. And as they walked away, tails between their legs, he shouted after them, 'Oh, and they're not hydrangeas, they're viburnums, you dicks.'

seemed off. No one could be that squeaky clean. I dispatched my assis-
tant to dig up some dirt.

When she filed her report three days later, it made for bleak reading.
Baker's only failing? It generally took him two attempts to parallel
park. Not that that was even a failing these days. In an age when the
motor car is fast becoming the devil, millennials see poor parking as a
plus. It's incredible but true.

Ultimately, though, an incident that happened over six years ear-
lier was to cost Baker his shot at the job. With the commissioning
editor poised to hand him the contract, a tip-off from an anonymous
source – who only identified herself as 'a female Baptist with the best
interests of the corporation at heart' – revealed that during the film-
ing of an episode of Countryfile *in 2015, a worse-for-wear Matt*
Baker had thrown sheep shit at some boys.

Less than forty-eight hours later I was unveiled as the new per-
manent co-host of This Time.

When you become a Big Deal, things change. Where previously a
smile at a pretty lady would have been met with a scowl and a tut,
now it's returned in kind. A blue joke in a business meeting, once met
with mild titters, is now embraced with full-throated laughter. You
no longer have to drive yourself to work. Or open doors for yourself.
Or brush your own hair (unless you want to).[100]

Point is, when you're a person with a public profile, people put
you on a pedestal. And though that sentence sounded odd because of
how many 'p's it contained, the fact remains that as co-host of This
Time, *beamed into living rooms five nights a week, I was now a*
figure of national prominence. As such, keeping my feet on the ground
had never been more important. My own way of dealing with this?
Daily affirmations. I'd stand in front of the mirror after my shower,

---

100 I did.

spread my arms and legs like the Vitruvian Man[101] and simply say: 'I am no better than anyone else. I am no better than anyone else. I am no better than anyone else. Even binmen and teachers.'

I'd change the jobs mentioned each day to expose my brain to the full range of menial workers. Dinner ladies, builders, Deliveroo drivers, tanning-salon receptionists, scrapyard monkeys, and so on. I found it to be an immensely powerful technique.

Humility became my watchword, both at work and at play. Once a month, rather than a runner getting my lunch, I'd get theirs. 'Take a load off,' I'd say. 'Today I'll be getting your lunch.' And while, as the show's presenter, I was typically too busy to follow through on that pledge and would have to get one of the make-up girls to do it for me, plus get mine, plus don't forget the change, the point was made, and powerfully so.

Out on the street? Same idea applied. If someone asked for my autograph I'd say, 'Uh-uh, you give me yours instead.' It was a neat and unexpected role reversal that showed me to be a man who wore my celebrity lightly, like one of those silk Japanese dressing gowns worn by women and the gay.

But being a sought-after figure also meant extra demands on my assistant, and I have to admit it took her time to adjust. Invites to openings, premieres and product launches began to flood in, and she would accept them all. It was lunacy. The idea that the opening of a community centre should have parity with the launch of an executive car was patently and morally wrong. In urgent need of guidance, I developed a simple flow chart to aid her decision-making, which she laminated and stuck to the wall next to her desk.

---

101 Look it up – I use these references for a reason.

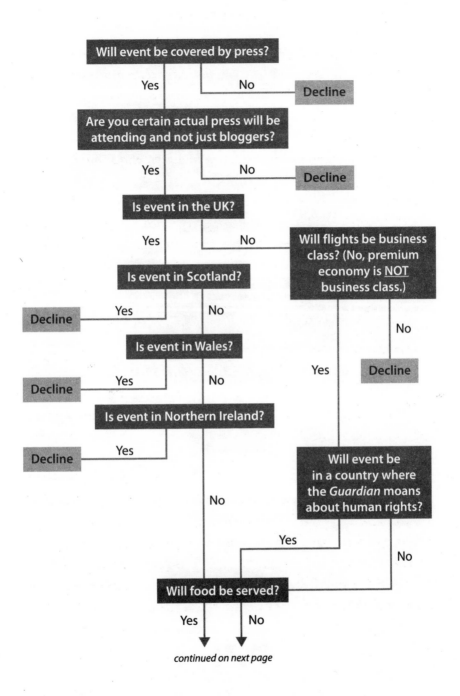

Will event be covered by press?

Yes   No   Decline

Are you certain actual press will be attending and not just bloggers?

Yes   No   Decline

Is event in the UK?

Yes   No   Will flights be business class? (No, premium economy is <u>NOT</u> business class.)

Is event in Scotland?

Decline   Yes   No   No

Is event in Wales?   Yes   Decline

Decline   Yes   No

Is event in Northern Ireland?

Decline   Yes   Will event be in a country where the *Guardian* moans about human rights?

No   Yes   No

Will food be served?

Yes   No

continued on next page

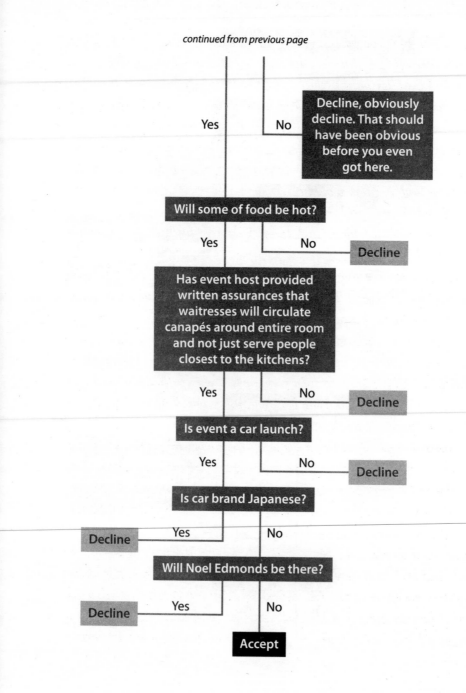

continued from previous page

Yes   No   Decline, obviously decline. That should have been obvious before you even got here.

Will some of food be hot?

Yes   No   Decline

Has event host provided written assurances that waitresses will circulate canapés around entire room and not just serve people closest to the kitchens?

Yes   No   Decline

Is event a car launch?

Yes   No   Decline

Is car brand Japanese?

Decline   Yes   No

Will Noel Edmonds be there?

Decline   Yes   No

Accept

Then there was the post bag. A gentle trickle when I was a DJ at North Norfolk Digital, it was now more akin to a swollen river that had bust its banks, with tens (sometimes dozens) of pieces of mail gushing in every week. They tended to be a roughly equal split between kind letters from elderly women, autograph requests and death threats. The elderly women would receive 'Pensioner letter 1' or 'Pensioner letter 2' (depending on whether or not they'd sent a gift), the autograph hunters would be ignored and the death threats would be collated, bound and dropped off at the local police station every Friday morning along with a thank you note and some homemade shortbread.

But perhaps the biggest change in my personal life at this time was my 'almost move' to London. Because though I'd always hated London and hated people from London and hated people who weren't from London but liked London, in a lot of ways it would have made sense. I was working there, socialising there, I'd found an excellent spin class and a masseuse who gave me weekly full- body massages (although she didn't touch my back because I don't like my back being touched). Maybe it was time to reassess.

I started the ball rolling by setting up appointments with a series of luxury estate agencies. We're talking a notch or two above your Winkworths and possibly even your Foxtons, though the latter remain my estate agency of choice.[102] Yet what I saw on the viewings appalled me. What they were calling townhouses were terraces with quite small gardens. In Norwich a nurse would live in a house like that, and they said they dealt in luxury properties? When one of the guys told me the rent was five thousand pounds a WEEK I had to ask him if he was having a laugh because he must have been having a laugh.[103] I also had to repeatedly point out to these people that luxury

---

102 Attitude.
103 He was not having a laugh.

homes were rubbing shoulders with council accommodation, which surely breached planning law. No, my first instinct had been right. The entire place is a shithole but no one dares say it. Well, I dares. I remained in Norwich.

On language

During this time, I also got to grips with the way the modern BBC talks to its audience.

The key word? 'Accessibility'. It's something BBC-bashers like to call 'dumbing down', but take the time to understand it, and suddenly, a way of talking that normally makes you want to kick the TV in makes perfect sense.

A particularly good example comes from the BBC's cohort of weather presenters. Imagine you tune in to a weather bulletin and hear the weatherman say, 'And later it's going to rain.' How is that going to make you feel? You don't want it to rain. You don't like rain. If it rains you might get wet and you don't want to get wet. And because the weatherman is the one who said it, you're a bit cross with him and you're a bit cross with the BBC. You're a hair's breadth from flicking to ITV. So what to do?

Well, BBC weather presenters have developed a clever solution. Instead of 'later it's going to rain', a weather person would now do two things. Firstly, they'd pull a sad face, and then they'd rephrase the sentence like so: 'Well, it's bad news for later on, folks. I'm sorry to say the sunshine won't last and it's going to rain.' See the difference? Let me walk you through it. On hearing these reformulated words a viewer thinks, That man just said it's going to rain, but I don't like rain and I don't want it to rain. Then again, he did say sorry about the rain, and when he said it he did a sad face, and I liked that because I had a sad face too.

The result? Our viewer isn't made to feel upset or cross at the BBC and is able to continue watching.

Job done? Well, not quite. You see, the weather presenter still made the mistake of saying 'it's going to rain'. Remember again: viewers don't like rain. But given that the key information is that rain is coming, how could this issue be solved? Could it be solved at all? Well, props here must go to the pioneering work of weather presenter Louise Lear (born Tracy Louise Barden, 1967). It was Lear who first realised that when she replaced accepted meteorological terminology with language used in books for the under-fives, a remarkable thing happened: viewers became less upset. So rather than 'it's going to rain', she would say 'and you might juuuuuuuust start to feel the pitter-patter of tiny raindrops beginning to fall'. It was a eureka moment for the weather team and was immediately incorporated into weather bulletins corporation-wide.

Yet within months, the humility had gone; melted like a snowman[104] in the sun. Instead, my behaviour was now characterised by a sense of entitlement only normally seen in Old Etonians. And while for them it is a perfectly understandable by-product of having to deal with the pressures of running our economy and leading our government, for me it was simply unforgivable. I had become a monster.

Around Broadcasting House, I took to wearing clacky shoes so people would hear me coming before I'd even got round the corner.[105] And when they did finally see me, I'd assert dominance by saying their name slightly before they'd finished mine.

'Ala—'

---

104 Or woman!
105 Doesn't work on carpet.

'Doug!'

If I was greeting a group of people, I'd shake one person's hand but already be looking at and saying hello to the next one; then when I was shaking that person's hand I'd be looking at and saying hello to the next, and so on. It was a technique that required split-second timing, but get it right and it was a quick and easy way to make people feel worthless. Arriving at work, I'd park my car so it straddled two spaces (only stopping when my assistant pointed out that people might think I couldn't park). In meetings I'd burp and sometimes not say 'excuse me'. If I was at a party and Tony Robinson was on the dance floor, I'd dance around him so aggressively that he'd get scared and have to go home. And while I don't regret that one, most of my behaviour was abhorrent.

But it was when I refused to return to Norwich to host the summer fundraiser for Norwich Conservative Federation and the Conservative Party in Norwich North and Norwich South that I knew something was badly wrong. It was just not <u>like</u> me. It was a blue-letter day in the local political calendar – we always had a Gordon Brown piñata which children could hit with sticks until sweets tumbled out of him; it was <u>that</u> kind of day! I hadn't missed the event in ten years, and even then it was only because I had a swollen face following a cosmetic dental procedure to reverse receding gums.[106]

---

106 As we age, our gums recede, hence the phrase 'long in the tooth'. The experimental procedure I underwent, which at the time of booking was just described to me as 'a procedure', was designed to reverse this, effectively de-ageing my smile by between ten and fifteen years. With an incision placed at either side of the tooth and blood flowing into the mouth, the gum was lifted, yanked downwards and anchored back into place. When the flap of gum didn't hold and Dr Chatterjee's working theory was disproved, he quickly pivoted and took grafts from the roof of my mouth to see if that would work instead.

The six-hour treatment, for which I paid £12,000 in a single upfront payment,

It's only now, looking back with the benefit of Heinzesight, that I can see what was happening. My behaviour was a symptom of a dissatisfaction I had for too long ignored, repeatedly squashing it back down inside of me like when you try to get a double duvet into a vacuum bag and there's no one there to help you because you live alone. The problem? I just didn't dig the BBC anymore.

That feeling of coldness after my first time presenting This Time? *That was a feeling I should have listened to; a feeling I should have sat down with, looked in the eye, and quite simply said, 'Wa gw'aaaaaaan?'*

But the volcanic eruption, the red–hot spaffing of those suppressed feelings was to come later. For now, and for nearly one hundred episodes of This Time, *I would be living life as a muddled-up feelings-squasher.*

---

is uncomfortable but not painful. The month after, however, is a different story. Searing pain in the gums and roof of the mouth are barely tempered by over-the-counter pain killers. Codeine is more effective but can only be prescribed for a short course and causes almost total constipation. Avoiding alcohol and eating only blended food fed into your mouth via a feeding pump, your face is so swollen you could genuinely pass for a cartoon hamster or Björn from ABBA. Facial deflation occurs in three to four days, and I'm happy to say the bleeding smile of a vampire soon gives way to the healthy smile of a TV evangelist – job done.

The procedure, the results of which I am largely happy with, is no longer available in the UK.

GUANO

March 2023

A man grunts and pants and huffs and strains. Bent double at the waist, in the honest throes of work, he stands suddenly, statuesque in the baking sun, proud and strong. Sweat glistens on his brow, cheeks and neck, and also on his tummy. His T-shirt has been removed and tied around the circumference of his head as a makeshift sweatband – like Stallone in *Rambo* or De Niro in *The Deer Hunter* or a lady action hero in a more modern film.

The man is me. I am labouring. If my contractors won't lift a finger, so be it. I've got eight of the buggers,[107] plus two enthusiastic thumbs, and I will simply lift those if need be. With the Lighthouse Board promising to come and see the renovated building, I am hellbent on getting the job done myself.

It's been a steep but rewarding learning curve, gleaning practical tips from a million YouTube videos and a hitherto-unopened DIY book I bought when I first married Carol called *The Practical Man: Handy Hints for the House-proud Husband.*

I have laid wooden flooring panels, I have sanded windowsills, I have screwed doors onto hinges and hinges onto doors. I have painted and hammered. I have damn near broken my back, but I sleep well every night (and for two hours after my lunch), my heart full with the sheer pleasure that comes of physical exhaustion.

---

107 Fingers.

And while I have no interest in joining a union and waging war on self-made employers who are just trying to create wealth that will trickle down to me anyway if I just bide my time instead of biting the hand that feeds me, I am in every other respect a working man. Mine is a life of honest toil, sore fingers, high-cholesterol processed foods (e.g. microwavable hamburgers), wolf-whistling, cans of Relentless and industrial language ('fuck a duck, someone pass me that shitting hammer').

I like to call myself Handy Alan or Alan the Builder. I drove to a branch of Screwfix and bought myself a hard-wearing pair of work trousers. I decided they looked too new, so I set about them with a cheese grater and spattered them with paint to create a pleasing careworn look.

Unfortunately, when I went to put them on I realised I had left my handprints in paint on the bottom. The trousers now look both cheeky and fruity, which is the one thing I didn't want to happen.

Still, the trousers I subsequently did buy have become scruffy through genuine graft, and I like the way I look in them. I was unloading materials from the boot of my car one afternoon and I was delighted to see Red walk past and notice me. Yes, I really did look great.

I have made some impressive headway with the rebuild. And while some days are frustratingly slow, and some days have seen me achieve little more than tracking down the customer-service department for Gorilla Glue and asking them why the nozzle has become jammed with hardened glue and how they must see that there's a design flaw there, like British Rail used to say: We're getting there!

'Scrub and clean and dust and polish! Soak and sponge and wipe

with relish! Scrub and clean and dust and polish! Soak and sponge and wipe with relish!'

My assistant is cleaning with gusto, we both are, swept along by her singing 'The Cleaning Song', a workmanlike ditty she appears to have penned herself. Leaving aside the fact that polish and relish simply do not rhyme, it's an unpleasant listen. Julie Andrews she ain't, managing not just to be out of tune, but almost *anti*-tune. Each repetition of the lyric seems to find new and unexpected melodic pathways, each of them bad and wrong, the overall effect being of someone who fundamentally misunderstands the accepted norms, the basic principles, the very *purpose* of music.

Then again, she's no great lover of music, not really. Her record collection is divided into the only two genres she knows: hymns and not-hymns.

'You should record this,' I say. 'They could play it in Guantanamo.'

'Thank you very much,' she smiles.

I have to say, though, it's keeping us motivated. We're making excellent headway, but there's still much to do, sprucing up a site that has become – and I hold my hands up – a bit of a shithole. Since the workmen withdrew their labour and I threw myself into completing the work myself, the ground floor has become a cesspit of unfinished sandwiches, fag ends, dirty boot marks and at least one pornographic magazine that I didn't even know they sold anymore. The walls are slick with candle smoke and grime. Outside, the walls need to be whitewashed, algae needs to be chipped off, and the smeared windows need de-smearing. All the soft furnishings need to be laundered and the finished rooms need to be rendered homely.

I would hate for anyone from the Lighthouse Board to see the place like this, so I've insisted we at least try to make the place presentable – hopefully spick/span enough for the fellows to suggest to their patron (Her Royal Highness the Princess Royal Princess Anne) that she could one day visit the finished' house.

Outside, the builders' equipment has been tidied and materials stacked. Sitting on a pallet is a recently delivered new lantern which will soon need to be crane-lifted up to the top of the structure. Verfoofen was meant to liaise with a crane-driver so we could get the installation booked in, but clearly he hasn't done that, so the new lantern lies wonky on the shore, like the Statue of Liberty at the end of *Planet of the Apes*. But aside from that, I am happy with our progress. Just goes to show what can be achieved with a bit of elbow grease and panic.

My assistant tableclothes the table, sets it for two, and pops a daffodil in a glass tumbler. 'There,' she says. 'Fit for a king. Or should I say princess!'

And she laughs, quite a lot. I have to concede, though, she is a damn good worker. She stands back to admire her handiwork.

I feel a breeze on my face and enjoy the coolness, imagining I am a bowl of custard and the breeze is a woman blowing on me. Suddenly, I open my eyes. A breeze?

I look round and notice my assistant has opened the door. 'I wouldn't do that if I were y—'

Too late. In, like the angel of death, swoops my trusty gull friend Likeworm. 'Uh-oh,' I say with colossal understatement, because Likeworm is about to make things very, very bad indeed.

The first few seconds are fine, as the bird enjoys a few laps of the circumference. But I can sense he is becoming distressed at being confined.

Kwaaaaak! Kwaaaaak!

He begins to zig-zag, his feathered, fingerless arms slapping down on the air like a single mum disciplining her kid's bottom. Swooping low, he nearly takes my head off. But as I bend the top half of my body back on itself to avoid a coroner's report that reads 'death by gull', I hear a tell-tale smash. The panic-stricken sky beast has flown into one of the windows.

I begin to lurch for the door, the residual fitness from several years of BodyPump with Dale and step aerobics with Debbie allowing me to hurdle a chair and run the remaining steps. In the blink of an eye – and I'm thinking Diane Abbott here, because hers stay closed for ages – I am at the door, and push it wide open, showing Likeworm a clear escape route. But no. In a scene eerily reminiscent of when I was in a car with my assistant and she got stuck on a box junction when the lights turned red, the gull is going absolutely berserk, or 'birdserk' – IHGTTSU![108]

He begins to defecate. Big, white sludgy dollops across the tablecloth and floor. My assistant screams and tries to cower behind a curtain, pulling it off the rail.

'No, please,' I wail. 'Please don't do this! Please!'

But Likeworm has not finished emptying himself, not by a long shit. He is in the midst of a carpet-bombing so intense that within seconds nearly every surface has been hit. What I am witnessing is nothing short of a faecal Dresden. Soon I have springed/sprung into action as fast as I had sprinted/sprunt to the door, flailing my fists in a desperate attempt to, and let's call a spade a spade, twat the bird out of the sky.

'Eat crap, bird brain!' But as the gull waste rains down, little do I realise how ironic those words will be. Because at the very moment they come out of my mouth, into my mouth drops some – no, a lot – of birdshit,

---

[108] I have got to try stand-up!

As it slips down my throat like a giant oyster, one thought enters my head: This is poison. Then another thought: I am going to die.

JENNIE GRESHAM

Jennie Fiona Margaret Gresham-Hartley, thirty-nine, is Britain's best-loved mid-ranking TV presenter. And with good reason! Armed with a winsome smile she practises in the mirror, Jen's a broadcaster I genuinely admire. If it's not verboten to say this in the current climate, she's the thinking man's thinking woman, and provides not just eye-candy, but ear-candy and even brain-candy too at times. She's that good.

From day one, it was clear Jennie and I enjoyed a chemistry that sizzled like liver in a hot pan and crackled like a genuine house fire.

Yes, I liked Jennie very much. And, when asked, she reciprocated warmly. 'I like you too!' she trilled, patting my upper arm and walking away. I shouted after her: 'Jennie? Jennie? Jennie. Jennie!' She turned. I said: 'In the words of Grease, *Jennie, we go together like rama lama lama ka dinga da dinga dong!' And we both laughed. Me first, followed by her. And while I had to find the clip on YouTube to assure a Malaysian researcher I wasn't mimicking her language, the good humour that would characterize my and Jennie's on-air relationship has been firmly established.*

It would be the start of a long and pleasant working relationship.

Privately educated and childless, Jennie enjoys being on both TV and Instagram. She always had a gift for presenting. Starting out fronting in-house videos for Lockheed Martin and Pfizer, she was soon snaffled by Bloomberg TV and later the BBC News channel, where she broke stories such as the Greek bailout, Prince William's second child and a capsized ferry. But there's much more to this news hound than that!

A keen tennis player and childless, she likes nothing more than catching up on the soaps, reading the Guardian *newspaper or shopping for the latest iPads in her white Tesla. She's modern, sassy and wants it all!*

Yes, Jennie enjoys tennis tremendously, and while I've never seen her play, it's not hard to imagine her as a rather handy female player, one who perhaps struggles to serve overarm but is a willing runner, scampering around the court like a young gazelle, a pleated white skirt bouncing and wafting in time with her legs.

From the start I took on a kind of mentor role, bringing my experience and know-how to bear on how together we could shape her career. It was just her bloody luck – oh, Jennie! – that she was caught in the no woman's land between two different eras of telly presenter. On the one hand, she was marginally too young to be grouped among the hairspray-and-teeth voice-of-the-Establishment ladies – Fiona Bruce, Katie Derham, Natasha Kaplinsky. But, heartbreakingly, she was a full age-group above the new wave – Stacey Dooley, Lauren Layfield, Storm Huntley – and no amount of being on Snapchat was going to change that. It's for that reason that we needed to manage her choices veeeeeery, very carefully.

From day one, I wanted to cultivate a friendship with her – partly because being a friend is something I happen to be good at (can provide testimonials if needed) and partly because I felt it would bring a tangible authenticity to our on-screen interactions. Get it right and viewers start to fixate on what they see blossoming before their eyes. A little glance here, a touch on the arm there, a wry smile at a private joke, a casually introduced pet name, even – could be as simple as Jen or as intriguing as Punky or Buggalugs. I suggested we could even move on to a will-they-won't-they dynamic after a few months, but Jennie didn't think that would fly. And I agreed with her.

One of the best ways to befriend a woman is to hang around her when she's upset. As luck would have it, the early weeks of our relationship were characterised by Jennie grieving the death of erstwhile colleague John. Ever the good guy, I stepped into the role of protector-in-chief, buzzing about and saying things like 'don't crowd Jennie', 'don't look at Jennie' or 'get Jennie a tissue'.

And I know that meant the world to her. Well, it would.

But doing the off-camera legwork needed to become friends proved difficult. We were just too bloody busy. I liked to unwind of an evening or attend a pub quiz. Jennie enjoyed dining at a private members club or hosting corporate awards for money. And on the occasions when she had agreed to come round for a spag bol followed by giggles in front of the telly, something would always come up and the Italian delicacy would end up slopped into the bin. Muggins here would be in front of Love Island *eating garlic bread and ketchup for one!*

Without these out-of-work get-togethers, our relationship's upward trajectory was built on shaky foundations. Ours was a precarious kinship; without a shared history or a shared Bolognese to look back on, we could easily be blown off course by professional niggles.

And so it proved. What was the turning point? Hard to say. I do remember we had sharp words over Jennie's poppy schedule that autumn. She started to wear one at the end of September, a full six weeks before Remembering Sunday, which I considered to be almost sarcastically early. I told her this was cynical and instructed her to take it off. She looked at me quizzically and laughed.

I said to her, 'There's a well-accepted timetable to the sporting of poppies: it goes, second Saturday in October for a cheap paper one; a week before Halloween, you can upgrade to a bigger, more flamboyant (no sequins, please) one; a larger plastic poppy can be fixed to the grill of your car from 6 November, and you can project silhouettes of the fallen onto the external walls of your home no earlier than the 10th.'

She said, 'You're only annoyed because I got in there first,' and yes, there was an element of that – her honouring the war dead night after night while I sit next to her, unable to follow suit for fear of appearing a copycat, and looking instead like a left-wing environmental agitator (Chris Packham).

But hand on heart, that wasn't what caused our relationship to fray. That came later, shortly before Christmas. It's a moment I have agonised long and hard about including in this book. In the end, I have decided, for personal reasons, that I will include it.

I'd been sent some homemade aftershave by a viewer – it was a Christmas fragrance called Cracker that supposedly had notes of frankincense, brandy, citrus, mulberry and Quality Street. Alone in a corridor after a show, I invited Jennie to smell it, and she stepped towards me so she could sniff my neck. And then . . .?

Then . . . there was a moment. Yes, a very definite moment. Our faces were close, in that position where the side of my nose is adjacent to the side of hers. There was something electric between us. And I'm almost certain she leant in for something more.

'No,' I said firmly. 'No, Jennie. No.'

She frowned and walked away. I leaned back against the wall, blowing my cheeks out so that they resembled two big balloons. Sometimes you have to be professional and do the right thing. She's a mixed-up kid, I thought. I've all the time in the world for Jen, but I also happen to believe some things matter more. I knew then and there something had fractured. It would have been the easiest thing in the world to scoop her up, pop her in a cab and take her to a nearby hotel to make sweet love at her. But I couldn't betray the professional code I have lived my entire life by.

As I say, I'm almost completely certain that she leant in for a kiss. And while you can never be sure about these things, I'm 99.9999 per cent confident it happened and have retained the 0.0001 per cent possibility I'm wrong not to give me wiggle room in the event of a legal challenge, but purely because, as I say, one can never be 100 per cent sure about these things.

Me, I didn't think much more of it. It had only been a fleeting moment, I reasoned, and my aroma had been very powerful. But looking back, I do think you can trace the beginning of the end to that day in the corridor.

People say, 'Did you find Jennie attractive?' It always makes me smile. I simply don't look at co-workers in that way – and that's to say nothing of the twenty-year[109] age difference between us! The thought of sullying a professional relationship in pursuit of base gratification, like a dog or fitness instructor, actually makes me laugh out loud. So, in answer to the question, no, of course I'm not in love with her nor have I ever been.

But things began to unravel after that day. We were never again the Alan 'n' Jen that the viewers had taken to their hearts. Might be that she was hurting. Might be that she was hurting real bad. Or, as I say, the whole kiss thing might just have been my imagination entirely. But she hardened.

Suddenly, she took less of an interest in the content of the show. I'd come to her dressing room with notes on the script before it was fed into the autocue – 'I think you should say "still to come" instead of "coming up"' or 'Can we say "Hello!" in unison and then giggle?' – and instead of engaging with the suggestion, she'd say 'yeah, fine' without even looking up from her phone. And that was hurtful. I told Howard on her but he advised me not to tell tales – I wonder if he'd have said the same to Harvey Weinstein's victims, or to the people of Ukraine when Russian troops were massing at the border. Just a thought!

---

109 Approx.

In time, I'd come to realise the reason for her distractedness. Jennie was developing 'outside interests', a common failing among younger presenters. She was working on a range of business interests, most notably a line of frocks for the fashion catalogue Very, plus a cosmetic range aimed at the school-gates market, mums who haven't quite given up and would like to reduce visible eye bags if at all possible.

Alongside this, she had embarked on an unwise dalliance with then-married TV presenter Sam Chatwin, who had attended a much more prestigious private school than she had and was able therefore to tap into the inferiority complex she had carried with her since being a day boarder in an otherwise full-boarding school. I have nothing against Sam. He's not perfect – like many posh men, his immense privilege means he sees nothing wrong with continually playing with his nose, and he clearly regards marital vows as beneath him – but their relationship was ill-advised, ending shortly after it began but still managing to upset the full trifecta of: 1) their friendship, 2) his marriage and 3) any relationship he might have had with his kids. Way to go, guys.

Somehow, she still managed to find the time to create and present her own podcast Listen Love with Jennie Gresham, *in which she has a chinwag and a cuppa (this is from the press release!) with free-thinkers and wisdom-dispensers from Malala to Jake Humphrey.*

Kindly, I took an interest and even agreed to be a guest myself some week – such that one afternoon I sat with her in her This Time *dressing room, shooting the shit and detailing my outlook on life, expounding on the blueprint I'd followed in order to meet my objectives (get back on TV), the importance of lists, as well as sharing some of my most intimate hopes and fears. After an hour and a half of chat (us), laughter (me) and tears (me), I sat back and asked when it was likely to air.*

'When is what likely to air?'

'The podcast,' I said.

Her brow crinkled in amusement. 'Sorry, did you think we were recording a podcast?'

My mouth guppied open and closed. Eventually, the word 'yes' dolloped out of it. Well, the thrice-engaged starlet roared with laughter.

Turned out the microphone I thought I'd been speaking into was just a make-up sponge, and she seemed to find that soooooo amusing. 'That's hilarious. God, I have to tell Holly [Willoughby] that,' she cackled.

'Why?' I said.

'Why is it hilarious?' she asked.

'No, why have you got to tell Holly [Willoughby]?'

She shrugged and went on to assure me that she wouldn't tell Holly Willoughby, an assurance that wasn't worth shit because I later learned she did tell Holly Willoughby.

Still, as the saying goes, from poor behaviour great results can spring. Because it inspired me to try my own hand at podcasting.

'Aaaaaaalan Paaaaartridge, from the oasthouse! Aaaaaaalan Paaaaartridge, from the oasthouse! From the oasthouse! With Alan Partridge! From the oasthouse. With Alan Partridge.'

It's a theme tune that will be familiar to more than four thousand podcast enthusiasts across the English-understanding world. In fact, after Going for Gold and Brush Strokes, 'Alan Partridge: From the Oasthouse (We're Having a Barndance) (Mumford mix)' is one of Britain best-loved theme songs.

It's 2020, and I, Alan Partridge, have created my own podcast.

The idea had come to me while sitting in the cubicle of a unisex toilet. A woman washing her hands by the basins was talking on the phone, seemingly unaware that anyone else was in the bathroom. As a result, I was treated to an incredibly intimate, unfiltered *confessional in which she divulged all manner of upsetting, highly personal matters. The woman – Debbie something – needn't fear: I shan't be spilling any secrets here, although her fiancé Stuart or Stewart might want to put his back into it when he's trying to satisfy her.*

That, I thought. That is what my podcast should be like.

I had toyed with the idea of podcasting for some time but didn't want to incur production costs until I was sure it could be monetised. But what if I could dispense with the hiring of a studio and frame the format as an intimate, behind-the-scenes piece of content which I could knock together in my own house?

That day, From the Oasthouse: The Alan Partridge Podcast *was born. In it, I would invite listeners into my home (not literally) to share in the most intimate moments of my superb life. People were shocked, of course they were. I'd always been a famously private man, yet here I was welcoming listeners into my home and audibly de-shrouding myself before them; letting the dressing gown of my life fall to the floor and saying simply, 'This is all of me.'*

Week after week after week, in each generously durated episode, I would siphon off some of my choicest thoughts, from wit to wisdom, from musings to moanings, and everything in between.

Listeners got to hear about my home life, my work life, my love life and the pond life who criticise me online.

To this day, people say, what's From the Oasthouse *like? Who are you inspired by? Well, I'm inspired not so much by other podcasts, as I tend not to listen to those, but by the excellence we see all around us: a dog leaping to catching a stick, a ballerina doing brilliant ballet, a forklift truck driver steering one-handed while smoking. And I think that comes over.*

Has it been a success? Yes, it has been a very good success.

By 2021, Jennie and I were two of the most successful podcasters in the UK – her by metrics such as numbers, me by metrics such as 'is it any good?'.

But there was tension on the set of This Time. Jennie had begun to grow distant. Whether that was because her business interests were struggling – one Amazon reviewer of her make-up range said the mascara felt like it was made of chip fat and Crayola – or some other reason, I don't know.

But I was keen to build bridges. I suggested we pool our talents. 'Why don't we do a joint podcast?' I said.

'Oh, I don't think I'd have time,' she chirped. 'I already have one to be getting on with.'

'So do I!' I laughed. 'I mean instead of those. We wind our own ones down and do something together. Alan and Jennie's Pizza Party, or Alan and Jennie's Coffee Morning . . .'

'Ha, no, no . . .' she giggled.

'Or Great Tram Journeys with Alan and Jennie? Or Sex Talk with Alan and Jennie?'

'No, Alan.'

'Jennie and Alan, then. Any of those but "with Jennie and Alan".'

Once again, she mysteriously put the phone to her ear as if someone had called. 'Jennie Gresham.' And off she strolled.

And that was that. As she walked away, I knew she'd gone. I'd bloody lost her. Any idea that we were teammates or partners or allies or buddies or chums or homies was well and truly gone.

I watched her after that day increasingly lose her way. Like Icarus, she became complacent, soaring too close to the Sun – and the Mail! – as she began to cavort and caper for the tabloids' approval, dancing the needy dance of the media darling, never quite grasping that soon they'll discard her like they discarded me all those years ago.

'Bye, Jennie,' I whispered.

But then I made a mistake. In a catastrophic error of judgement,

I goaded her with the news that I had secured an interview with Her Royal Highness the Princess Royal Princess Anne. As she walked away, the thinnest of smiles on her lips, little did I realise that she was plotting; plotting to use my oft-trumpeted devotion to H.R.H.T.P.R.P.A. to destroy me.

THE POISON INSIDE
(OF) ME

March 2023

'How much did you eat?' my assistant wheezes, her hands gripping the steering wheel and constantly turning it left and right
like they used to do in old movies when they weren't actually
driving, except she is.

'Eat?' I exclaim, panicking. 'I didn't eat it, it fell in me.'

'How much fell in you?'

'I don't know. It felt like a lot. Maybe four ketchup-sachets-
ful? Maybe more. He's a big animal and he'd had a *very* big meal.'

'Oh, God.'

'Why are you saying "oh, God"? Is that bad?'

'I don't know. You're the one who said it was bad.'

'Yes, because I read in a magazine in a hairdressers in America
that it can be fatal. Guano can contain bacterial bodies, fungal
bodies, viral bodies and parasitic bodies. The big four.'

'What's guano?'

'Bird shit! What do you think?'

'Put your fingers down your throat.'

'I can't do that. I've tried and I can't.'

'I feel sick now.'

'Drive, woman!'

For ten more minutes we wind along country lanes and down
dual carriages, during which she is never once in a high enough
gear for the speed we're going. When we get to the hospital,

she screeches to a halt in a way that sounds quite cool but will definitely have been accidental. Hoisting my lifeless body across her shoulders with an ease that is almost bizarrely effortless, the dog-loyal septuagenarian carries me to the door of A&E, hands me to two porters and weeps.

I'm weeping too. I am all too aware of the risks I'm facing. As well as the article in a magazine in a hairdressers in America, I once saw a report on local news of a child whose kidneys had failed after ingesting bird droppings. This is real and it could easily be the end. An awful way to die as well. For weeks my mind has been addled with Britain's greatest maritime heroes – Shackleton, Scott of the South Pole – good, burly men who had succumbed only to the very worst nature could throw at them. Me, I am about to die at the hands – nay, the backside – of a seagull.

I can feel myself getting hot, as if my throat is constricting. The bright ceiling lights of the hospital, the rush of healthcare professionals, the rapid exchange of information. I am starting to spin out.

'I am poisoned,' I say to everyone and no one.

'Poisoned? With what?' says a doctor.

'E. coli; salmonella; listeriosis; campylobacter; psittacosis; toxoplasmosis . . .'

'You need to calm down. Tell him he needs to calm down.'

'A gull did a poo in his mouth,' my assistant blurts out. 'Please don't let him die.'

'You need to calm down as well, madam. He's not going to die from a bit of bird poo.'

The words land in my ear canal quite deliciously. How do I feel? As a sensual guy unafraid to talk about feelings and blessed with a rich vein of emotional intelligence, I can tell you I feel three distinct emotions swell inside of me: I feel happy, I feel good and I feel *very* nice.

I turn to my assistant. 'Get a couple of Bounty bars from the machine and go and start the car. We have a lighthouse to finish.'

I swing my legs off the gurney and set about unfastening the inflatable blood-pressure collar from my arm muscles, but the doctor puts his hand on my mine to stop me. He looks at the blood-pressure read-out. What he says next leaves me reeling, but as it also strikes me as a good way to end a chapter in any future memoir that might cover this medical emergency, I decide not respond.

'I'm afraid you're not going anywhere, Mister Partridge.'[110]

---

110 See what I mean? Good ending, isn't it?

SELDOM

'Can I help you, mate?'

'Yes. I'd like the most dangerous dog you have, please.'

The story of how I came to own my beloved dog Seldom is a moving and nine-hundred-word one. In the exchange above I've just arrived at the house of one of East Anglia's most unorthodox dog-breeders, but the thought process behind coming to own the world's best (angry) dog began four days earlier . . .

I'd spent the evening at a recently divorced friend's house watching a blue movie. With me on the sofa and him in an armchair on the other side of the room, we'd watched in intrigued silence, only choosing to speak once the credits rolled, at which point we ordered a Thai takeaway, turned the lights back on, took our glasses off, and had an honest chat about what we had and hadn't liked about the film. My friend found it sexy, but I had to admit it had left me cold. Had I expected to find it sexy? You bet I had. But, I dunno, maybe it would have been better if I'd watched it alone.

Maybe then I'd have been able to fully immerse myself in the groundbreaking CGI and heart-rending story of James Cameron's magical 3D creation.

As I wandered home that night – I say 'wandered', I drove – I tried to work out why Cameron had bothered making Avatar when for the same money he could surely have made another two to three Robocops. It was certainly a headscratcher, and as I scratched mine (friend had had heating on all night), I just couldn't work it out. No,

Cameron had made an error of judgement and that was that. I liked the idea of fit aliens as much as the next man, but to dedicate ten years of your life to it? Well, that was a bit pervy.

I arrived back at the oasthouse, drove marginally past it, then reversed smoothly back into the drive without even needing to put my arm behind the passenger seat headrest, and that's not even a lie. But what greeted me as I got out of my car was the sight every homeowner fears: an open front door. I had been burglarised.

Putting all risk to my personal safety aside, I charged into the house once the police had arrived and done a full sweep of the property. No damage had been done, no possessions taken.

Suddenly, it all became clear. This wasn't some opportunist robbering person; this had been done to scare me.

'As I've already told you, I was at a friend's house. He's recently divorced and we'd agreed to watch a blue movie together.'

'I see. Actually, would you mind just repeating that for my colleague? Craig, come and hear this.'

No offence to frontline bobbies, but sometimes they just don't get it. And as I recounted what had happened for the umpteenth/second time, my mind had already moved on to potential suspects. The list was made up of four categories: people I'd had a run-in with at traffic lights or box junctions in recent years; people I'd had a run-in with in the car parks of retail parks or multiplexes; those who feel I have wronged them on my radio show; and Noel Edmonds. Yet with no forensic evidence to go on – no fingerprints on the door, no blood stains and not so much as a trace of the perp's spunk – I was stumped.

And while the police said there was no suggestion of an imminent threat and that maybe I'd just forgotten to close the door when I'd gone out, my view was that maybe I hadn't. No, screw the cops, it was time to circle the wagons: I convened an emergency session of my cul-de-sac's Neighbourhood Watch group. As the three of us (Paul couldn't make it) began to wargame possible approaches, my view began to solidify: what was needed was a round-the-clock watch on my property. Clive disagreed, feeling that keeping watch during daylight hours was pointless. Unfortunately for him, though, that's not even what I'd said. If I'd meant 24-hour surveillance I'd have said we needed a 'twice round the clock watch', because to the best of my knowledge, a full revolution of a clock only takes 12 hours. Either way, Clive said he hadn't been sleeping well so wouldn't be able to help, while Phil said he'd have to bow out too because he had to set an alarm for 3 a.m. every morning to do Judy's insulin injection.

With my plan A scuttled, I needed another solution. My assistant suggested I get a gun because it's 'what Jesus would have done'. And while it was certainly an interesting thought, and one she argued for with passion and by standing too close to me, I disagreed. Jesus had never been a homeowner, and though my assistant didn't like hearing it, the fact of a life spent wandering around Galilee meant Christ was, I'm afraid, a vagrant. So while a firearm often is the answer, on this occasion it was not. No, what I needed was a guarding dog.

Hence and thus I had found myself at 35 Speke Street, Norwich. Prodding at the doorbell with a ginger finger, I was here to invest – in cash money – in one of the most dangerous dogs in Norfolk. I'd been put on to this place by a friend of a friend's wife's friend's friend. The guy who lived here – Happy Ferguson – was apparently just the person for me. Something of a eugenicist, word had it he'd dedicated his life to trying to breed the perfect unhinged dog. Yet as I explained I was here to buy a dangerous dog, he regarded me suspiciously.

'Don't even know who you are, mate.'

'I'm Alan Partridge. You must be Happy.'

'Not especially. How did you find out about me?'

'Your friend is a friend of a friend's wife's friend's friend.'

'What?'

'Basically, do you know a fat fella called Barry?

'*Yeah.*'

'*Him.*'

'*Right. You coming in, then?*'

As I followed him into his house, now unsure if he actually was called Happy or if that was just a friend of a friend's wife's friend's friend's chubby little joke, I clocked the pooches straight away: a dozen big puppies dozing on the floor of the kitchen as their dangerous mother and dangerous father patrolled the back yard.

I was about to ask him what breed they were but quickly realised that would have been silly. They were no breed. Their breed was indeterminate. They were, by design, a biological mash-up, a genetic smorgasbord; they were a Frankenstein's dog. A pinch of Rottweiler, a dash of Pit Bull, two heaped tablespoons of Staffordshire Bull Terrier, and, judging by the size of them, several entire St Bernards. And Happy? Well, he was the mad scientist at the centre of all this, although unlike most mad scientists he had a shaved head and a West Ham tattoo.

I began to weigh up which puppy to take as my own. I've always enjoyed watching the way the judges at Crufts assess dogs. Rough without being violent, at the kind of level where if they did it on a person, that person would take it for a little bit then snap and say, 'What are you doing?!' At Crufts, though, the judges have a God-like authority. If those dogs dare to show even the mildest hint of irritation as their hind quarters are felt, their gums are inspected and their tails are lifted to one side to allow their bumholes to be seen and scored, then they have absolutely fucked it. No rosette. No favourite treat. And certainly no mussing of the hair accompanied by a, 'Who's a good boy? Who's a good boy?' then a pause before, 'Who's a good boy, then?'.

It was then that I noticed one of the mongrels was by my feet, specifically my left one.

'*Oh, I wouldn't bother with him. He's a pathetic little runt.*

Wouldn't say bark to a goose,' said Happy, adapting the well-known idiom in a way that was actually quite clever and I wouldn't really have expected given the standard of his house.

But there was something about the way that puppy stared at Happy that was chilling. I decided to leave and come back another day for a second viewing. And though Happy complained that second viewings were only normally for houses, he nevertheless agreed.

I bid the man good day, headed for the door and took a final glance back at that odd little puppy. His eyes remained fixed on Happy, and a small smile seemed to be playing on his jet-black dog lips.

I strolled away, sauntered up the path and shouted, 'Bye!' over my shoulder. No reply. 'I said, "Bye!"' Still nothing. I took a few steps back towards the door. 'Bye!' I said again, since good manners cost absolutely nothing. This time, Happy grunted a long, slow grunt. That'll have to do, I shrug.

When I got to my car, however, I was greeted by a surprise. The puppy was waiting there for me. I boop-beeped, opened the door with a single finger, and blow me if the cheeky little scamp didn't just hop right in and plonk himself on the passenger seat!

My God, I thought to myself. Me driving and him alongside? This is exactly like Every Which Way but Loose, *for those of us who remember that film. Except rather than a Jeep, mine is a Vauxhall Vectra, and rather than an orangutang, mine is a dog. But other than that, yeah, exactly like* Every Which Way but Loose, *for those of us who, as I say, remember that film.*[III]

I remember those early days with Seldom through rose-tinted

III To this day, something else that still puzzles me is how Seldom got out of the house. Happy refuses to talk about what happened. All I know is that ever since, he's had to pee sitting down. The only positive about the whole story, and it is a positive, is that I never had to pay for the dog, saving me a cool two grand. And that, as the saying goes, will do me nicely.

spectacles, although thinking about it, the tint was actually more peach.[112] They say dogs grow fast, but Seldom rewrote the rule book. By the time of his first birthday (we celebrated at Frankie & Benny's) he was fully grown. And by golly he was big. Clearly, he wasn't going to submit to being weighed and I wasn't stupid enough to try, but judging from the welt marks left by his paws when he sat on me, he must have been easily seventeen stone.

From there, life settled into a comfortable enough routine. Seldom wasn't what you'd call an affectionate dog, but then we all express fondness in different ways. Yes, if you thought you could waddle over and give him a stroke that was unsolicited, you needed your head examined, but when the moment came when he did want a bit of love, it was vital you were ready. Because he required you to stroke him for up to an hour, I tended to keep a foam kneeling pad in every room of the house (you can pick them up for around £5 from any good garden centre). That way, if his need arose, I could quickly grab the pad, begin to stroke his tummy while holding his paw, and ensure I wouldn't be in too much pain.

In life, friends come and go. They let you down, they betray you, they send a message slagging off your new bright red coat to a mutual friend without realising they've accidentally sent it to you instead. My old mate Seldom, though? He was always there, and provided the butcher didn't miss a delivery and you didn't look him in the eye, you could generally get through the day without too many mishaps.

On Sundays he liked to go for a drive. I'd wind down his window, head to the town centre and let him spend a good few hours indulging in his favourite pastime of staring people out. He seemed to have a particular issue with workmen and Sikhs in wheelchairs. But I just

---

112 The glasses in question were the protective specs you wear at the oral hygienist. Used in my case as a way of keeping off the meat spatter that flew my way when Seldom was eating his meats.

kept one finger on the button that operated his window and we rarely had a problem. And if things did get a bit heated, I was often (but not always!) able to distract him with the emergency mince I kept in the glovebox.

Suffice to say, ours was a blissful existence. My best friend? Try timesing that by a hundred thousand trillion and you'd be about one billionth of the way there.

Then came the night at the funfair. The night described so arrestingly in the opening chapter of this book.[113] A dog now dead. An owner now sad. A life that would never be the same. Three short sentences that could very well form the subtitle of a film about that night.

As I arrived back at the oasthouse, my cleaner Rosa was just leaving. She said, 'Where Good Boy?' Which was what she used to call him. And I had to say, 'Rosa . . . Seldom, he didn't make it. He passed away at a funfair. He ain't never coming home.' And she just crumbled. Rosa could be quite rough with Seldom because she used to own oxen back in the Philippines and I think he respected that, so as a result they'd become quite close. Telling her he'd gone was . . . hard.

But it was as she drove away in her van that it really began to hit me. Thoughts tumbled round my head like dogs in a washing machine. Memories of Seldom's likes, his life, his feeding habits. Never one for water, Seldom was one of the few dogs I know who'd love to drink a big salad bowl full of Coca-Cola. I'd never seen a dog burp before then, but my God. He'd burp with such gusto, his eyes would water. I'd just pat him and say, 'Easy, boy.' And it had to be Coca-Cola. I once gave him Fentimans Cola and he just put his foot on my foot, and shook his head as if to say 'don't do that again, mate'.

I didn't even bother going up to bed that night. I knew I wouldn't

---

113 It really is a quality bit of writing – keep a particular eye out for the use of the word 'rambunctious' in paragraph four.

sleep. I just slumped myself down on one of Seldom's giant bean bags, opened a tube of sour cream and onion Pringles, opened a family bag of Kettle Chips, opened a tub of Jen & Berry's cookie-dough ice cream, opened a packet of flame-grilled steak McCoy's and wept until my snacks were soggy.

They say the death of a dog helps you focus on what really matters in life, and if they don't, it's certainly plausible that they might. In my case I came to be aware of the constants, the ever-presents, the things that would always be central to who and what I am — my commercial deals, my profound respect for the Royal Family and Her Royal Highness the Princess Royal Princess Anne, a good head of hair, and, of course, my broadcasting career. As long as I had them, all would be well. Little did I realise that all four of those constants were about to blow up in my face in front of 1.2 million viewers, or 1.4 if you adjust for catch-up.

UNDER PRESSURE

March 2023

The news that I have high blood pressure immediately causes my blood pressure to rocket – something a medical professional must surely have foreseen.

An oxygen mask is placed over my face. Ordinarily I'd attempt a Darth Vader voice but panic has set it in. I am making a heeeeeee noise every time I inhale.

Soon, I'm being surrounded by concerned medics. It seems the reading the doctor saw once he'd blown up the inflatable armband was so concerning that I was immediately admitted. I am taken to a private room, given a set of 100 per cent cotton hospital pyjamas, and told to wait for the doctor.

What happens next is, I'll be honest, a fog, as medics fight to bring my blood pressure under control. Cries of '98 over 30!', '110 over 65!', and '88 over 60!' or whatever it is they shout, fill the room, competing with the urgent beeping of the various monitors-on-wheels to which I am hooked up like a (female) cow at milking time. I am given drugs. I am peered at by consultants. A young blonde nurse called Katie holds my hand and feeds me small sips of organic apple juice. Nothing is making a difference.

The stress of the build, spiralling costs, fear of death and now my worries about what being stuck in hospital will mean for the already-slipping schedule/schedule[114] are pushing me to the very edge of a heart collapse. But just as the doctors are considering their options and I am asking Katie if I can have another little sip of juice, please, my assistant rushes in with news.

James Martin has appendicitis, and bad. He's been taken in for an urgent operation and his lighthouse restoration put on hold. Like the warm jets of water surging into a hot tub, relief seeps deliciously into every vein, artery, nook and cranny of my beleaguered body. I am instantly soothed. Within minutes, my numbers start to level out and the danger passes.

To this day, I still don't know if Martin was actually having his appendix out or if it was a lie from my assistant, and I've never bothered to find out. But that wave of relief, that sweet crumb of goodness has remained a touchstone for me. Whenever I feel my anxiety rising, I imagine James Martin clutching his side and wincing, and that brings me enormous comfort.

Thirty-six hours later. I am still in hospital. The worst has passed, but my blood pressure remains too high and the effects of medication on my hypertension are being monitored. One problem, though: this is an NHS hospital.

Bringing me here had been an honest mistake by a het-up assistant, but now it needed rectifying. She puts in a call to Tony-Tom Ridgely, an old friend of mine (with a double-barrelled Christian name in which the names are so similar it's almost impossible to remember which way round they go) who works for the East Anglian Air Ambulance service. Hearing of my predicament, TT, as you'd imagine he'd let us call him but doesn't,

---

114 To assist American readers I have included the US as well as the UK version of the word.

has immediately agreed to airlift me to my private hospital in Norwich.[115]

After a ninety-minute wait, during which my assistant 'tries to distract' me by telling me an interminable story about Michael Ball, Tom-Tony pulls up, loads me into the passenger seat of his Range Rover[116] and we set off for the airfield.

Three hours into the drive, it transpires that he's heading to Hardwick Airfield, which is only a 25-minute drive from my destination, rendering the helicopter flight quite pointless. He drives me to the hospital instead, which I guess was quite good of him, but I did want to go in the helicopter, that's the only thing.

I later learn that Tony-Tom had lost his pilot licence a few months before. The incident that cost him his licence, flying his plane too close to a Scout hut, followed the discovery that his wife was having an affair with a local Akela.

Nothing against the NHS, but the Spire private hospital in Norwich is a terrific place to be poorly. Cable TV with on-demand movies, a call button nurses don't pretend they didn't hear, and a snack trolley at 11 a.m. and 3 p.m., just some of the reasons it really is a cut above.[117]

---

115 Like many middle-class people, I am a passionate supporter of the NHS. And while you're obviously not going to muck about when it comes to your own health or that of your family, the principle of health services free at the point of delivery certainly feels right for the general population. But no, this was important, it was *my* health, so I went private.

116 Which, ironically, he *does* call his RR. Quite thick, really.

117 I know my assistant was similarly pleased with it. It had been a tough few days for her, seeing me so unwell, but I knew she was on the up because her frowl – the half scowl, half frown that was her near-constant expression – had returned. Being private, the hospital paid higher wages than the NHS and was thus able to attract a higher percentage of nurses and doctors who were British.

My stay, in a private double room with views over the well-tended gardens, was organised through AXA Insurance. It lasted ten days.

By about the fourth day there is no medical need for me to be there, but after a quick word with the Clinical Director (whose husband is a friend of mine), my stay is extended and I settle down for fish pie and *Schindler's List*.

And I sensed that, for whatever reason, that meant she just could breathe more easily.

HOPPING MAD

June 2021

In the two weeks after Seldom perished, I threw myself into my work. With no dog to care for, This Time *became my pet and – this bit's a metaphor – I treated it lovingly, tickling its tum, feeding it raw bacon and saying 'I wuv woo' in a gruff doggy voice, all through the medium of good broadcasting.*

Things were going well. But they truly reached a zenith when I received a message from Gatcombe Park, the residence of Her Royal Highness the Princess Royal Princess Anne. An invitation for her to appear on the show had been accepted. This was a real coup, although I made sure not to use that word around the royal party in case they think you're talking about an uprising and worry they'll be beheaded.

News of the royal visit spread like wildfire or Covid-19[118] around the town. In the shopping centres of Norwich, old ladies would squeeze my hand excitedly (with my permission), taxi drivers would grunt their support, even market-stall holders, traditionally the most belligerent people in Norfolk, nodded at me.

'It's nice that it's you doing it,' said Ethel, ninety, a retired butcher from Holt, as we chatted outside a branch of Dunelm. 'Usually, if it's not one of the Dimblebys, it's Paddy McGuinness. Either too clever by

---

118 Covid fans may have noticed the topic has not been mentioned in this book. I have chosen instead to monetise my views about the illness by turning them into a children's book. Due to be published when I can find a publisher, the book will be called either 'Viral Boy', 'Kid Covid' or 'Poorly Ben'.

half or too thick by double. People like me, we just want—'

'Something in the middle?' I offered, wryly.

'That's exactly the right phrase,' she said.

I went inside and bought some pillowcases.

The day soon came when Her Royal Highness the Princess Royal Princess Anne would be joining us in the studio. I awoke, breakfasted on fresh fruits, a handful of nuts, some Greek yoghurt and bowl after bowl of Golden Grahams. I was alone in the house but I felt good. My assistant would be travelling to Broadcasting House separately, as she had an early morning hair appointment to get to.

I could tell this was a big deal for her, as she was going not to her usual salon, but to the gay hairdresser in town, something she, as a committed Baptist, was deeply uncomfortable with. But if you want 'sophisticated glamour', Barbara from Snippy Kutz just ain't gonna give you that.

Me, I also wanted to look my best. I had my tailor knock up a suit based on one I'd seen in a painting of King George VI shooting a deer between the antlers. My shirt was lightly checked and the tie looked like an old school tie, even though it had come from M&S just a week earlier. On my lapel, my trusty tooth brooch.

I opened the front door, grabbed my jacket from the coat hooks quickly and well, then noticed Seldom's lead hanging from a hook. I smiled. He would have liked this a lot. He'd been an ardent royalist who would sometimes stand when he heard the national anthem, although it's possible he thought it was an ice-cream van coming.

I touched his collar, and noticed it still had tufts of another dog's fur in it from Seldom's last proper walk, when he'd partially eaten a Spaniel during an altercation. In his case it really was a dog-eat-dog world.

Little did I know, I was about to enter one of my own.

You see, on the day of what should have been one of the crowning moments of my career, I was about to be slain. You may remember a scene in the 1990 film Goodfellas in which a guy gets all dressed up thinking he's about to be 'made', which is Mafia for promoted, but on arrival at the ceremony, he's shot in the head. That was exactly what was about to happen to me.

Simon and I drove into London together. Simon is a committed anti-royalist and was doing his best to explain why. Well, I just roared with laughter. These republicans give it the big 'I am' in peacetime – 'Oh, we don't need a king or queen, we support the Liberal Democrats' – but if an aggressor invades, we're gonna need leadership and hierarchy like never before. If this green and (largely) pleasant land is one day besmirched by jackboots – or, let's face it these days, sandals – we'd see another side to His Majesty the King. Gone would be his focus on making superb organic food products for Waitrose; instead, a commander-in-chief would emerge, marshalling the troops and barking orders: Scramble the jets! Prime the missiles! Man (or woman) the barricades! Get me a coffee – white, two sugars! And ready my steed, for today we lay down our lives that Britannia, the greatest nation on God's earth, may rise again! Now, who's going to do that in a world with no monarchy? Zac Goldsmith? Fuck off.

Simon tried to push back, but he gets quite carsick, especially if I razz it on the corners, and his tummy began to get the better of him. He went quiet, and I smiled, satisfied the argument was won (by me).

We arrived and parked up. I sang the full theme tune to the eighties sitcom Bread then out we got. It would be the last time I sang for many weeks.

I fairly bounced into Broadcasting House that day. I didn't even mind getting my bag checked by security, although I gave them a few pointers on how they could look smarter. Incredibly, they didn't even know how to do Windsor knots on their ties, but a crash course in the *foyer using a willing receptionist as a dummy soon equipped them with the necessary know-how needed to know how to knot nicely.*

I headed up to the This Time *office. Jennie was in unusually early and I patted her on the arm. 'Big day today!' I said.*

She smiled but her eyes didn't meet mine.

FREEZEFRAME!

In that moment, in the split second when she looked at a kettle instead of me, I knew something was afoot. I've always been blessed with superb intuition, especially when it comes to women – on a date a tight smile, a dart of the eyes, a stiffened jaw can furnish me with substantial intel. She doesn't like me stroking her ear, she wants me to compliment her blouse, she needs the toilet and wants me to busy myself doing something else so as not to be cognisant of how long she's taking. It's just one of the things I'm good at. When you're alive to tiny details like this you notice when things smell a bit off. And today, this show stank. I realised then and there, this was a hit, they were going to try to finish me.

Why?

One theory is that Jennie and the producer Howard Newman were sleeping with one another. And while there's no evidence to support that, it would explain their eagerness to eliminate anyone who might draw attention away from Jennie. Me, I choose not to get involved in tittle-tattle, so I'm not going to take a view either way. You can draw your own conclusions. It's not even something I personally have heard, but if others are saying it, as you suggest, then who knows.

Another theory was that I was too old, too past it, too uncool for BBC One. But I quickly dismissed that as a big bowl of bullshit. No, this was something else – this was politics. Sometimes a presenter just outgrows the show he's presenting. He begins to swell and rise, the parameters of the show no longer able to contain him, like a muffin cascading out of the cake tin as it bakes.

No programme wants to admit it's too small for its presenter – that the star has outgrown the show. Instead, they find a reason to engineer an exit. It's transparent and it's petty, but I understand why they do it.

Did the BBC fire Jeremy Clarkson just because he hospitalised a producer for not supplying a hot meal and called him a lazy Irish cunt? I seriously doubt it. If that were a sackable offence Joan Bakewell would have been toast long ago. No, the BBC saw that Clarkson's star was beginning to eclipse the car-focused ethos of Top Gear, *realised he was destined for bigger things, and, yeah, it scared them.[119] Same thing was going on here.*

Fine, though. I accepted it, dusted myself off emotionally and instantly moved on. No fuss, no crying, no recriminations. An observer might have assumed I'd been trained by the SAS (I haven't!). I remained happy, resilient and professional.

UNFREEZE!

The production meeting went ahead in a blur. I felt quite, quite serene, as if I'd done some light meditation or heavy medication. When Howard floated the idea that Jennie and I should interview Her Royal Highness the Princess Royal Princess Anne together, and glanced away like a big chicken, I just shrugged. Whatever.

That surprised a few people, I could tell. After all, it was me who had brokered the deal to get Her Royal Highness the Princess Royal Princess Anne to come along. It was me (I) who had briefed the crew on the correct way to address a royal. It was I (me) who had written a list of questions for the interview: What's it like to be keen at

---

119 As ever, though, Jez has come up smelling of roses. Yes, on the one hand he ruffled a few *Guardian* readers' feathers when he said he was dreaming of the day when Meghan Markle is made to parade naked through the streets of every town in Britain while crowds chant, 'Shame!' and throw lumps of excrement at her, but on the other his series about a farm has been a huge success and is now appointment-to-view television for white, right-of-centre, middle-aged men everywhere.

equestrian? What's it like to have a daughter who's a keen equestrian? As someone who shakes hands with lots of people, what's your hygiene routine? What's all this about Prince Andrew, then?

Moreover, I'd long been a fan of Anne, an Anne fan. She's the best royal by a country mile,[120] managing to embody the very best of British, although I know she has Germano-Greek heritage. No, Anne has stiff upper lip and stiff upper hair and I like that a lot.

To now have to share the interview with a co-presenter who, at a push, should have been interviewing one of the younger royals – let's face it, to all intents and purposes she is Kate Middleton – should have been a slap in the face. But I wasn't going to let them goad me.

The show went relatively smoothly. Nothing it seemed could penetrate my cool exterior. Later, moments before Her Royal Highness the Princess Royal Princess Anne was to be interviewed, Howard would take me to one side and ask me to sit this one out, handing sole responsibility for the interview to Jennie Gresham, who, as I say, he may or may not have been boffing. It was all I could do not to laugh. Let's call it what it was: constructive dismissal. But was I going to react and give them the excuse they wanted? Sorry, amigo, ain't gonna happen. If anything I was in cheerier form than normal, even indulging in a bit of off-air horseplay with Simon where we pretended to have a fight resulting in one of us getting a bruised cheek. All good fun, though, all good fun.

Why was I being so zen? Well, this show was never the be all and end all to me. I had plenty of other projects I was talking to the BBC about. I'd recently paid a five-figure sum at auction for the now-lapsed format rights to ITV holiday show Wish You Were Here ...?, *which I believed could be updated and pizzazzed for a BBC One audience. I had recently pitched 'Bencher', an unapologetically inclusive drama about unconventional criminal barrister Ben*

---

120 And as a keen equestrian it's a measurement she knows all too well.

Cher busting a gut to defend the seemingly guilty while a prescription drugs addiction threatens to jeopardise his marriage to a bisexual wife of colour, as well as his relationship with disabled non-binary teenage child Cassie who's also autistic. A factual series, 'Inside The Killing Machine', was conceived to be a heart-warming docusoap following the lives, loves, hopes, dreams and execution methods of the employees of Britain's biggest abattoir. So, as you can see, I had irons in the fire – coincidentally one of the execution methods I just mentioned – and the future was rosy.

Nah, it was all good, baby. It was gravy. But as the show reached the twenty-minute mark, something began to dawn on me. I might be fine with being cast aside – but what about the viewers? Didn't I owe it to them to speak up? As the seconds ticked by, I became conscious that to ordinary people – from Norwich taxi drivers to market stall-holders with dirty fingernails and Ethel, ninety, a retired butcher who exists in Holt – I was the one person holding the BBC on an even keel. I was the keeper of the flame, the guardian of correct tone. I don't want to get into hot water here, but I couldn't help but think of the teen Christ telling the moneylenders that if they insisted on screwing people who were cash-poor, they should at least have the decency not to do it in an effing temple.[121]

I could feel their eyes burning through the screens. Please, Alan. Do something. Say something. I was, after all, more than a man on the telly. To ordinary people, I was a conduit, an outlet, a sluice pipe through which their own views could be expressed. Granted, I wasn't bothered. But even though I wasn't bothered, I had a duty to pretend I was bothered to reflect the fact that they were bothered.

---

121 Christ Jesus, God Almighty, the Holy Ghost, if any of you are reading this (?), I've got good news and bad news. The good news? Christianity is still really popular, despite a few bumps. The bad news? Money-lenders are doing even better. And that's gotta hurt.

And so, calmly and clearly, I took issue with a few points regarding the editorial direction of the BBC. It felt like a perfectly reasonable call to arms. Yes, I also issued some home truths about BBC executives not appreciating viewers' feedback, but that didn't feel like a bombshell revelation any more than if I'd said BBC managers are rude to the canteen staff or they wish Claudia Winkleman would cut her fringe or you'll find cocaine on the top of the cistern in staff toilet cubicles. It's not exactly news. Of course they talk down to the dinner ladies. Of course they get razzed off by Claudia's fringe. Of course you'll find cocaine on the top of the cisterns in staff toilet cubicles. And of course they're not bothered if viewers write in.

And then I said the words: 'I'm hopping mad and I want something in the middle.'

The stars twinkle in the sky like tiny diamonds, even though up close they'd be really big. I'm outside the BBC, and the show has ended.

I had at least signed off the show with a bit of oomph. Perhaps I was a touch overzealous. The culmination of the show saw me summon a cameraman (Terry, good guy, unless you're a woman) to join me on the street to gauge whether the central London public were getting behind the idea. I can't remember how many viewers shouted the slogan from their windows. Some say it was two, I seem to recall it was about forty. But I admit, I had encouraged the general public to bellow 'I want something in the middle' from their windows, and apparently that played badly among Mumsnetters because it aired at a time when young mothers were trying to get children to sleep. Fine, I apologise, move on.

But from the reaction of the local residents, I really do think I have tapped into something special. I have captured something. The powers that be cannot ignore that. They cannot, and I'm confident they will not. Sure enough, I get a text from my assistant: 'They want to see you now.'

Bring. It. On.

Cut to me striding down the corridor, a man with almost rhinoc-
erine confidence: 'I'm gonna need breath mints, a big banana and
some coffee.'

If these words sound familiar, good. They appeared at the begin-
ning of the book as well. Because this is the point where the strand
about my TV career connects with the chronologically later strand of
the whole lighthouse business.

You'll notice that the italics previously used to delineate the older
strand of the story from the new gradually begin to disappear in the
course *of t*his *paragraph. H*as *th*at been done be*fore? I'm* certain
that is hasn't. And before we know it, yep, the italics have gone
and we are out of flashback and into the more recent stuff, which
is also flashback, but more recent than the material that had
been, but is no longer, in italics.

I hoik up my shirt, extend my arms like Christ on the cru-
cicross, so that my assistant can apply roll-on deodorant. And
then I enter the meeting, ready for the new chapter of my life.
I'm crying my eyes out as I write this. This is incredible.

THE FRIENDS OF
ALAN PARTRIDGE

April 2023

I'm discharged from hospital by the doctor, who talks as if he's doing me a favour, although he concedes that I was free to leave at any time, so in a sense we're *jointly* discharging me. Still, I'm in good fettle and for that I have to thank the healthcare practitioners.

So, I do. Gone are the days when you can give a nurse a peck on the cheek or a squeeze round the middle, so I gather them at the booking-in desk, ask for a bit of hush then quite simply 'clap for carers'. The room falls silent save for the meaty sound of my palms colliding. Then, after the allotted two minutes, the nurses smile and make their way back to work. *I* feel good, *they* feel good.

I've been advised not to drive, so my assistant settles me into the passenger seat, takes residence on the driver's side, moves the seat *right* the way forward then pulls away. I could point out that as a result she now has to rotate her head nearly forty degrees just to see the rear-view mirror, but that's for another time.

Having experienced her driving before, I have learned a number of techniques that allow me to enter what I call a 'mind spa', a place deep within me where I can simply relax and let all my worries – e.g. why is she indicating a mile before the turn off? – just slip away. These techniques essentially take the form of distractions. I might try to recall the names of the Bourne films in order (harder than you think!) or I'll play a game of 'What is the worst house on this street'. And before long, I've whiled away huge chunks of journey time.

Which is how, before I know it, we've arrived back in Kent. Not to continue the build – no, that dream is over, an old ticker like mine clearly isn't up to the ravages of seaside renovation – but to collect my things, hook my assistant's caravan to the towbar and leave the lighthouse for good, ready to be sold.

Abbot's Cliff looms over the horizon and we loom towards it, until we've pretty much loomed together. I sigh a sad, sad sigh. Once again, there's a black cloud over the sea, and once again it reminds me of my former dog (now dead dog) lying down, having died.

I think of Seldom, of how he'd appeared to me from beyond the grave all those months ago, his way of saying this is what he wanted for me. 'Well, old friend,' I say in my head. 'I said I'd do it for you, but it seems I've let you down.' And for a second, I'm relieved he's dead because, my God, he did not like it if you didn't do what you said you would.

Just as I'm thinking, Thank God that animal is dead, I hear a sound. It's the wisps of a shanty, almost certainly a sea one, on the breeze. I look to my assistant, confused. There's a smile playing on her lips, or it's indigestion, one of the two. She stops the car. 'Let's walk the rest,' she says.

We get out and now I can hear the shanty more clearly. The singers are pretty good. A little loud on the bass, maybe, and the female altos are a touch pitchy, but pretty good.

I come over the hill/mound and see the lighthouse. Its walls are freshly whitewashed, the door resplendent in shiny pillar-box red. The windows gleam and the brass door furniture also gleams.

Whaaaat? It's finished. My lighthouse is finished. The Abbot's

Cliff Lighthouse in association with Alan Partridge is finished.

My assistant gestures towards a small gathering of people, with a sweep of the arm she's slightly over-practised in her head. There are the local shanty group, singing that Wellerman song. The builders smile and chat. A few selected locals enjoy cider from a small stand which technically doesn't have a licence, but I don't say anything.

She tells me they've come together in the last week to finish my work for me. And if you stop to consider it, that is *incredibly* moving. These are the *very* people, remember, who had taken against me earlier in the book. And now, here, right near the *end* of the book, those *same* people have done a full one-eighty and have come together to work towards a common goal with the man they had *previously* antagonised – completing a truly un-expected reversal of sentiment (see fig. 1), which is all the more impactful *because* it's unexpected (see fig. 2).

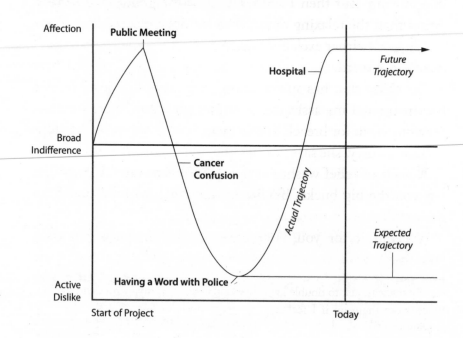

272

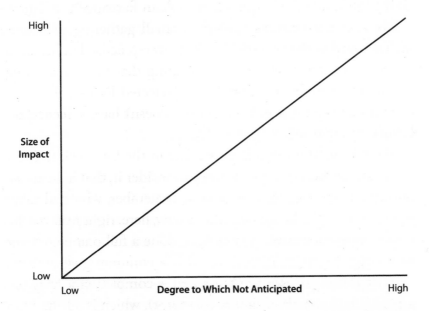

And now they're all here in the same scene. It really is incredibly moving. But then I suddenly chill (the going-cold version rather than the relaxing one). I've remembered something.

'Oh, no!' I either exclaimed or declaimed, depending on which is the right word.

The thing that has splooped into my head? The legal writs I had instructed my assistant to hand-deliver to the builders the previous week for breach of contract.

'Don't worry,' she says, reading my mind. 'I didn't deliver them.'

A wave of relief washes over me. I want to say, 'That's why I pay you the big bucks,' but for obvious reasons I am unable to do so.[122]

'We did it for you, Alan,' they all say in perfect unison,

---

122 By the way, just to double back, 'splooped' is one of my own words. I sometimes make them up if I feel existing vocab doesn't quite offer the sense I'm looking for.

certainly in my recollection, as the shanty soars towards its key change, again in my recollection.

'Thanks,' I shout, and I walk inside my house. I close the door behind me and my assistant soon follows.

'Don't you want to go and mingle with—?'

'Get a press release out,' I splutter. 'I want you to contact publishers, TV channels, whatever. Quickly, please.'

'Now, then. It doesn't do to gloat.'

'Who's gloating?' I say. 'I happen to think the preservation of our architectural heritage is something to be celebrated, and who knows? Maybe getting the word out will inspire another man – or even a woman – to take on a similar project, that's all.'

My assistant does make me laugh sometimes. She can hold a grudge against someone in her church for decades, just because they baked biscuits for the vicar on his birthday and didn't tell the other ladies in advance, and she seems to think we all think the same way. No, if anything, I felt a twinge a sadness for James Martin and the BBC's flagship magazine show *This Time*. I have finished my build and James Martin hasn't. I have beaten the BBC. I have won. They have lost. And that *has* to hurt.

I turn back to her: 'Oh, and call a structural engineer.'

'Why?'

'They did all this in a week? I guarantee it doesn't meet building regs. Ask Nick Knowles. Apparently, on *DIY SOS* a wall fell on a grandma, and they had to shelve the whole episode . . . and what is that?'

In front of me is a painting on the wall. It depicts a stricken fishing boat being scooped out of the water by a pair of giant hands, as a beam of sunlight shines down through stormy clouds. Above the ship are the words, 'Behold, God is my salvation'.

'One of yours?' I ask my assistant.

'Oh, yes,' she says proudly. She's become quite the watercolour enthusiast in her dotage, which is bloody commendable, although I've sought assurances that it doesn't impinge on her work, and reserve the right – as her employer – to do spot checks by turning up at her address in the middle of the day to ensure she's not in her smock.

'Well! Lovely hands. They are possibly your best ever knuckles. And is this eczema or a smudge?'

'Smudge,' she replies.

'You should auction that for charity.'

'Don't be silly. It's yours to keep.'

'Are you mad? You have to auction that!'

'I did it for you to keep.'

'Trust me, that painting belongs at auction.'

'No, no, keep it.'

'Auction, I think.'

'I think keep it.'

'Auction.'

'Keep.'

'Auction!'

'Kee—'

'I'll put it in the guest bedroom, alright?!'

A truce. I have avoided upsetting my assistant, which I *hate* to do. As I say, she's a commendable worker. No, more than that – she's a commendable *woman*. Oh, and 'she' has a name. Her name is Lynn. Lynn Benfield. And I am fond of her.[123]

'I do think you should buy these people a drink, though.'

And generously, I did, going back outside and offering each attendee one free cider. If they didn't drink cider, they could give

---

123 By which I mean, professionally fond.

theirs to someone else, and that person could have two, but there were to be no exchanges for a soft drink. I wasn't getting into all that.

I drink my cider – it's kind of like apple juice but a wine – and look at my house. Then I remember: *There's someone I've forgotten, someone I ought to be with.*

Cut to me running. Running along the beach. I'm going at quite a lick, although the undulation of the sand makes me flail and stumble, diminishing the *Chariots of Fire* vibe I was hoping for. Still, I run, the sides of my hair flapping in the breeze like the clumps of fur on a horse's legs. My lungs are bursting as I run – fetlock, that's the word I was after – but I press on.

A woman on the beach up ahead turns. It's Red. We've not spoken since she informed on me to the contractors. She smiles when she sees me. I'm getting closer, closer and then I . . .

. . . run right past her. She frowns and goes, 'Hmph!' Or I assume she frowns (she's behind me at the time). She sees I'm running toward someone else. Or something else. A kindred spirit. Maybe the only person in these parts who truly understands me. It's a seagull. A seagull by the name of Likeworm.

I throw my arms around the large seabird, embrace it as I would a long-lost pal, and fondly whisper, 'Never shit in my mouth again.' The gull doesn't fully reciprocate my hug and I suffer lacerations on my cheek and ear from the frantic jabbing of its beak. I take it by the wing and walk it veeeeery slowly back to the lighthouse. To home.

The sun is going down now. I look at the lighthouse, at the cliffs, at the smattering of houses up above, at the locals I am proud to call my friends. It's a new life, but it's one I'm looking forward to, with both hands.

And, just as I had when I arrived at BBC Television Centre

all those years ago, I find myself shaking my head wistfully for about ten to fifteen seconds.

* * *

When the last of the locals have got off my property, and I am about to usher Lynn to her caravan, I see something shiny in the corner of my eye.

It's a plaque. A plaque bearing the words 'HML Seldom (formerly known as Abbot's Cliff Lighthouse). Opened by Her Royal Highness the Princess Royal Princess Anne, 13 April 2023.'

'Lynn,' I stutter. 'Is this . . . real?'

'Oh, yes,' she replies, but with a noticeable smile.

'Keep talking,' I instruct.

'Well, it wasn't an official engagement. She was on her way to Portsmouth naval base, but she very much enjoyed it. So I had a plaque engraved in town.'

I look at her, waiting for a smirk to break out and give the game away, but she holds firm.

'You would have taken photos,' I say.

She hands over her phone and I spool through her photos, but she's managed to flip to the front-facing camera again so the only photos from that day are ones of her own torso and neck. 'That's a shame,' she says. 'I suppose you'll never really know now.'

'Then I'm afraid I can't believe you,' I tell her.

'Well, that's up to you, isn't it?' she replies. 'You could always just choose to believe. Like I choose to believe in God. Night, night.'

God bless Lynn. In her efforts to make me feel better she's forgotten about the existence of social media. It would take me mere seconds to check if Her Royal Highness the Princess Royal

Princess Anne had opened my lighthouse, the home in which I will spend the rest of my life.

And yet . . . I choose to do no such thing. Because my assistant is right. It is up to me. And I'm choosing to believe.

EPIDOGUE

It's May 2023 and I'm back in Norwich – yeah, decided not to do the living-in-a-lighthouse thing in the end – and I'm also back to being clean-shaven. I'm glad I let the beard grow for a while: in arable crop rotation, a field gets to remain fallow one year in every three. This helps to improve the fertility of the soil. And the same is true of my face. With my facial hair left unharvested and wild for so long, the follicles underwent a reset and now, well-rested and with their vim replenished, they are able to produce high-quality hair that grows more quickly and evenly than ever before. It means that if I'm going to be attending a music festival in the Cotswolds or speaking to a mechanic in a few days' time, I can allow the stubble to do its thang, knowing it will emerge swiftly and neatly rather than in fat clumps like it did before.

Why did I leave the lighthouse?

I made some good, good friends there, but it was impossible to ignore the potential rental yield for a historic coastal building. A simple benchmarking exercise, looking at similar properties in similar seaside locations, suggests I can expect a median nightly rate of £400, assuming you can get more like £500-550 in high season. An occupancy rate of even just 70 per cent (around 250 nights per calendar year multiplied by the £400) means you're looking at annual revenue of around £100k.

They say owners should apply the '50 per cent rule', where you set aside half of the rental income for property maintenance. Now, that's obviously ridiculous, but if we spend a quarter of that (roughly £12k a year) on cleaning, pest control, mowing the grass, replacing damaged items, taking legal action against guests who have damaged items, and the upkeep of smoke and carbon monoxide detectors, etc. etc., that's still almost £90k of clear revenue.

With half of the purchase and renovation bill kindly supplied by crowdfunders, my mortgage repayments amount to just £18k a year. Subtract that from the £90k and, oh look, I'm bringing home £72,000 per annum. Not bad. Not bad at all.

Does that detract from the selflessness of my renovation work? Not really. It's not as if I've sawn the lighthouse from its foundations, winched it onto a low-loader and hauled it back to Norwich with me – that would have been too costly and the house would have suffered chronic structural damage in transit. No, I wanted to restore this lighthouse for the people of Kent, and in Kent it remains, there for the whole community to enjoy, albeit from the outside – although they're free to rent it on Airbnb if they're that fussed about getting inside.

I also plan to open the house to the public for three days in every calendar year, with one of those set aside for school children and the disabled.[124]

Returning to Norwich has been joyous. I've been treated like a prodigal son, with a feast in my honour and a friend's prize calf slaughtered that same day.[125]

The oasthouse is looking impeccable. Apparently, we forgot to inform my housekeeper Rosa that I'd be moving to Kent for more than a year, and she's been turning up five days a week and

---

124 Wheelchairs must be left at the door.
125 Accidental tractor collision.

cleaning it, a financial outlay that has been seeping out of my bank account every month and which my assistant really should have noticed. And she will be spoken to about that.

Not that I'm worried about the cash. God, no. On top of my rental income (seventy-two thousand, remember), my financial health isn't just rude, it's positively pornographic. I'm *coining* it in right now. I left my broadcasting career behind, *a decision I have never once regretted*, particularly because I've since returned to presenting work, enjoying a steady stream of lucratish corporate work from clients in the Middle East and Belarus. Whether it's hosting an online Q&A for a beachside property development in Oman, voicing an essential guide to Ramadan for Home Office diplomats visiting Muslim countries, showcasing the latest hand cream available for all passengers using the Air Emirates lounge at Heathrow, or just showing off a new product line for an ethical munitions manufacturer, I'm back, and I wish peace be upon you. *As-salamu alaykum.*

I also have a girlfriend.

As for James Martin, it transpired that he hadn't fully understood the nature of his golden handcuffs deal with ITV. Under the terms of the arrangement, he was and still is precluded from working with any other UK broadcaster for the duration of the deal, which meant the BBC, and by extension *This Time*, couldn't have used any of the material it had shot even if he had completed his build before me. James is now trying to find a buyer for the lighthouse, and *This Time* is no doubt both licking its wounds and kissing my arse.

As I write, I'm walking through the funfair at Chapelfield Gardens in Norwich, which has returned to the town for the first time since that fateful weekend in 2019. In my hands[126] are

---

126 I've put my pad and pen away now and am writing this later.

two fresh candy flosses, although there's an argument to be had about whether candy floss can ever be described as fresh.

I eat the fluffy pink meal as I walk, nodding at visitors and hawkers alike. The two fairground Morrisseys are there too, though they don't seem to remember me. Then again, I'm sure dogs die at their funfair all the time.

And before I know it, I'm at the lighthouse-shaped spiral we know as the helter-skelter. I look around, trying to identify exactly where Seldom breathed his last. I find what I think is the spot and crouch down.

'I did it, Seldie. You wanted that lighthouse? Well, I've gone and bloody did it,' I say, slightly mangling my tenses but I doubt he'd mind. The guy was a dog, it's important to remember that.

Then I plant the rod of the candy floss into the earth, by way of tribute.

And then, something quite, quite incredible. A single white balloon descends from the sky and comes to rest by my side – just as Seldom used to do if he wanted companionship or my dinner. The very same balloon that had risen skywards when Seldom passed away.

'Surely you're not saying it's the same one?', you're thinking. Surely this is just you allowing yourself a big slice of dramatic licence because it's the end of the book and you think you've earned it? After all, the fair gives out hundreds of identical balloons every day and this one would have had to have stayed airborne for four years.

Ah, yes, but this one has a bit of dirt on one side, and I distinctly remember the one that day had a bit of dirt on one side, which proves not only that it's the same balloon, but also that you are wrong.

Yes, just as I have returned to Norwich, it seems Seldom's soul has returned to me. How do I feel? Again, always hard to precisely articulate a feeling, but I can tell you I feel nice and I feel good.

Buoyed by the undeniable presence of my former pet, I stand and look at the twirly chute of the helter-skelter. Sod it, I think, I'm going to have a go. And have a go I do, handing over my pound coins and bounding the stairs one, sometimes two at a time. Then I place my mat on the rim of the slide, sit myself upon it, and push myself away while saying the word 'Awaaaaaay!'

I speed downwards, hurtling along like a luge champ. I'm laughing, my hair flailing behind me. I feel free! Would I have done this on my last visit to the fair? No, but maybe the light-house build has changed me. Maybe rising to that challenge has given me new vim and shown me you can do *anything* you set your mind to.[127]

But then . . . what's this? I've stopped. On one bend, the walls of the chute must have tapered slightly, perhaps because the makers didn't know how to use a set square, and the narrowing has funnelled my hips into a bottleneck. This surprises me. I'm actually quite slender around the hip, certainly no wider than some of the bigger-backsided children you see these days. I try to push off again but I'm jammed, my haunches wedged in the chute like a big human stopper.

I sit helpless on the slide, looking at the mums and dads with a look that says 'sorry about this'. Unfortunately, their children are oblivious to my plight, and before long one, two, three kids have slammed into the back of me, unable to get by.

As I wait to be rescued, I imagine the chute is a visual met-aphor representing the pipeline to professional success. The wailing children are younger TV presenters, coming up behind me, only to find that I'm not going anywhere. I'm at the head of

---

127 Within reason.

the pack; they wait for me. And with that, a huge smile breaks out across my face.

Oh, and if you're wondering about my one-time bed and breakfaster Cynthia and if she ever learned to cook a decent egg? The answer is I don't know, we didn't stay in touch. Thank you!

INDEX